Gender, Sexuality and Subjectivity: A Psychoanalytical Perspective

Gender, Sexuality and Subjectivity: A Psychoanalytical Perspective

Jensen Wallace

MURPHY & MOORE
www.murphy-moorepublishing.com

www.murphy-moorepublishing.com

MURPHY & MOORE

Cataloging-in-publication Data

Gender, sexuality and subjectivity : a psychoanalytical perspective / Jensen Wallace.
p. cm.
Includes bibliographical references and index.
ISBN 978-1-63987-712-6
1. Gender identity--Psychological aspects. 2. Sex (Psychology). 3. Subjectivity--Psychological aspects.
4. Queer theory. 5. Social psychology. I. Wallace, Jensen.
BF692 .G46 2023
155.3--dc23

Murphy & Moore Publishing
1 Rockefeller Plaza,
New York City,
NY 10020, USA

ISBN 978-1-63987-712-6

Contents

Preface ... VII

Chapter 1 **Gender and its Social Transformation: An Overview** ... 1

Chapter 2 **Exploring the Feelings of Gender** ... 23

Chapter 3 **Methodology and its Temporality** ... 41

Chapter 4 **Changing Historical, Cultural and Political Contexts** ... 65

Chapter 5 **Gender Complementarity in People born between 1900 and 1920** ... 91

Chapter 6 **Gender Equality and the Struggles of People born in 1940s** ... 130
Monica Rudberg

Chapter 7 **Welfare Society, Gender and Individuality** ... 173

Chapter 8 **Generational Patterns Across Time and Space** ... 220

Chapter 9 **Gender: A Study of Continuities and Psychosocial Change** ... 243

Chapter 10 **The Processes of Degendering, Gendering and Regendering Across Three Generations** ... 276

Appendix: The Women and the Men in the Study ... 296

Permissions

Index

Preface

This book was inspired by the evolution of our times; to answer the curiosity of inquisitive minds. Many developments have occurred across the globe in the recent past which has transformed the progress in the field.

Gender is a central characteristic for social organization, which encompasses attributes related to masculinity, femininity and their differences. The term gendered subjectivity indicates a critical formulation by diverging from the idea of natural sexual identity characteristics that differentiate human beings into male and female. Sexuality refers to the manner in which humans express themselves sexually, and encompasses to the emotions and attraction that people feel towards another person. It also covers the biological, psychological, physical, erotic, social, or spiritual feelings and behaviors. Developments in gendered subjectivity and sexuality are studied within the disciplines of transgender studies and queer theory. The book aims to shed light on psychoanalytical perspectives of gender, subjectivity and sexuality. It is appropriate for students seeking detailed information in this area as well as for experts. The extensive content of this book will provide the readers with a thorough understanding of the subject.

This book was developed from a mere concept to drafts to chapters and finally compiled together as a complete text to benefit the readers across all nations. To ensure the quality of the content we instilled two significant steps in our procedure. The first was to appoint an editorial team that would verify the data and statistics provided in the book and also select the most appropriate and valuable contributions from the plentiful contributions we received from authors worldwide. The next step was to appoint an expert of the topic as the Editor-in-Chief, who would head the project and finally make the necessary amendments and modifications to make the text reader-friendly. I was then commissioned to examine all the material to present the topics in the most comprehensible and productive format.

I would like to take this opportunity to thank all the contributing authors who were supportive enough to contribute their time and knowledge to this project. I also wish to convey my regards to my family who have been extremely supportive during the entire project.

Jensen Wallace

1

Gender and its Social Transformation: An Overview

Feelings of gender at different times and places are a relatively neglected aspect of the social transformation of gender.[1] Feelings represent a certain kind of personal and embodied meaning that belongs to the immediacy of the present, but which also integrates the past and the future (Chodorow 1999). Feelings integrate past experiences as they are shaped over time through a specific biography, and they make imprints of the future as they are part of a person's capacity to act and infuse life choices with personal meaning. Feelings are personal, but they are also thoroughly social since they are created in social contexts and social institutions in a given historical period. In this way, feelings can be seen as a central psychosocial link.

Feelings as Social

Erik H. Erikson, one of the first psychoanalysts to take an interest in the intertwinement of subjectivity and culture, says that people who share a historical era, class or ethnicity are guided by common images of the world,

[1] See, however, Layton (2004a), Aarseth (2007, 2009a, 2016), Roseneil (2007) and Walkerdine and Jimenez (2012) for some recent examples.

but that these images also take a specific individualised form in every person: 'Infinitely varied, these images reflect the elusive nature of historical change; yet in the form of contemporary social models, of compelling prototypes of good and evil, they assume a decisive concreteness in every individual's ego development' (Erikson 1959: 18). Individual experience is always unique, but shared or similar life conditions may produce social patterns in feelings across the individual singularity: we often understand the feelings of our contemporaries much better than the feelings of those who belong to our parents' or our children's generation, and we recognise more immediately the feelings of those who belong to our own social groups than of those who do not. Different patterns of feelings reflect relational experiences and opportunities characteristic of the time and place of living. Hence, feelings are no less social than cultural meanings or social structures, but they represent the social in another form. Stephen Frosh says that people 'express in their feelings the dynamics of the social order itself' (Frosh 2011: 9). This includes, I would add, the dynamics of change of this social order.

My concern in this book is that the social transformation of gender also involves the work of feelings. Gender attains emotional meaning through the life course and in the transmission between generations at a particular time. I want to explore the link between generational transition and the negotiations and calibrations between women and men belonging to the same generation. To understand this dimension of social change, we must look into subtle and gradual historical processes working on the level of gender identities and gendered subjectivities, including motivations/capacities for autonomy in women and emotional intimacy in men, which may have provided a psychological readiness for structural and cultural changes and political interventions. The empirical basis for the analysis is a longitudinal research project that explores the feelings of gender across three generations of a sample of white, heterosexual women and men of different class backgrounds as they moved from childhood and youth to adult life, and what impact these feelings had on changing gender practices. New life projects gradually came into being, not only as outcomes of externally imposed norms, but also as the work of subjective feelings of gender.

The personal and the social are often thought of as complementary, mirroring the academic disciplines of psychology and sociology, as if individuals could exist without a society or a society could emerge without individuals thinking, feeling and acting in certain ways. The mutual and dynamic character of the process in which both societies and individuals come into being makes it meaningless to use the word 'social' as a contrast to the 'personal' or the 'cultural'. Conceiving of the social or the societal as a totality that may be differentiated and expressed in many different forms seems to be a more fruitful approach. Such forms should neither be radically separated nor levelled out and reduced to each other. As the American anthropologist Michelle Z. Rosaldo once wrote, even though culture and personality cannot be separated, culture is not 'personality writ large', nor is personality 'culture in miniature' (Rosaldo and Lamphere 1974: 141). Different concepts and theories may be needed to grasp the specific dynamics of personal meaning, cultural meaning and larger social structures, but they will always emerge analytically as 'mutually constituted and fundamentally intertwined' (Roseneil 2007: 86) because, in different ways, they all make their marks on concrete acts and practices that can be made objects of study. The British cultural critic Raymond Williams argues that one needs to start from 'the whole way of life', from the whole texture, and from there one may go on to study 'particular activities, and their bearings on other kinds' (Williams 2011: 59). In accordance with this, I understand feelings as a specific kind of social 'activity' that takes place in persons, but not in isolation from other kind of experiences, other persons, other kinds of social activities or the historical situation. By analysing the meanings and feelings that are generated through the gendered practices of three generations and trying to understand how each generation strives to find ways to do gender that feel right in terms of their experiences, desires and circumstances, I seek ways to think about the inner and the outer world, desire and reality, structure and agency, and the subject and the object in ways that do not start out by separating them.

Gender Relations in a Process of Change

The life times of the three generations analysed in this book coincide with huge structural and cultural changes in gender relations in the Western world and beyond. There has been a sea change in the gender-normative assumptions about who 'cares' and who 'works', who deserves what kind of rights and protection (Kessler-Harris 2003: 159). From the late 1960s onwards, there was a strong increase in women's education and employment in Europe. From the 1970s and 1980s, women with young children also entered the labour market in increasing numbers, and the percentage of women has increased in higher education, high professional and political positions during this period as well—although with important variations according to the sociocultural context and the kind of political support and interventions seen as advisable and legitimate within these contexts (Walby 1997; Pfau-Effinger 1998; Lewis 2001; Leira 2002; Crompton et al. 2007). Parallel to these processes, but at a slower pace, men's participation in childcare and household work has increased (Hobson 2002; Brandth and Kvande 2003; Kitterød and Rønsen 2012; Brannen 2015).

All this has had a significant impact on the gendered division of labour in society as a whole, but has evidently not eradicated all inequalities in women's and men's responsibilities, opportunities and privileges in work and family. Cross-nationally we find persistent gender gaps with regard to pay, work hours and career tracks (Crompton et al. 2007; Skrede and Wiik 2012). Attitudes to gender equality and actual practices do not always overlap and this inconsistency may be related both to cultural and structural factors (Knudsen and Wærness 2001; Bühlmann et al. 2010; Usdansky 2011; Hansen and Slagsvold 2012). Thus, the issue of who works and who cares—and more generally of what gender means or should mean—is still filled with unanswered questions, tensions and feelings, something that may be visible in the high divorce rates since the 1970s. The changing gender relations have also increased differences *between* women. Whereas the majority of women in the Scandinavian countries around the middle of the twentieth century lived comparable lives as housewives, although with different material standards and security, the lives of professional middle-class women and the lives of working-class women, and the few women who still chose to be housewives, have become more differentiated, as have the priorities among women (Melby 1999).

Seen from a bird's-eye view, these changes in gender relations and family models must be understood with reference to broader historical processes of modernisation and modernity, and the way in which these processes have materialised in different national contexts. Processes of industrialisation, urbanisation, education and secularisation have had a profound impact on gender relations, class relations and generational relations. This development has increased trends of individualisation where the self and society are understood at large as reflexive projects and where 'standard biographies have become elective biographies' (Beck and Beck-Gernsheim 2002: 4, 24). On the one hand, this process has amplified individual life choices and social mobility; on the other hand, it has 'condemned' people to individualisation within standardised institutional settings and unpredictable and insecure labour markets where people are seen as responsible for their own success or failure. Theories of modernisation and individualisation have been met with questions regarding to what extent detraditionalisation runs parallel to increased reflexivity (Adkins 2004b) and to what degree it dissolves or maybe rather transforms social and emotional bonds between people (Giddens 1992; Jamieson 1998; Morgan 1999; Brannen et al. 2004; Roseneil 2007; Aarseth 2007). It is, however, beyond doubt that processes of individualisation have had a strong impact on gender relations. Gender differences have become less defined and legitimised by religion, tradition and family. Beck and Beck-Gernsheim (2002) point to three important trends in women's lives in modern society: the gradual changes in education, work, and sexuality and relationships. It has not been the major systemic changes, power struggles and revolutions that have changed the 'new normal biographies' of women, but rather the many little steps in education, work and the family. It is such 'trivial matters' that make history and society: 'It is perhaps only by comparing generations that we can perceive how steeply the demands imposed on individuals have been rising' (Beck and Beck-Gernsheim 2002: 76, 4). The Norwegian social anthropologist Marianne Gullestad has described this generational process in terms of a change in the moral imperatives, from 'being of use' to 'finding oneself' (Gullestad 1996). An example of the intertwinement of individualisation and gender from my study is the shifting relationships between mothers and daughters: as young women, the oldest generation of rural women felt it to be self-evident that their duties to their parents had an absolute priority over their own inclinations to take up paid work.

They would have felt like bad people if they had let their parents down. However, in the middle generation a rural mother who asks her young daughter to stay at home and help out may elicit self-pity or even rage in the daughter, and the daughter does not feel like a bad person at all. She feels she has the right to her own life. In the youngest generation the idea that the daughter should stay at home and help out is close to unthinkable both for mothers and daughters, and therefore not emotionally charged in the same way as for the two older generations. Here the young daughter would instead feel like a bad person if she did not pursue a good education and become independent of her parents, as successful young women should. The example also lends support to the claims that personal bonds are not dissolved, but rather transformed in this process, and that the process is not guided only by reflexive considerations.

Processes of modernisation are dependent on timing and the particular route from agrarian to industrial society, as well as the roles that various social groups have played in this (Duncan 1995; Birgit Pfau-Effinger 1998). The ways in which different national welfare regimes frame family and equality policies have been given particular attention in order to understand different developments in family models and the choices made by women and men in different national contexts and by different social groups (Esping-Andersen 1990; Lewis 1992; Korpi 2000; Leira 2002; Den Dulk and Doorne-Huiskes 2007). Feminist scholars have analysed these welfare regimes with emphasis on gender and unpaid work, childcare facilities, leave arrangements, availability of flexible working arrangements and the ways in which taxation systems encourage or discourage men and women to share paid employment (Lewis 1992; Leira 2002; Den Dulk and Doorne-Huiskes 2007). These structural, economic and political conditions are important framings for changing gender relations; however, they do not by themselves explain the changes or stabilities in these relations. Research has concluded that gender arrangements depend on a complex interplay between structural conditions, cultural values, institutions and agency—for instance, cultural ideals concerning motherhood/fatherhood that are incorporated into existing social policies (Acker 1989; Duncan 1995; Pfau-Effinger 1998; Den Dulk and Doorne-Huiskes 2007).

Gender Contracts and Agency

The changing work and family articulations may be seen as expressions of shifts in broader societal 'gender contracts' (Hirdman 1988; Duncan 1995; Hagemann and Åmark 1999; Lewis 2001). This perspective aims at grasping the hegemonic normative assumptions about gender relations in a given historical period and place, the underlying norms about what women and men should do, think and be. Such implicit cultural norms feed into state politics and institutions, as well as into regulations of the labour market interpretations and negotiations between individual women and men in the family and beyond (Haavind 1984a, b; Hirdman 1988; Duncan 1995). The Swedish historian Yvonne Hirdman sees the breadwinner/carer family model as an expression of a societal housewife contract that was hegemonic in most European countries between 1930 and 1965, emerging in the wake of the private patriarchy of the nineteenth century. In the following decades she identifies an equity contract that is realised in the full-time/part-time family model, and an equality contract that is the basis of the dual-earner/dual-carer family (Hirdman 1990). During this process, gender differentiation becomes increasingly culturally illegitimate and socially irrelevant with regard to citizenship in all its dimensions (Hagemann and Åmark 1999). From the field of political theory, Nancy Fraser has suggested that different normative visions may be seen as operative in the new gender contracts: in the universal breadwinner model, women are upgraded as citizens and workers on par with men, and care is moved from the family to the market and the state; in the caregiver parity model, care work is kept within the family and normally carried out by the woman, but is culturally upgraded and supported by public funding; finally, in the universal caregiver model, women's life pattern is also taken as the norm for men so that the couple will share both care and breadwinning (Fraser 1997). What unites the different approaches to cultural change is that they all indicate a normative move away from a gender order characterised by unquestioned differences in norms, rights and obligations for women and men towards a situation where women's and men's lives have become more alike and where gender equality has gained an increasing foothold as a common norm. This change in normative ideas does not necessarily coincide with all ongoing practices, instead sometimes disguising them. As the Norwegian psychologist Hanne Haavind's studies of negotiations in married couples indicate, what was earlier understood in terms of gender obligations may now be legitimised as free choice, loyalty, love, attraction and so on. She says that the essence of the new femininity is to 'make inequalities appear as equalities' (Haavind 1984b: 147). Thus, the fundamental tension between the abstract assumption of equality in the public sphere of Western capitalist societies and gender difference in the private sphere is not solved through democratisation and individualisation alone. Gender remains a persistent element of 'disorder' in modern society (Pateman 1989; Hirdman 1990; Hagemann and Åmark 1999; Solheim 2007; Melby et al. 2008).

The gender contract frames the ways in which women and men are integrated in society. It accentuates the reproductive force in a given hegemonic social and cultural order, working as the unnoticed background against which gender arrangements are negotiated and decided upon. However, the concept may also open up for an understanding of gender arrangements as complex and variable historical outcomes of many interacting societal processes. In this way it also leaves room for agency.[2] As is the case with other social contracts, gender contracts do not presuppose equality between the partners, but a certain amount of voluntariness and active participation without which the concept of agency would lose its meaning. This agency is also present in relationships and practices in daily life, within the varying constraints and opportunities given by class, ethnicity and age at a given time and place (see also McNay 2004 and Adkins 2014b). An important dimension here is the gradual and multilevel reciprocal shifts between women and men when it comes to paid work and care: 'the process whereby women's behaviour has changed in

[2] In some versions gender contracts are seen as a reproductive force working along with historical change: new gender contracts are basically new expressions of the same underlying, patriarchal gender system, at least until further notice (Hirdman 1988; Haavind 1984a, b). Other versions (Hagemann and Åmark 1999; Duncan 1995) find that the value of the concept lies precisely in its opening up for agency and (real) social change. My use of the concept is based on this latter understanding.

recent decades, requiring reciprocal change in men, which in turn will require reciprocal change in women, and so on, in a cycle of continual adaption and change' (Gamles et al. 2007: 17; see also Thompson 1997). Such reciprocal interchanges in daily life do not only rely upon perceptions and reflexions, but also involve feelings of gender: What kind of personal experiences—understood as feelings, meanings and practices—were behind the increasing support of the change in the gendered division of work in the family and beyond? By looking into how practices, meanings and feelings of gender are reconfigured over time and how such 'micro histories' Walkerdine (2012: 86) contribute to the larger history of the development of new gender contracts, we may gain more insight into the mutual dynamics between structural, political, cultural and psychological change. Since the concept of feeling incorporates meaning and process, it may in some respects be better suited to comparison over time and place than more specific and isolated dimensions of behaviour like women's employment patterns or changes in dominant family models, which say little about the underlying processes or the context of the phenomena.

Generational Transition and Transmission

Intergenerational transmission has a dynamic and open character and covers much more than the sheer adaption to or protest against parental values, norms and models of behaviour (Bertaux and Thompson 1993; Bertaux and Bertaux-Wiame 1997; Thompson 1997). As will be elaborated in Chap. 2, relational experience in families are loaded with emotional meaning, with 'projections and identifications, love and anger, symbols and desires' (Bertaux and Thompson 1993: 7). Issues of gender identification play a special role in intergenerational transmission, and feelings of gender originating in the familial context may be in tension or even contradiction with other gender lessons of the same family and beyond. There are several reasons why socialisation is not about mechanical learning or has deterministic outcomes. One is that the context for action changes over time—what is learnt will be put to use in new situations. Another is that experiences are processed psychologically and reconstructed over time in the light of new experiences. And, finally, this reconstruction or work of integration exceeds a purely reflexive or articulated level. What is transmitted may consist of more or less articulated feelings of self and others (Benjamin 1995; Layton 1998; Chodorow 1999; Chodorow 2012) or it may be a kind of knowledge embedded in everyday practices and relationships (Bourdieu 1990; Morgan 1999). Transmission may result in generational breaks and ambivalences, as well as in continuities and reproduction (Brannen 2015: 12; see also Bertaux and Bertaux-Wiame 1997).

The interviews in the project on which this book is based focus on childhood, youth and the transition to adulthood in each generation. This means that two temporal perspectives are combined: the process of *transition* from child to adult in each generation and the processes of *transmission* between generations. Seen together, these processes connect different historical moments of the life course, as well as different dimensions of meaning and practice within and between generations.

The ongoing dynamic in life transitions between societal change and a person's psychological reconstruction of cultural and emotional gender will be approached as an interchange between *gender identities* (how I see my self as gendered), *gendered subjectivities* (the kind of person I am, how I feel) and *sociocultural contexts* (which potentials of my current gender identity and gendered subjectivity that are possible to express and pursue in a specific sociocultural context) (see also Nielsen and Rudberg 1994; Nielsen 1996, 2015; Thomson et al. 2011). Gender identities involve dimensions like belonging to a gender category, which can be felt as more or less certain or secure, the specific content of what it means to be a man/woman, and whether this is felt as positive or not. Gendered subjectivities denote particular ways of being and relating produced by relational experience. It includes psychological capacities and orientations, for instance, the extent to which one is able to see others as separate subjects, the ability to be alone and close to others, or the kind of activities one feels drawn to. It also includes the intrapsychic conflicts that may exist in these matters and the defences that are mobilised. To the degree that such capabilities and conflicts are culturally gendered, the subjectivity can be relatively single-gendered or relatively multi-gendered. If multi-gendered subjectivities are lived with few intrapsychic tensions and defences, they may also be understood as degendered subjectivities. Gender identity and gendered subjectivity cannot be entirely separated empirically, but the concepts represent an analytical effort to grasp gender as both reflexive and non-reflexive. The floating border between gender identities and gendered subjectivities are taken into account by the comprehensive concept of 'feelings of gender'.

As the interchange between gender identities, gendered subjectivities and sociocultural constraints and opportunities continues during the life course, relationships between parents and children will become part of it, and the personal stories of the parents and those of their children will cross each other at several points in time (see also Morgan 1999). In the empirical chapters (Chaps. 5, 6 and 7) we explore these interchanges through an analytical model that combines different aspects of the *experiences* of gender—practices, feelings and meanings—with the trippel *temporal* dimension of transition from childhood to adult life, from one generation to the next, and in changing historical contexts. Thus, on the one hand, the analysis connects different dimensions and areas of experiences *within* each generation and *between* women and men in this generation, and, on the other hand, *links* the generations to each other. The analytical model explores six areas of experience and how they are connected to each other within each generation, and how feelings, reflections and life choices[3] lead to the gendered practice that became the point of departure for the next generation. For each of the three generations, we look at the connections between:

1. WORK: the perception of the division of work and care in their childhood families.
2. RELATIONSHIPS: the feelings of gender that grew out of the relational experience connected with this division of work and care.
3. BODIES: the feelings of gender with regard to sexuality, and to one's own gendered body and those of others.

[3] The concept of 'choice' is in this book used to indicate a dimension of agency, but does not imply that agencies or choices are based on purely cognitive or rational deliberations (as in 'rational choice' theory). Life choices or life projects are seen as complicated outcomes dependent on many sources, some of which are the emotional or even unconscious meaning that the choice has for the acting person.

4. REFLECTIONS: the ways in which these feelings of gender found their way into articulated reflections on gender.
5. PRACTICES: the way in which one's own family as an adult was organised, and the gendered division of work and care this implied.
6. ATTITUDES: finally, how all these experiences are reflected in thinking about gender equality as a contemporary personal and political issue.

By combining intergenerational transmission with the changing sociocultural context, I am bringing together two meanings of generation.[4] One is the *genealogical* meaning, which points at the kinship position of being children, parents and grandparents. The other is the *historical* meaning, which sees generations as groups of people who share a distinctive culture or a self-conscious identity by virtue of having experienced the same historical events at roughly the same time in their lives (Alwin and McCammon 2004: 27). The idea of historical generations goes back to Karl Mannheim, who argued that people who share a common location in the social and historical process might establish such generational identities in the period of youth. In every such location, Mannheim says, there is 'a tendency pointing towards certain definite modes of behaviour, feeling and thought' (Mannheim 1952: 291). According to Mannheim, this plays a decisive role in historical change, as it will provide refreshed views at the passing on of social and cultural traditions, even though not all generations will be equally active and visible. In my analysis I focus more specifically on how different genders and generations display different patterns of feelings through the way they act and talk, directly or indirectly, about gender. Is it possible to see patterns that are more typical for one generation than for another? Are they equally clear and do they have the same consequences across social class? What is the connection between patterns within and between generations? I do not claim that the identified patterns fit everyone equally well, but that they may still crystallise into a shared feeling of 'the way things are', or a sense of life, in a given period of time (Williams 2011; see also Ellingsæter and Widerberg

[4] The relationship between generation and cohort and how these concepts may be related to social change will be further discussed in Chap. 3.

2012: 21). For instance, the generally positive relationships daughters had with their mothers in the eldest generation, and the generally much more negative relationships between mothers and the women in the middle generation emerge as a marked shift in the life-world between these two generations of women, in spite of the variation in mother–daughter relationships that is also always present. My aim is to trace the experiences during the life course that made women and men in different historical generations feel differently about gender and how this became a drive towards new life projects and changed gender relations. These feelings may also have consequences for what cultural values and political issues different people tend to identify or disidentify with. In the words of Raymond Williams, this is the real indication of change:

> the absolute test by which revolution can be distinguished, is the change in the form of activity of a society, in its deepest structure of relationships and feelings. (1979, p. 420)

Generational Patterns as Normative Creations

When many people in a generation share the same feelings towards something, they tend to react in much the same way to new societal opportunities, for instance, investing in the same kind of new family model. In this way the model gradually becomes a social norm, which may be experienced as hegemonic or even coercive for those who do not feel at home in it. Hence, if new life projects are shared by many in the same generation, they may contribute to the social transformation of gender, although often in more incremental and less obvious ways than the kind of changes that are articulated within political contexts or public cultural discourses. The North American historian John Modell argues for a social-historical approach to the life course, which can grasp the two-way relationships between large-scale historical change and the way in which individual lives are lived: individual experiences during periods of change may *aggregate* to constitute a new *context* for others living through these changes: 'Even "kids" can make history, as their choices aggregate into behavioural patterns and, rationalized, become normative' (Modell

1989: 22). Thus, cohort effects may indirectly constitute normative patterns and feed into new generational identities. Bertaux and Thompson argue along the same lines when they say that 'a sufficient minority' can contribute to the momentum of change: by 'voting with their feet, they can transform the structures of social space or demography' (Bertaux and Thompson 1997: 2). Beck and Beck-Gernsheim make a similar point when they talk about how 'new normal biographies' are produced by numerous small steps that simultaneously may have a dimension of adaption and yet over time aggregate to a challenge of the existing conditions (Beck and Beck-Gernsheim 2002: 55, 76). This excludes neither variations and tensions within such patterns, both in accordance with class difference and individual variation, and between women and men in the different generations, nor the existence of other patterns in different subgroups.

Social and geographical mobility is characteristic for times of industrialisation and post-industrialisation. There have been typical *social pathways* understood as trajectories of education, work, family patterns and places to move from and to (Elder et al. 2003: 8). As many studies have indicated, there are often personal costs associated with a class journey (Walkerdine 1990; Mahony and Zmroczek 1997; Lawler 1999; Trondman 2010). In particular, studies from the UK emphasise that class travellers experienced their families to hold them back and not being supportive to their upward mobility (Bertaux and Thompson 1997: 23; Lawler 2000: 112; Brannen 2015: 143). The sample analysed in this book is taken from a Norwegian context and the Scandinavian story appears to be somewhat different here. Due to the cultural and political emphasis on equality and the relatively high social security provided by the welfare state (see Chap. 4), the Scandinavian version of the class journey associated with industrialisation and de-industrialisation came to resemble a 'group travel' rather than the individual travels depicted in the British studies, and this collective character may have allayed some of the cultural and psychological ambivalences. The Norwegian sociologist Ivar Frønes has compared this kind of mobility to a lock chamber: you are lifted onto a new level together with many others in your cohort and thus never leave the space perceived as 'normal' (Frønes 2001). The foremost example of this kind of collective class journey is the generation born after the Second World War. A large number of young people could at that point take advantage of an expanding and free educational system, rising material standards in their families and a restructured labour market, and become urban middle class. The process altered the class composition in Norway from being a society of mostly small farmers, fishermen and workers to a society where the most 'normal' is to be middle class or lower middle class (Ringdal 2010). The difficulties for those who were not part of this collective journey may have increased, but it reduced the strain on those who left: 'Many made a small class journey without giving it much thought', as the Swedish sociologist Mats Trondman expresses it (Trondman 2010: 252). Furthermore, the process of geographical and social mobility took place over two or three generations and was characterised by a sequence of short-distance moves (only one move up in relation to the class of origin) (Ringdal 2010). Even if the class journey did take you away from your family of origin and could be marked by a sense of dislocation, it was simultaneously often part of a generational 'relay race' in the family. The compressed story of modernisation in combination with these gradual moves and the support from the welfare state have contributed to a perception of the journey as a move from rural to urban culture rather than from working class to middle class, as was the case in the UK. Thus, the character of this particular period of social mobility in Norway meant travelling *along with* and not *against* the shifting notions of what was considered normal and expected. Another way to say this is that we have here a case where staying within the hegemonic pattern and at the same time contributing to social change have been two sides of the same coin. The collective class journey provided a bigger space and a more privileged position in relation to contributing to new cultural forms, often complex and heterogeneous, reflecting both the culture of origin, the impact from educational institutions, new demands in work life and other current cultural and social impulses (Frønes 2001; Nielsen and Rudberg 2006). Some of the new things to be invented on the way were the norms and practices of modern gender equality. Thus, the generational sample in our study aggregates into normative patterns not only because it belongs to the majority with regard to ethnicity and sexuality, but also because it is typical for the specific type of urbanisation and social mobility that took place in Norway during the twentieth century.

Whereas our sample is geared towards illuminating incremental changes taking place in majority groups, it is important to keep in mind that many aspects of the social transformation of gender may not be covered. The design does not include people who in the course of these three generations did not move to the city, and only to some degree those who did not enter a generational process of social mobility. The sample cannot say anything particular about the situation of people who stayed single, who did not have children, or who identified as gays, lesbians, bisexual or transgender, or the new immigrant population, who started to arrive in limited numbers in the early 1970s. What the sample *can* say something about is how majority groups who live the normative and hegemonic gender order of its time and class, in the course of generational transmission, may also contribute to the social transformation of gender. It is the significance of the changing patterns of feelings of people living different kinds of 'normalised' lives at different points of time that I explore here.

Changing the Norm from Within

What may a generational and psychosocial study of the social patterns feelings of gender add to the understanding of the social transformation of gender? I will end this chapter with a short discussion of this in relation to three perspectives on change in contemporary feminist theory taken from political theory, poststructuralist/queer theory and practice theory. In contrast to feminist work in the 1970s and 1980s, which put emphasis on structural change, contemporary feminist theories are more oriented towards agency, practices, processes, symbolic power and meaning. With regard to this, my view is that including the feelings of gender would contribute to improving the understanding of how gender norms and practices are both connected with larger social forces and, at the same time, may be transformed 'from within'. Feelings find their ways into people's agencies during their life course and at specific historical times.

Political theory works with the assumption that in order to be political, identities must be explicit and articulated, and that political action is characterised by having a collective and public form. Politics is about participation and about making claims to be included and recognised, to have a voice, to participate and be able to pursue one's social and economic interests in the public sphere. It is about strategic choices made by social actors representing social groups and movements (Hobson 2003: 2). However, changes in gender relations can and often do take place outside the sphere of articulated political claims and collective political identities. They may be consequences of changing historical, structural and cultural conditions and the way people feel, reflect and respond to these by making other choices in their own lives—for instance, a woman deciding to take up paid work or a father wanting to spend more time with his children. What I see in our sample is that such choices and negotiations can be based on more or less conscious reflection, but they need not be articulated *as* political projects or take the form of individual struggles in order to happen. It may be sufficient that they appear necessary or possible, meaningful or desirable for people. Among our informants, we also find several who distance themselves from feminist politics, and even some who distance themselves from gender equality politics, but who nevertheless have made choices in their own lives that increased gender equality in their families. This may partly be explained by the contributions of feminist politics and discourses to new senses of normality without making gender an explicit concern for people. Kate Nash, for instance, argues that women who say 'I'm not a feminist, but…' and then articulate norms that would have been unthinkable without feminist politics still embody a social resistance against women's subordination (Nash 2002: 323). However, the connection between new practices and new political claims could also go the other way: the emergence of new feelings and practices in everyday life may work as silent conditions for the cognitive framing chosen by the actors in a movement or in a political process. As argued above, when many do the same thing, it is also in effect a collective force as it changes the horizon of what is perceived as normal and justifiable. An exploration of how feelings change in the course of generations may thus help to illuminate this 'inverse' mode of processes of change.

The approach to change in *poststructuralist and queer theory* works on the level of cultural categories and representations: normative categories of gender and sexuality need to be deconstructed and destabilised so that it becomes clear that they are not natural or innocent entities. Since categories are seen as constituted by processes of exclusion, they will always be products of power struggles (Butler 1990; Corbett 2009). As categories in this way are internally dependent on what is externalised, they will also be internally unstable and targets of continual resignification. In Judith Butler's version, the poststructuralist point of the constitutional instability of norms is combined with a theory of performativity, which is defined as 'the reiterative and citational practice by which discourse produces the effect that it names' (Butler 1993: 2). The constitutional instability of gender, in combination with its performative character, is what provides the possibility of change for Butler (Stormhøj 2003). This opens up for the possibility of changing the norm from within, but as such resignifications are merely coincidental consequences of the indeterminacy of language, triggered by unconscious processes in the speaker, their effects are also undetermined.[5] Raewyn Connell (2009) has questioned the value of Butler's idea of generalised instability because it cannot take into account that in some historical periods, gender identities and relations change fast, while in others they change slowly. Nor does the concept explain why some people would want to change gender arrangements, while others would resist (Connell 2009: 90).[6] Without a concept of change connected to their broader social uses, norms are in practice often only analysed as becoming more and more restrictive every time they are repeated (see, for instance, Corbett 2009: 13).

Queer theory is understood as transformative in itself by intervening in the politics of knowledge. The idea is that theoretical and practical critique are intertwined. The inquiries begin from the margins, with people

---

[5] Butler here combines Derrida's theory of the instability of signification with Lacanian psychoanalysis: something had to be repressed in order to become a subject within the symbolic order, and this produces psychic excesses that may surface and disturb an otherwise obedient gender performance. This gives her theory a dualism of adaption (the subject) and protest (the unconscious, the psyche), which will be discussed further in Chap. 2. Since the protests are unconscious, the incorrect performances may disturb the power, but hardly rearticulate it (Stormhøj 2003: 132).

[6] See also McNay (2004) and Stormhøj (2013) for similar critiques of Butler's ahistorical and abstract concept of agency. In her work within queer theory, Butler has engaged more explicitly in political discussions, and argued that deconstruction and resignification alone are not enough to make social and political transformation happen: 'Something besides theory must take place, such as interventions at social and political levels that involve actions, sustained labor and institutionalized practice' (Butler 2004, 204).

who are engaged in non-conforming gender and sexual practices and who do not feel like they fit into whatever 'we' is being articulated as a norm (Stormhøj 2013: 65). However important this approach is, it also has a tendency to conceptualise the dominant norm as monolithic and undynamic (McNay 2004; Stormhøj 2013). The dominant norm emerges as a static background to non-normative gender performances and the question of what motivates some people to adhere to this norm moves out of focus (Hollway 1984; Layton 1998). But gender norms are neither deterministic nor monolithic or static. They vary between men and women and between classes and generations, and this creates internal incoherencies and contradictions within prevailing gender norms. The norms also change historically, and often also within the life course of individual people, without necessarily being dependent on destabilising discursive interventions from non-normative groups. Thus, the 'dominant norm' is a moving target, and some of the movement may be explored by looking into the feelings of gender in those groups that adhere to these norms or through their behaviour modify them or create new ones.

Feminist approaches departing from Bourdieu's *practice theory* have a structurally and historically based understanding of change, combined with an emphasis on the ways in which such change also takes place as 'lived relations'. Practice is motivated by people's perceptions, feelings and representations, not just abstract social structures and economic forces (McNay 2004: 184). It is necessary to enter the 'phenomenology of social space', a space that is relational in its structure and tied to experience in specific contexts, in order to understand how reflexivity and agency work as elements in both societal reproduction and change. Such reflexivity could be understood as an ongoing transformative practice '*simultaneous* with the normal course of daily life, but also *constitutive* of how life is lived in history, across generations and in personal interactions' (Silva 2005: 96). By producing gender in ever-new ways, new 'normalities' also come into being. Thus, change does not necessarily imply normative constraints, individual resistance or collective mobilisation, but can be located 'in regard to a shift in the conditions of social reproduction itself' (Adkins 2004a: 9). Gender does not dissolve through this reflexivity, but is constantly in a process of *reconfiguration*. It is reflexivity itself that becomes 'a habit of gender in late modernity' (Adkins 2004b:

192). Whereas Bourdieu mainly sees changes in the habitus as a non-reflexive bodily practice, scholars like McNay, Adkins and Silva emphasise the interaction of reflexive and prereflexive dimensions of meaning, especially in relation to modern rearticulations of gender.

These perspectives are close to my approach, as I also focus on the gradual reconfiguration of gender over generations that draw on practices, reflections and feelings. However, the emotional or prereflexive dimensions of agency, reflections and motivation are not particularly elaborated in practice theories (see Aarseth et al. 2016). Feelings are seen as direct effects in the individual body and mind of a restricted social context, and social and psychological explanations of behaviour tend to be seen as alternatives (Skeggs 1997; McNay 2004). Emotional responses are primarily connected with experienced social inequalities, in particular class differences: feelings of shame, fear or anxiety in working-class people and feelings of resentment, pity or guilt in middle-class people emerge when they become aware of 'the others', feel devalued by them or feel they must defend themselves psychologically against them. Psychological tensions are here understood as a direct response to perceived injustice, and it is not taken into account that different people will experience this conflict in different ways depending on their previous relational experience (see, for instance, Reay 2005, 2015; Skeggs 2005).[7] Since the psychological concepts are primarily used to describe pain and psychological defence, the emotional aspects of agency also become tied up with these negative sides of experience, whereas the positive and formative potentials of feelings are insufficiently explored. Furthermore, the prereflexive or emotional dimension is used to understand how the past becomes part of the present, biographically and generationally, but not how it may also anticipate the future as social change is seen as connected only with the reflexive dimension. The Norwegian sociologist Helene Aarseth has argued that this division between prereflexive belonging and reflexive distance makes it difficult to understand what actually motivates change. She suggests instead trying to capture the *resonance* between prereflexive

---

[7] More psychosocially oriented work on class includes how class relations may also permeate the interaction between parents and children long before the children have become aware of class differences (see, for instance, Walkerdine and Lucey 1989; Layton 2010; Lucey et al. 2016).

and reflexive appropriations of new meanings (Aarseth 2009a: 7). The analysis of how women and men in generational chains rework gender lends support to Aarseth's more general claim. What they both tell and live, practically and emotionally, not only connects with the past, but also provides them with agency to change the future. Thus, what I want to add to the feminist theories of practice is a more historicised conception of psychological structure, a more psychologically informed understanding of the mutual creation of the social context and feelings, and an understanding of how biographically anchored emotional meanings may sometimes be drivers for change, not merely resisting or delaying it.

New norms are not necessarily more inclusive or pluralistic than old ones, since it is not only individual variation presses towards change but also changing patterns of similarities between individuals that may contribute to emptying an earlier norm of its meaning by disconnecting gender from what used to be gendered practices. This raises a question about the relation between *destabilising* a category and *weakening* its significance in different areas of life. Does a destabilisation of the binary structure of gender and of sexuality lead to fewer social inequalities between people of different genders or different sexual identities? And, conversely, does increased social equality between women and men or between people with different sexual identities make the gender category less important, constraining and exclusionary? Is it gender as practice or gender as category that is the root of evil? These are also questions I keep in mind in my analysis of what aspects of gender are done, undone and redone across the three generations.

The Structure of the Book

In the following three chapters I will elaborate some of the theoretical and empirical assumptions for my analysis. *Chapter 2* will discuss the concept of feelings in connection with theories of subjectivity, identity and affect. It will look specifically at theories about gender and subjectivity, and in what ways it makes sense to talk about social patternings of feelings. *Chapter 3* will dive into the methodological aspects of the study, the design, procedures and presentation of the data. It will discuss how one can 'read' feelings from qualitative interviews and will look at the many methodological challenges that arise when studying and comparing generations. *Chapter 4* will set some of the societal context for the three generations of the study, particularly the Norwegian context and in what ways it is similar to and different from other European countries. The structural, economic and political conditions for family and work, and the changing cultural contexts for the youth of each of the three generations will be chief areas of focus. The subsequent three chapters—*Chaps.* 5, *6 and 7*—are dedicated to an inductive analysis of the dominant patterns within each generation organised along the six thematic issues mentioned above: work, relationships, bodies, reflections, practices and attitudes. In the three last chapters the patterns found in the different generations are seen and analysed from different methodological and psychosocial angles. *Chapter 8* is a methodological interlude where the results from the analyses are discussed along the dimensions of time and place. It includes reflections on how the effects of age, generation and historical period are intertwined with the production of social change. Furthermore, it includes a comparison with selected generational studies from the UK in order to see what may be specifically Scandinavian in the patterns detected and what might have wider applicability. *Chapter 9* summarises the changes and continuities of gendered subjectivities across the three generations and examines them in terms of different historical theories of psychological gender. *Chapter 10* summarises the changing social patterns of feeling gender and how they have fed into new life projects and ideas about gender and gender equality.

2

Exploring the Feelings of Gender

Three points are important to understand the concept of feelings as I use it in this book: first, feelings are understood as a kind of personal and embodied *meaning* which lingers between the conscious, the preconscious and the unconscious, and between inner and outer objects. As such, they are central to human creativity and agency. Second, feelings stem from our *relationships* with others, and from how this relational experience is processed by the subject who comes into being and is continuously reshaped by these relational processes. Thus, feelings have a temporal dimension connected to the historical and social context of the relational experience, as well as to the subject's life course in time and space. Feelings live in socialised subjectivities. Third, this means that feelings, even though they are always personal, may also display *social patterns* characteristic of a certain class, gender or generation. These points also apply when feelings are expressions of gendered experiences.

In order to elaborate upon and combine these three points, in this chapter I will connect theoretical perspectives from and inspired by the German Frankfurt School with some of the more recent psychosocial work, which, drawing on object-relational approaches,[1] aims at combining psychoanalytic theory with societal context and change. What characterises both the older 'grand' theories from the Frankfurt School and the younger, more detailed psychosocial approaches is the effort to find ways to think in non-reductive ways about the connections between the outer and the inner world, between structure and meaning, and between object and subject. However, there are differences in their main questions and preoccupations, and also in the ways in which they proceed analytically. The old approach of the Frankfurt School seems to have a better grasp on the wholeness of the intertwinement of culture, individual and society, providing a framework to think about the social patterns of feelings, but not elaborating to any great extent upon the psychological processes in individuals. Conversely, the younger approach often focuses more on what goes on in the inner world of singular persons (and definitely with a more explicit emphasis on gender than the old approach), but sometimes with less attention to how psychosocial interchanges may also amount to more general social patterns of feelings. Where the old approach is occupied with social patterns, the younger approach concentrates on the multiple individual variations on and tracks to such patterns. I think we need both approaches to grasp feelings as an element in social organisation and change.

Feelings as Socially Patterned

The understanding of feelings as the emotional aspect of *meaning* makes the approach in this book different from the turn to affect that has occurred in a broad range of fields within the humanities and social

[1] The main characteristics of object-relational approaches are that they work with a broader concept of human motivation than drive theories tend to do, asserting that attachment and recognition by one's loved ones is as primary a human force as the sexual drive. There are many versions of object-relation theory, not least in relation to how much the social and historical dimensions are drawn into the analysis of the inner psychological object world. Melanie Klein, the founding figure of British object-relational theory, works only on the level of the inner, unconscious world, whereas more contemporary feminist psychoanalysts as Nancy Chodorow, Jessica Benjamin and Lynne Layton, whose work I rely on in this chapter, place emphasis on how social relations affect the inner psychic processes. It is the latter version I draw on in this chapter, whether I name it 'object-relational theories' or the psychosocial approach of 'relational feminist psychoanalysts'.

sciences as a response to the discursive dominance in poststructuralism (see Leys (2011) and Wetherell (2012) for critical reviews). In many theoretical versions of this turn, affect is seen as the opposite of meaning, as a 'formless, unstructured, non-signifying force or "intensity" separated from cognition': Leys 2011: 442). Contrary to this, I see feelings as an aspect of meaning and as part of the human capacity to understand and act in the world: feelings are enmeshed in stories, biographies and history (Chodorow 1999). This does not imply that feelings have to be verbalised in order to be felt and present in what is said and done. From psychoanalytic theory, I draw the basic assumption that feelings can be conscious, preconscious and unconscious, and that they work in ways that may be more or less known to the person who harbours these feelings. Feelings can be meanings that are existential rather than representational, 'a form of deep memory' (Bollas 1987: 50), but they may also be symbolised in words. Sometimes we reflect on and verbalise what we feel; at other times feelings just play an unacknowledged part—conflictual or not—in how we perceive the world, making themselves present in the ways we talk and act. I understand feelings as personalised meanings floating through inner and outer relations and through time. It is something the subject carries with him or her, but is also something that is continuously reinterpreted and reconstructed as he or she experiences and acts in the world together with others in shared contexts.

The idea that feelings are socially patterned is not new. Erik H. Erikson has already been mentioned as one psychoanalyst who wrote about the ways in which culture, history and ethnicity emerge in unconscious fantasies, symptoms and conflicts (Chodorow 1999: 227). A more sociological approach to this is found in the efforts of the Frankfurt School to integrate psychoanalysis and Marxism by studying the connection between social and economic structures, cultural patterns and individual psychological development. The main concern here is not the individual psychological story, but the social form of subjectivity and agency in a given historical context. One of the terms for this was Erich Fromm's concept of *social character*, the emotional attitude common to people in a specific social class or society in a given historical period. Erich Fromm defined a social character as the psychological reactions typical for a social group, which have developed as a result of common experiences and life conditions for that group. The emotional matrix of cultural ideas is seen as rooted in the character structure of individuals, and this is key to understanding the spirit of a given culture, according to Fromm. What is seen as 'normal' in a society has an emotional foundation in the typical social character of this society. It is the similarities in individual responses of most of the members, not the differences between these responses that the concept frames. The differences are important if we want to understand the single individual fully, Fromm says; however, 'if we want to understand how human energy is channelled and operates as a productive force in a given social order, then the social character deserves our main interest' (Fromm 1941: 278). He engages with the cultural patterns in the subjects' psychological organisation not only as irrational adaption based on repression, but also as something that may work as a social and generative force, a dynamic psychological adaption of human needs to a particular mode of existence in a given society.[2] Thus, the social character has both adaptive and creative sides—it internalises the external necessities, but in a way that also appears as sensible and often emotionally satisfying and motivating for the person. Fromm's ideas about the social character, moulded in specific social spaces where the individual 'by adapting himself to social conditions … develops those traits that make him *desire* to act as he *has* to act' (p. 283) can also be linked to Bourdieu's much later concept of habitus and his idea about 'a socialized libido' which combines necessity with the person's engagement in the field (Aarseth 2016). However, since Fromm understands society as not merely repressive, it may also meet the human striving for freedom and growth. In this way the psychological organisation of the individuals, which develops as a result of the social process, also becomes 'productive forces, moulding the social process' (p. 13).

A problem with Fromm's concept of social character is that it works on a very general level, combining grand societal formations like Protestantism and modern authoritarianism with general traits of psychological reaction and defence, and thus leaves us with a rather massive image of the character as a fixed internal template that more or less

[2] It is important to be aware that the concept of 'socialisation' in this German tradition is not the functionalist one from Parsons with which it is often identified in the English-speaking world, but a concept that, like the concept of 'subjectivity', integrates societal moulding and adaption together with the constitution of personal agency.

stays as it was made, or gets defensive and destructive if the societal formations that produced it change. In this sense, Fromm offers a 'grand theory' working with jigsaw pieces too big to really understand continuing social transformations. The concept of character is also contested in modern psychoanalytic theory to the extent that it is based on assumptions about fixed and coherent identities. More process-oriented concepts like 'identifications' or 'subjectivities', indicating that a person have multiple versions of selves in his or her internal world, have gained foothold compared to theories of identity and character as fixed psychological structures (Benjamin 1995). Modern psychoanalytic theories would agree that developmental processes connected to biographical trajectories are formative, but not that such formations of subjective structures are unchangeable, coherent and without internal conflicts (Layton 1998). Instead of talking either about character and identity as reified entities, as in the case of Fromm, or about fluidity with no core or continuity, as is the case in postmodern theories, we may talk about historical *patterns* of identification, desire and subjectivity in individuals as well as across social groups.

The concept of pattern is central in the work of the British cultural critic Raymond Williams, who has expanded on Fromm's ideas with the concept *structure of feeling* in a way that maintains both the formative and the transformative dimensions of subjectivity and cultural practices. The structure of feeling is not an overall psychological organisation of the subject's inner world, but patterns in the subject's feelings:

> The term I would suggest to describe it is the structure of feeling: it is as firm and definite as the 'structure' suggests, yet it operates in the most delicate and intangible parts of our activity. In one sense, this structure of feeling is the culture of the period, it is the particular living result of all elements of the general organisation … I do not mean that the structure of feeling, any more than the social character, is possessed in the same way by the many individuals in the community. But I think it is a very deep and very wide position, in all actual communities, precisely because it is on it that communication depends. And what is particularly interesting is that it does not seem to be, in any formal sense, learned. (Williams 2011: 69)

Williams describes the structure of feeling as a felt sense of the quality of life at a particular time and place, and he connects it to gradual change and to generation: 'We are usually most aware of this when we notice the contrast between generations, who never quite talk "the same language"' (2011: 68). Structures of feeling may change over generations, they may take on different forms in different segments in society, and there may be several structures of feelings in a society at the same time.

In spite of its holistic character, Williams' concept seems to provide us with some smaller jigsaw pieces, explicitly detached from the idea that the material structures necessarily 'come first'. He insists emphatically on the interconnectedness of different processes in society: historical processes are complex wholes where each part needs to be understood for what it is, but it is the interaction, interpretation and feedback between them that leads to transformation: 'A keyword is *pattern*—it is with that any useful cultural analysis begins, and with its relationships to other patterns, which may sometimes reveal unexpected identities and correspondences in hitherto separately considered activities' (Williams 2011: 67). He opposes the idea of separating a concept of 'reality' from subject—as subjects are in themselves realities and expressions of society, not something that should be related to a social world *outside* itself. Thus, human experience is both objective and subjective in one inseparable process:

> It is right to recognise that we became human individuals in terms of a social process, but still individuals are unique, through a particular heredity, expressed in a particular history. And the point about this uniqueness is that it is creative as well as created: new forms can flow from this particular form, and extend in the whole organisation, which is in any case being constantly renewed and changed as unique individuals inherit it and continue it. … In practical terms I think such approaches will be the kind of study of patterns and relationships, in a whole process, which we have defined as the analysis of culture. There, in the practice of creation, communication and the making of institutions, is the common process of personal and social growth. (Williams 2011: 125–126)

Williams is primarily writing about art and culture; however, he also includes the psychological organisation of the subject in this constant renewing of society. The re-creation of meaning is done both by the society as a whole and by every single individual. The idea that changes can happen on any level of society is particularly relevant to my argument about the generative role of feelings of gender. No structure has priority and subtle changes may take place before they are properly understood. Williams offers the example of gradual changes in literary style. Such small elements of qualitative changes are not necessarily epiphenomena to institutional changes or just accidental variation. They are social in two ways: they are 'changes of the present' and they are effective before they are classified and understood (Williams 1977: 132–133). Williams' concept of structure of feeling, his take on incremental changes and how they can happen anywhere in a system are highly generative ideas for my analysis of how patterns of feelings in different generations, genders and classes represent an agency that may contribute in creative ways to the gradual change of gendered practices. However, the concept of feelings needs more psychological elaboration in order to become operative in a study of lived lives.

Socialisation and Desire

In psychoanalytic theory, on the level of individual psychology, we find compatible ideas about the connection between the self and the world in the work of the German-American psychoanalyst Hans Loewald. Loewald does not start by separating the inner world of the subject from outer reality. On the contrary, in the psychological organisation of the subject—ego, reality, objects and drives—they are created at the same time, in a process where a unitary whole is gradually differentiated by the subject. In this process many versions of both ego and reality will be created and, unless fixations happen, this will allow for a flexible ego-reality integration where earlier versions will remain alive as dynamic resources in later versions (Loewald 1980: 20). This means that the qualities of inner and outer are not given in any direct empirical sense, but are elaborated by the subject in 'a lifelong process in which not only the meaning but also the constitution and organization of inner and outer are negotiated' (Chodorow 2003: 903).

It is the work of Hans Loewald and Nancy Chodorow who in particular have informed my understanding of the continuous and creative interchange between the conscious and the unconscious. In their perspective the unconscious is not entirely equated with dynamically repressed emotions and fantasies, since the unconscious is also seen as a creative and generative part of our psychological organisation. This makes us co-creators of meaning and reality, not passive victims of the world. Neither Loewald nor Chodorow's vision is to replace unconscious life with conscious, but rather to infuse and integrate unconscious life in the conscious. It is this infusion and integration that gives conscious life its depth, texture and richness. Fantasy and reality come to resonate in a way where fantasy deepens and enriches the experience of reality, and reality keeps us rooted and connected in the world (Chodorow 1999: 248). The constant intertwining of the conscious, the preconscious and unconscious, of past and present, self and reality, subject and object are captured by the concept of transference. In Chodorow's words, transference is the phenomena 'that we personally endow, animate, and tint, emotionally and through fantasy, the cultural, linguistic, interpersonal, cognitive, and embodied world we experience' and, by this process, 'any single thought or feeling simultaneously creates and embeds itself in both realities' (Chodorow 1999: 244, 14). Thus, feelings are always part of experienced meanings, of the ways in which the subject makes sense—or cannot make sense—of things.

Nancy Chodorow has argued that Hans Loewald together with Erik H. Erikson and others can be seen as representatives of a specific American 'intersubjective school of ego psychology', which combines an understanding of the ego functions as integrating and synthesising experience in a creative way, with a relational perspective that sees the self as developed through interpersonal relations and by processes of transference between subject and object (Chodorow 2004). This ego-psychological and object-relational perspective where development is not only seen in terms of instinctual drives or universal conditions for subject formation, but also in terms of relational attachment and culture, and where the unconscious is not only understood as the dynamically repressed, but also as a part of the self that organises and may enrich experience and inform creativity and agency, has been criticised for severing the critical potential in Freud's theory of desire. Psychoanalytic perspectives indebted to Lacan reject the notions of ego and reality, and talk instead about a radical difference between the conscious and the unconscious. The unconscious is here seen as a site formed by the prohibition and repressing of desire, and it can only express itself in enigmatic and symptomatic ways that are not translatable to consciousness. Whereas conscious identity is doomed to be expressed through language, social categories and norms, 'the unconscious constantly reveals the "failure" of identity' (Rose 1986: 90). As subjects, split and cast in socially defined identities, we will always lack something, and the pressure from unconscious desire will push us towards activity, but we do not know what we are looking for and we will never find it other than in momentary and partial ways.

A problem in conceiving of consciousness and the unconscious as radically separated systems of meaning is that it leads into a dualism of conformity and non-conformity. The possibility of reflection and agency as sources for change is dismissed as it is only unsocialised and unsocialisable desire that may represent resistance against the social because it is outside the symbolic realm (see also McNay 2004; Layton 2004 and Woodward 2015 for similar critiques). But as Erikson, Fromm and Williams insist, society not only represents pressure and pain for the subject, it also represents possibilities and pleasure. Conversely, Lynne Layton has argued that the unconscious is also infected by the social: it is neither a space free of norms nor a space that can solely be conceptualised as resistant to norms (Layton 2002, 2004). Her concept of 'the normative unconscious' refers to the splitting-off of feelings, behaviours and thoughts when they conflict with particular social norms connected to gender, class and ethnicity, and therefore are deemed unacceptable to those on whom one depends for love. Williams also argues that most human actions will combine conformity and non-conformity in a way that does not fit into a model of either/or of conscious confinement and unconscious protest, and these actions must be analysed concretely and over time to decide their character and outcome (Williams 2011: 117). Such combinations may represent small but desired steps of action, and even when they look rather conformist, they may still lead to change in a more long-term perspective. In particular, the dynamics between generations indicate how a series of actions that, seen independently, look only adaptive may in the long run become one of the conditions for change. Instead of understanding socialisation and desire as opposing forces, we may think in terms of 'socialised desire', which places the subject in a generative and creative role that combines adaption, defensive reactions and change. Within this framework it is possible to understand the conscious, preconscious and unconscious as different levels of meaning that can float into each other, without also dismissing the existence of unconscious conflict and forbidden desires. By seeing self and reality as an original unity that is later differentiated and continuously reshaped throughout life, it is possible to see the subject not only as either conforming or protesting, but also as continuously in search of and as a creator of intermediate solutions in his or her life. In this view, the subject is simultaneously socialised, desiring and agential.

The blending of the conscious and the unconscious, of meaning and feeling, of conformity and non-conformity, of subject, identity and reality represents a perspective that renders a flexible and useful way to think about my data. What I see here is that feelings of gender change over lifetimes and between generations, and become part of the specific agency we see in each generation. A radical critique of the repressive society or an accidental acting-out of unconscious conflicts is seldom what informs agency and change of the generations in my study, but is rather a more gradual and varied response to the historically framed experience and possibilities and new ways of adapting to a given context, whether it is done with inattentiveness, hope, ambivalence or pain. This perspective makes it possible to describe and understand the strivings of the subject in a cultural and historical context instead of analysing it in terms of universal conflicts between the social order, power regimes and unruly desire.

Feelings and Relations

In an object-relational perspective, feelings stem from and are shaped in and through relations. In particular, but not exclusively, this begins in our first relations of love and dependency. Early identifications with caretakers, or aspects of them, are the way in which the human subject and psychic reality first come into being: Melanie Klein stated that object-relations are the centre of emotional life. The subject's feeling of its own self and others is differentiated from these early experiences with relations through processes of transference, projections and introjective fantasies—feelings of who I am, who I can or cannot be in relationships with others:

> The child, by internalizing aspect of the parent, also internalizes the parent's image of the child—an image that is mediated to the child in the thousand different ways of being handled, bodily and emotionally ... The bodily handling of and concern with the child, the manner in which the child is fed, touched, cleaned, the way it is looked at, talked to, called by name, recognized and re-recognized—all these and many other ways of communication with the child, and communicating to him his identity, sameness, unity, and individuality, shape and mould him so that he can begin to identify himself, to feel and recognize himself as one and as separate from others and yet with others. (Loewald 1980: 229–230)

The basic feelings of self and others are prior to mental representations and language and will become part of what Christopher Bollas has coined the individual's 'unthought known' (Bollas 1987: 280). The unthought known is an operational logic of 'being and relating': through countless intersubjective exchanges with the infant and its object world, 'sometimes in tranquillity, often in intense conflict', the unthought known comes to constitute the subject's ego-structure. Thus, 'ego-structure is a trace of a relationship' (Bollas 1987: 51–60). This also means that agency is formed and takes shape in relationships (Layton 2004: 47). Layton's concept of the normative unconscious refers to relational conflicts where the child split off aspects of itself to maintain love, and where these aspects will survive in the unconscious and be seen in behavioural tendencies to split, disavow or idealise what the child was refused to be. Thus, splits are produced by unmourned losses. Self-esteem problems generally reflect difficulties in negotiating a sense of agency while maintaining connections to others (Layton 1998: 17; 2004: 32). However, in contrast to Lacanian theories, where processes of splitting and disavowal of the other are seen as the universal conditions for subject formation, the relational and temporal perspective inherent in a object-relational understanding includes an intersubjective space that opens up the possibility for communication, mutual love, recognition, creativity and agency (Layton 1998).

The tension between self and others represents a developmental logic where the child learns to navigate between the intrapsychic worlds of object-relations and the interrelational world of real subjects (Winnicott 1971; Benjamin 1995). Thus, the relational world gradually becomes both internally object-relational and interpersonally intersubjective: we may become both 'love objects' and 'like subjects' to each other, as Benjamin (1995) coins it. This means that whenever two people interact, there are at least two self–other psyches at play. If the inner objects do not overwhelm and invade us, we may experience a non-narcissistic interaction based on mutual recognition. The more we are able to see the other as a whole and separate subject, the more we can also integrate negative feelings we may have towards the inner object. Coming to terms with the internal and external parents is a major developmental project and a life-long internal process for most people (Chodorow 2012: 47). Winnicott points out that for the child, it is the intrapsychic aggression towards the object that makes it possible to recognise the other as a like subject, as it gives the child the possibility to experience that the other continues to exist in spite of the child's aggression. Through this, narcissism or omnipotence is broken: there are others out there with a separate centre of existence and their own agendas. Benjamin states that in this way destruction is 'the Other of recognition' (1995: 48). The capacity to deal with both kinds of relationships is developmentally intertwined and therefore the pains of loss and the pleasures of attachment are equally determinant in subject formation (Layton 1998: 18–19). It never becomes a harmony, but implies continuous disruption and repair.

In the intrapsychic as well as in the interpersonal space, the sense of self and others is constructed through transference, which includes the universal psychic capabilities of the human mind like positive and negative *identifications* (I see myself and the other as alike in some respect—and I can like it or not like it), *introjections* (I see something of the other as part of myself), *projections* (I place something of myself in the other), affective *ambivalence* (I love and hate the other at the same time), *disidentifications* (this is not me!), *splitting* (dividing things into only good and only bad and projecting the aspects onto others or myself), *disavowal* (refusing to recognise the reality of a traumatic experience) and *idealisation* (aggrandising and exalting the other and thereby also enlarging myself).[3] These

[3] See Laplanche and Pontalis (1973) for more detailed definitions.

processes continue to create and re-create our psychic reality throughout life. Some of them exist to defend us from anxiety and pain; others, like identification and introjection, may also enrich our agency or sense of subjectivity. Furthermore, identifications are not a coherent relational system—we may identify with aspects of different persons, in negative and positive ways at the same time (Laplanche and Pontalis 1973: 207–209). They are ways of taking parts of the other into our selves.

If feelings come from and are reworked through relations, this adds a dimension of temporality to the different sociocultural locations. This is a point that has been developed especially by Lynne Layton (1998, 2004), who underscores how relatedness, agency and feelings take shape in particular cultural fields framed by class, race and gender. This makes some versions of subjectivities acceptable and others not, and generates particular patterns of conflicts and defences:

> We are born into families with their own histories and ways of mediating culture, and so we immediately engage in particular patterns of relating. The ways those patterns are internalized is conditioned by the accidents of gender, race, and class and by the power differentials that structure them at any given moment … It is also conditioned by the bodies and temperaments of individuals and those with whom they come in contact. The meanings these bodies, temperaments, and other individual identity elements take on are not outside of culture; they are culture … Subjects idiosyncratically make meaning of, identify with, disidentify with, take up parts of, or modify these positions in accord with on-going relational experience. (Layton 1998: 27–28)

An object-relational perspective is intergenerational in itself: it concerns change and transmission between generations in the light of changing sociocultural contexts which encounter the different generations at different points in their biographies. This means that the feelings that are experienced by the subject in any given situation will be historical in two ways: in the *biographical* dimension, where feelings from earlier points in life will be carried with the individual into new situations and continuously reworked; and the *contextual* dimension, where a specific historical and political context will frame the reworking of conscious and unconscious feelings in the individual.

Gender and Feelings

Feelings of gender are also products of intrapsychic and intersubjective relations. From an object-relational perspective, gender involves both sexual object choices and the emergence of a gendered self, which again has multiple constitutive components that may vary from individual to individual and also over time. Gender is a 'soft assembly', as Adrienne Harris has called it, constructed, assembled and maintained differently in different persons (Harris 2008: 40). Chodorow (2012) suggests four components that are often central: the psychic creation of *bodily* experience, the experience of intrapsychic and intersubjective *self–other* relations, the transference of linguistic and *cultural categories*, and the *affective tonalities* explicitly connected to gendered fantasy content. These components will come together in each individual's personal animation of gender, 'with a characteristic emotional tonality and an organization designed to manage and contain particular anxieties and defenses' (Chodorow 2012: 146). Relational feminist psychoanalytic theories maintain that gender is a cultural as well as a personal construction (Layton 1998; Chodorow 1999). It is seen simultaneously as an effect of discursive positions and as elements of each individual's sense of self and his or her specific relationships with others. The personal images of gender gained through relational experiences, and the emotional qualities that are invested in them, do not necessarily conform to dominant cultural norms. Continuous and ongoing identity work is necessary to make the inner and the outer world connect (Nielsen 1996, 1999; Chodorow 1999). Every psychological formation of gender is unique, but it is also the case that a shared social and historical context may create social patterns in gendered subjectivities—between or within gender groups—because the society and the kinds of families where subjectivities are created are gendered in historical and cultural ways (Layton 2004; Roseneil 2007). As Chodorow (2012) formulates it, gender development is characterised by clinical individuality, universal psychic processes and social patterning.

The move towards thinking in terms of processes of identification rather than of identity mentioned earlier has been prominent in gender theory over the last 25 years. In particular, constructing gender identities in a binary system with different developmental routes for women and men has increasingly been seen as outdated, also in versions where they are not understood as universal, but historically contingent stories (Chodorow 1978; Nielsen and Rudberg 1989). The focus is not on gender identity as a specific content, but rather on processes of identifications, which may more often than not traverse biological and cultural gender dichotomies. In addition, relational psychoanalyst feminists today question the presumption that internally consistent gender identities are possible or even desirable. However, the rejection of the binary gender identity model has in this strain of thought not led to a dismissal of ideas of development or the significance of gender differences in such developmental processes. As Jessica Benjamin (1995) has argued, if the category of identification is seen as relevant for theories of gender, it must also be taken into account how such gender categories take hold in the psyche. The question has rather moved from taking difference as the point of departure to seeing how difference is constructed, not only culturally, but also personally. In Benjamin's words, the notion of psychologically 'coming to terms with [sexual] difference' has given way to exploring the ways in which perceptions of the body and the sense of self and others 'come to *figure* difference' (Benjamin 1995: 49). This places the question of gender differences in a relational space, which also includes how gender was built into the parents' own psychic worlds:

> Any term that a child learns is learned in the context of the parent's unconscious and her or his own particularized femininity and masculinity, which is itself emotionally cast, shaped by fantasy, and includes many elements of affective tonality and context that the parent has built into gender. (Chodorow 2012: 145)

The generational perspective makes visible that gender also emerges in same-sex relations, not only within the gender polarity. For instance, a women's positive or negative experience of her body may be organised around reproductive issues or sexuality, or both. A man may feel his 'masculinity' threatened when confronted with powerful women or because he feels inadequate in relation to other men, or both (Corbett 2009; Chodorow 2012). By locating the formation of sexuality and gender in a relational space, 'sexual difference' in fact becomes less absolute and more complex than when differences lead back to a single principle of binarity, whether based on anatomy (Freud) or commanded by language (Lacan). The relational roots imply that even though personal gender identities will always have multiple components and represent some kind of psychological compromise formations, they are not always or necessarily defensive and pathogenic symptoms of splitting and repudiation of otherness, which is the dominant perspective in poststructuralist accounts (Butler 1990; Goldner 1991; Corbett 2009). Gender identities may, depending on the way they are culturally constructed and personally formed, be more or less hurtful, and in benign cases they may contain pleasurable elements that people may want to hold on to (Benjamin 1995; Layton 1998; Harris 2002, 2008).

Temporality in Theories

Psychoanalytic theory places sexuality and gender among the most important dimensions of human development. How this should be understood has been the target of heated debates ever since Freud first formulated his theory about the Oedipal phase, where the incest taboo installs masculinity and femininity as complementary psychological structures based on the identification with the same-sex parent and love of the opposite-sex parent. As is well known, this model has been heavily criticised for its inherent biologism, universalism, binarity, phallocentrism and heteronormativity. Later theories have challenged the Freudian idea that psychological gender differences are non-existent before the Oedipal phase and argue that differences in heterosexual masculine and feminine personalities are better explained by early object-relations and the ways in which gender arrangements frame processes of separation-individuation for girls and boys (Dinnerstein 1976; Chodorow 1978; Benjamin 1988). Newer gender theories have questioned the binary opposition between desire and identification and have argued that both fathers and mothers alike may be 'love objects' and 'like subjects' for the child (Benjamin 1995; Chodorow 1999). The different models have emerged as theoretical alternatives in academic debates about psychoanalysis and gender, and the latest one is more in tune with recent relational thinking as well as with recent gender theory. However, one important point to notice in the context of a generational study is that different models of gender development have been formulated at different historical points in time. To what extent do different theories of psychological gender match different and historically delimited patterns of feelings? May psychological theories (and other theories about the social world) be seen and used as historical formations, not only in the sense that they reveal the cultural, normative and theoretical assumptions of their time, but also as sources of information about empirical patterns that later disappeared or became less poignant?[4] Psychological theories are made not only for internal academic use, but also as tools to describe clinical situations. Hence, theoretical models of gender and heterosexual development can also be seen as attempts to describe different figurations of gender that emerged in different historical and familial contexts. Such figurations represent what in the context of this book I call differently historically shaped 'structures of feeling' connected to gender. Maybe gender identities were, in fact, more binary and less fluid if we go back half a century? Is it the theoretical idea of stable identities that is wrong or have such identities simply become less frequent?[5] Because the childhoods of the three generations in our study took place in the same span of time as when these psychoanalytical models of gender development were formulated, criticised and dismissed, these questions beg to be asked.

I will return to the question of the possible connections between psychology, history and theory in Chap. 9, where I present some of the most influential theories of psychoanalysis and gender conceived in the historical period of our three generations, and see to what degree they fit

[4] See also Layton (2002) on this experience of how 'outdated' theories may fit some patients in the clinical setting well.

[5] Stable identities are not the same as coherent identities, which no psychoanalytic theory would assume. It was Freud who with his concept of the unconscious was the first to argue that the human psyche is internally contradictory. Thus, the self will always be in discord with itself in more or less painful ways.

the changes and continuities in psychological gender that emerge from our study. In raising these questions I am neither saying that we should assume that all theories will always be empirically true during the period in which they were conceived, nor that theoretical and normative critique is redundant or worthless. Rather, I am arguing that it may be useful to include historical perspectives in the ongoing theoretical, philosophical and normative debates. The current focus in feminist theory on the situatedness of knowledge that emphasises the importance of place, space and variation quite often appears to be oblivious to the dimension of temporality. Without historical framing, critiques of universalism and essentialism, for instance, may become universalist and essentialist themselves.

3

Methodology and its Temporality

Temporality is a crucial dimension of the topic and methodology in this book. The book is based on interviews that are up to 25 years old and most of the issues the informants talked about had taken place many years prior to the time of the interview. The oldest informant was 92 when we interviewed him in 1991, while the youngest informants were 18. The generational transmission is in itself temporal and so are the different ages from which the generations talk about themselves and each other. Also included in the study is a longitudinal dimension of lived time as the youngest generation was followed over a timespan of 20 years (1991–2011). Finally, time has infiltrated the research process itself. The initial research questions and the interview guides were conceived in 1991 and the interview guides were extended and modified in 2001 and 2011. The interviews have been interpreted at different points in time and through different foci influenced by changing theoretical paradigms, by having been presented to different audiences and by the ageing of the researchers themselves. This chapter will dive into these temporal issues, provide information about the sample and the way it is presented in the book, discuss the concept of pattern and, finally, how it is possible to know about feelings of gender from old interviews.

The Study and the Sample

Monica Rudberg and I began the study 'Young Women and Men in Three Generations' in 1991. The focus of the project was to explore how cultural modernisation had been associated with the psychological project of becoming adults in three generations. We wanted to understand more of the interactions between cultural and personal gender in a process of change in order to grasp how not only cultural norms but also subjectivities are historically embedded and, more specifically, how generational relationships in the family contributed to these changes on a psychological level. We also wanted to understand more about what different class cultures and youth cultural identities meant for these processes.[1] It originated as two partly independent projects: one about young women (conducted by Monica Rudberg and myself) and one about young men (a PhD project conducted by Kari Vik Kleven).[2]

The project was initiated by two weeks of ethnographic observation in five classrooms in two high schools in Oslo in 1991. One school, old and centrally located in Oslo, had a very good academic reputation and the students mainly came from middle-class families where the parents received higher education, but there were also a small number of students from working-class and lower middle-class families. The other school was a suburban school with a broader recruitment profile. We found middle-class students here too, but the majority were working class and lower middle class. All the students were in their last year of high

[1] The study has been presented earlier in a book in Norwegian (Nielsen and Rudberg 2006) and in several English articles, among others Nielsen (2003, 2004), Nielsen et al. (2012), Nielsen and Rudberg (2000, 2007), Rudberg and Nielsen (2005, 2011, 2012) and Rudberg (1995, 2009).

[2] As mentioned in the Acknowledgements, the PhD project was not completed. For many years the interviews with the male chain laid untouched as Monica and I had more than enough to do with our own data. For this reason, most of the previous publications from the projects are about women only. We did, however, take care to get the youngest men included in the second round of interviews in 2001. In around 2008 Monica started to work with Kari's old data. Not all data was possible to retrieve and for this reason we have less information about the men in some respects. Three articles about the male chains appeared in the following years (Rudberg 2009; Rudberg and Nielsen 2011, 2012). However, the analyses in this book are the first to see the dynamics *between* women and men in a generational perspective.

school and following the general academic track.[3] The vast majority of high schools in Norway are free and, at the time we did our study, admission depended partly on grades from junior high school and partly on where the students lived, giving priority to students living nearest to the school. In 1991 almost 40 per cent of the youth cohorts in Oslo attended the academic track in high school and another well 40 per cent attended the vocational track or other schools; thus, the students in our classes can be described as ordinary Oslo youth of that time, but selected from among those who took the academic track in high school and with variation according to social background.

The classroom observations will not be used in this book, but they are still important to mention since they were the basis that we used to select the informants in the youngest generation. After the observation period we invited approximately half of the students, selected in order to secure a variance in relation to social class, marital status of their parents, choice of academic subjects and activity profile in the classroom, for a life historical interview. Later we interviewed the girls' mothers and maternal grandmothers, and the boys' fathers and paternal grandfathers. Because the focus of the study was generational changes in the youth period for women and men, the single-gendered chains made sense. As we later became more interested in the family dynamics, it made less sense. However, as all generations were interviewed about their relationships with both of their parents and their spouses (where relevant), the relationships with the other gender is not absent.

Since it turned out that not all in the two older generations wanted to take part in the study (in particular, many of the fathers declined, and fewer of the grandfathers than of the grandmothers were still alive), we ended up with a sample of 22 female and 12 male chains consisting of either two or three generations.[4] In 2001 many of the youngest

[3] Norway has nine years of compulsory school and three years of voluntarily high school which is specialised into different tracks: some academic (the general academic track preparing for university admission) and some vocational. All the students in our study followed the academic track, but a few boys (among them Erik and Glenn, who are analysed in this book) were recruited from the sports track, which also counts as academic. The students enter high school at the age of 15–16, so the students were 18–19 when we interviewed them.

[4] A total of 32 women and 25 men in the youngest generation were interviewed in 1991 at the age of 18. Of these, 19 girls and 17 men were re-interviewed in 2001. In this book, however, we have

Table 3.1 Overview over the informants and interviews on which this book is based

88 informants / *121 interviews*	*Oldest generation* 21 informants, born 1899–1927	*Middle generation* 33 informants, born 1919–1953	*Youngest generation* 34 informants, all born 1971/1972
Interviews 1991 (88 in total)	14 women 7 men (between 64 and 92 years old)	21 women 12 men (between 38 and 72 years old)	22 women 12 men (18 years old)
Interviews 2001 (25 in total)	–	–	19 women 6 men (30 years old)
Interviews 2011 (8 in total)	–	–	5 women 3 men (40 years old)

See the Appendix for a more detailed overview over family chains and distributions on social class

informants, now approaching 30 years of age, were interviewed a second time, and in 2011 eight informants, now approaching 40, had a third interview. All together this added up to 88 informants and 121 interviews (Table 3.1):

In 2001 we interviewed all the informants we managed to get in contact with and who consented (some of the men declined). In 2011 it was our own work situation that limited the number of informants we could interview. It would have been better to include more, but research projects running over several decades must live with compromises. We prioritised at that point to achieve a balance both in relation to gender, the schools they had attended and their class background. All those we approached in 2011 agreed to be interviewed once more.

The interview method consisted of semi-structured life-phase interviews focusing on childhood, youth and the transition to adulthood.

---

only included the cases of the 22 young women and the 12 young men whose parents and/or grandparents were also interviewed.

Biographical narrative interview methods had not yet gained the attention as a method in the social sciences that it received during the 1990s (Josselson and Lieblich 1993; Chamberlayne et al. 2000; Hollway and Jefferson 2000; Wengraf 2001). However, we also deliberately chose a semi-structured interview format because we wanted to compare information about childhood and youth from the different generations more systematically. For the two oldest generations of women, the interview started with filling in lifelines and genealogical trees.[5] The interview guide used in the 1991 interviews was the same for all generations (with some adaption to their age and stage of life) and focused on how they remembered their childhood and youth in terms of family life and relationships with parents, grandparents, siblings and friends, as well as activities, play, school, choice of education and political and cultural engagement in youth, description of self and others, the coming of age, the body, youth culture, courtship, love and sexuality, attitudes to gender and gender equality, and how they shared the work in their adult family. The interviews of the youngest generation at 30 and 40 years of age had three aims: to get information about what had happened in their lives since the last interview; to see whether they answered differently to some of the same questions that they were asked in the interviews at 18; and to check whether they could remember what they had answered to selected items at 18. In this way we could partly compensate for the methodological problem in the design that the two oldest generations were interviewed about their childhood and youth as adults, whereas the youngest generation was interviewed while they were still in the midst of it. As will be discussed further in Chap. 8, the concurrence between what they said at 18 and later was surprisingly good, and even though they had forgotten

[5] The interviews typically lasted between two and four hours and were tape-recorded. All interviews from 1991 were fully transcribed, while the interviews in 2001 and 2011 were summarised and only partly transcribed. The lifeline technique was simply that we drew a line on a piece of paper starting with the year the informant was born and ending in 1991. Then we asked the informant to fill in important life events and life transitions. The genealogical tree was a chart of names, years of birth and occupations of parents, grandparents and siblings of both the informant and the spouse(s). The lifelines and genealogical trees turned out to be of incredible value for orientation in relation to what was told later in the interview. It was Hedvig Ekerwald who taught us these techniques, for which we are still grateful. Unfortunately the lifeline and genealogical chart do not exist for the male chains, so for this reason our information about the men is sometimes less exact (for instance, we have less information about the jobs of their wives).

some of the details they had provided at 18, very few came up with completely new stories.

The way in which the study was designed and the time and place it was carried out had some consequences for the sample that should be kept in mind because it delimits the range of validity of the study. First, Norway is a small country with a population that was ethnically rather homogeneous until the late twentieth century and until recently the absolute majority of people were of Norwegian and European descent. There were (and still is) a small minority of indigenous population of Sami people from the northern part of Scandinavia and a varying but small number of people of Romani descent. As late as 1970, only 1.5 per cent of the population consisted of immigrants and their children, most of them from other European countries. The figure had risen to around four per cent when we did our interviews in 1991.[6] This specific demographic history explains why there were very few immigrants and non-white students in Norwegian schools at the time we did our study and why, as a consequence, the sample in the youngest generation consists of only white people of Scandinavian descent.

Second, it turned out that all the students we picked for interviews identified as heterosexual both in the first, second and third interviews. In the pre-queer times of the initial interviews there was generally little attention paid to sexual diversity or fluidity. Homosexuality was not illegal in Norway at this time, but it was seldom disclosed in classrooms either.[7] Thus, it was a dimension that was difficult to take into consideration when selecting our sample, but we have to admit that it was not something to which we as (heterosexual) researchers gave much thought either (see also Griffin 2000 on this). Issues regarding sexual orientation were not touched upon in the interviews in 1991, but were taken up in the 2001 interviews with the youngest generation. Here we asked about

[6] From 2000 the immigration numbers increased rapidly. In 2015 15.6 per cent of the population consisted of immigrants and their children, and only half of them were from other European countries (Statistics Norway https://www.ssb.no/en/).

[7] Sex between men was prohibited through legislation in Norway until 1972, which was very late compared to the other Scandinavian countries. In practice, however, it was only subject to prosecution in cases where there was a big age difference between the men or if the sex was exposed publicly. Sex between women has never been illegal in Norway (Rydström 2011).

their experiences with and attitudes to non-normative sexualities, and what they remembered about this from the time when they were in high school (see Chap. 7).

Third, since we chose classes of the academic track in the two city high schools, the sample turned out to be characterised by a high degree of social mobility across the three generations. Whereas the vast majority of our youngest generation received higher education, many of them had parents who grew up in working-class or lower middle-class families, most of them in Oslo. A majority of the grandparents (12 out of 21) grew up in the countryside as sons and daughters of farmers, fishermen and smallholders, and only three grew up in the bigger cities of Norway (see the Appendix for details). Thus, the geographical mobility happened with the oldest generation and the mainly upwardly social mobility happened with the middle generation. This is not an unusual generational trajectory for these generations as Norway was late to be industrialised and urbanised (see Chap. 4). In particular, it illustrates how close in time traditional rural life is to modern urban life in Norway. Many of our young informants had grandparents who had grown up in environments that reminded us of rural life in the nineteenth century. Given the character of our data, the research question was extended to explore how processes of cultural modernisation *and* social mobility had been associated with the psychological project of becoming adults in three generations.

Analysing Patterns

In psychosocial studies today the most used methodological approach is to employ either biographical narrative interviews or clinical vignettes and explore single cases in their richness and complexity in order to see how specific societal conditions are processed, adapted to or protested against by the person in question (see, for instance, Roseneil 2006; Layton 2010; Rudberg and Nielsen 2012; Hollway 2015). I have chosen another approach in this book: to look at the whole sample and find the commonalities in patterns of feelings between the singular cases, and then try to see the connection between these patterns and societal conditions that formed them and on which they also may have a transformatory effect.

As argued with Eric Fromm in Chap. 2, analysing the individual case and analysing patterns are not mutually exclusive alternatives, but the choice of focus depends on the purpose of the analysis. Both approaches have their limitations: the single-case approach may lose sight of the general patterns that in their aggregated form may become a social force, while the whole-sample approach does not explain the variation and may lose out on the individual context and specificity. However, since the single cases are the foundation of the patterns of meanings and feelings, they must first be summarised and analysed in their individual specificity in a whole-sample approach. Thus, the patterns that emerge in the analyses in Chaps. 5, 6 and 7 were preceded by thorough work on the level of the singular cases. But in order to make visible the shared patterns, much of the individual context and variation had to be excluded in the subsequent process. Any found pattern can always become more specified by highlighting the differences within; however, categories are analytical constructs and their usefulness will depend on the theoretical potentials of the category in combination with the research question rather than the degree to which they grasp empirical variation in any absolute sense.

So what is a pattern in a whole-sample analysis? A pattern in the context of this study means similarities across individual cases along a certain dimensions of meaning, like feelings about parents, bodies and sexuality, ways of organising work and care, ways to reflect on gender, and the ways in which all these things may interact. A pattern may exist even if it does not cover everything or is contextual-dependent. This is obvious in quantitative studies, but in my view the same is the case for patterns of meaning in qualitative studies (Nielsen 1995). It may be equally important to see the similarities in the seemingly different as seeing the differences in the seemingly alike. As illustrated by chaos theory, levels of order and disorder in complex and non-linear systems are dependent on the scale employed: in a close view, patterns may disappear, but they may re-emerge when seen from a greater distance and vice versa (Kamminga 1990). In this way identifying patterns is both dependent on regularities in the studied object itself and a view from the outside that makes the patterns visible. Here I take a critical-hermeneutic position, trying to avoid both the extreme naturalist and extreme constructivist positions. The object of study has its own ontology, but the scale or the approach of the researcher also conditions the result of the analysis (Nielsen 1995, 1999).

In our analyses of the narratives of the three generations, much of the work has been about finding the distances from which significant and meaningful generational patterns emerge. Sometimes a pattern becomes visible because there are marked quantitative differences between the generations. An example of this is the mother–daughter relationship, where nobody in the oldest generation and very few in the youngest generation have negative descriptions of their mothers, compared to the middle generation, where this is the case with more than half of the informants. However, since we are working with a qualitative sample, significant quantitative differences do not in themselves give evidence of general patterns, as they may be purely accidental. Thus, also a numerically based pattern must be argued to make sense in connection with other dimensions of the data or find support in relation to what has been found in comparable studies. In the case of the shifting mother–daughter relationships, the found pattern makes sense with regard to both the structural changes in women's lives in these three generations and the ways in which they engage in heterosexual relationships. These things also fit with bits and pieces of other studies, even if these other studies do not describe all three generations. Since numbers in themselves are not the main argument in qualitative studies, it is consequently possible to argue conversely that a pattern can also be significant in cases where it is only found in a limited number of informants. An example of this is the way some of the men in the oldest generation talk with compassion about their too-hardworking mothers. Less than half of them mention this. However, seen in relation to the invisibility of the mothers in the narratives of the other men and compared to the generally elaborated description of fathers, the connection between femininity and weakness emerges as a generational pattern among the oldest men. The arguments almost all the men have about not wanting their wives to work makes this connection even clearer, and this pattern is not seen in the younger generations. Since frequencies are only—and not even necessarily—part of identifying patterns of meaning, I have abstained, also for the sake of readability, from operating with exact numbers in my analyses, but instead have used rough amounts like 'few', 'many', 'a majority' and so on. When it comes to comparing details in the empirical Chaps. 5, 6 and 7 with other studies, I have mainly used other Nordic studies, whereas the whole 'gestalt' in Chap. 8 is compared with selected generational studies from Britain. The many 'see also…' references are used to indicate when a found pattern of our analyses matches findings in comparable studies.

Comparing Generations

Generational studies have several methodological issues to them that need to be addressed, but to which it is not always possible to find good solutions. The notion of 'historical generation' is not the same as the concept of 'cohort', as a generation will most often include several cohorts and not necessarily with any clear border: generations tend to be 'clearest at their centers, but blurred and fuzzy at the edges' (Rosow, cited in Alwin and McCammon 2004: 41). The concept of generations becomes even more fuzzy when they are used in generational studies, partly because the design itself separates what is a gradual historical development into more or less incidental 'generations' and partly because these generations will be broader the longer the distance to the anchor-generation. In our study, the youngest generation that is our anchor-generation represents a birth cohort (1971/1972), whereas the two older generations cover approximately 30 cohorts each. Most of the informants in the oldest generation are born between 1910 and 1925, most of the middle generation in the 1940s, but there is also an overlap among the men in the two eldest generations as two men from the middle generation in terms of age could have belonged to the oldest generation. Furthermore, as women tend to be younger than men when they have their first child, the mothers and grandmothers in our study belong on average to younger birth cohorts than the fathers and grandfathers. Yet, the middle generation may also be seen as a parental cohort since they all had a child within the same year, something that may have given them some similar experiences from the period in which their child grew up, despite their different ages. But this cohort effect is, of course, not relevant prior to their parenthood.

It has been argued that the imprecise concept of historical generations makes it difficult to connect it to social change and that the operative concept of cohort seems to be more straightforward. However, Alwin and McCammon (2004: 25, 27) also make the opposite argument: the concept of generation has more potential for understanding the origins and nature of social change as generations are more a matter of quality than degree. Even though cohort and generation are not the same, it may still be the case that cohort effects are 'given life' though interpretative and behavioural aspects of the generation. In this way the combination of cohort and generation may also contribute to a better understanding of the agency of a given cohort. This inclusive approach to cohort and generation makes sense in relation to our study. Some patterns emerge from informants in a generation clustering around certain birth cohorts, while others may emerge from informants sharing similar conditions or formative experiences as children and youth. Informants who are on the margins of these main clusters may show something important about the gradual character of the process of generational change: the oldest informants in the middle generations often combine patterns from the oldest and the middle generations, for instance, when it comes to obligations to their parents or the work ethic. This again leads to a perception in their children of having 'old parents' with different ideas and values than other parents, and by this the child may also have a modernising effect on the parents and contribute to further modifying them as border figures between historical generations. In this way one can argue that a generational data set with 'fuzzy edges' may actually be an advantage to understand the gradual emergence of generational patterns. Used with methodological precautions, the value of the study of intergenerational transmission in a historical context is that it may grasp some of the more elusive aspects of social reproduction and change. As Alwin and McCammon (2004: 42) conclude: 'Generations lack specific boundaries and are meaningful in their distinctiveness largely as subpopulations, but offer the potential of being used as powerful explanations in and of themselves for distinctive patterns of attitudes, beliefs, and behaviors'—and, once again, I would add feelings.

Another consequence of not being able to control the characteristics of the generational samples derived from the anchor generation is that the class composition of each generation becomes unequal. In our case the social composition of the different generational groups reflects the process of social mobility of these three generations: a majority in the oldest generation grew up in rural areas, the majority in the middle generation grew up urban working class, and the majority in the youngest generation grew up urban middle class. The slightly higher social profile among the women compared to the men in the youngest generation may illustrate that upward social mobility through the school system was a track generally used more by working-class girls than by working-class boys in the middle generation (see Chap. 4). Even though the imbalance in social profile between genders and generations reflects general aspects of the process of social transformation, it also indicates that comparisons between groups must be made with caution, in particular when it comes to distinguishing class differences from generational differences There is no doubt that the differences we found between the generations are accentuated by the imbalance of the geographical and social composition of the different generational groups. However, since the demographic movements in society during these three generations did increase the urban population and the number of people belonging to the middle classes, the class differences in fact reflect a generational change.

A third issue that complicates generational studies is determining what items it makes sense to compare. Because of structural and demographical changes, such as those related to increased standards of living, the increased level of general education and the increased prevalence of divorces, the same experiences in different generations of not getting an education, being poor or having divorced parents attain very different cultural and emotional meanings. It may make more sense to compare different items that address the same dimension of experienced meaning to achieve more relevant comparisons. Instead of comparing single items like the level of wealth or the number of divorces in the childhoods of the different generations, working on the level of context and meaning of the experience of poverty in the oldest generation and the experience of divorces in the youngest generation may be a more relevant comparison: as the oldest generation knew that poverty and the deaths of parents were calculated risks in life, so did their grandchildren know that parental divorces were, and that there were no relational safety nets against it. They learnt how to handle divorces in much the same way as their grandparents learned to handle the hardships of their childhood. The increased consciousness of the fragility of human relationships became the backdrop of life in the youngest generation. Whereas the conditions of life taught the oldest generation skills of frugality and modesty, the youngest generation learnt, for good or ill, to take different perspectives, to differentiate between different social relationships and norms, and to handle ambivalent feelings. As 18-year-olds, most of them had come to the conclusion that their parents were just not the right match.

Narratives in Time

All biographical interviewing raises the question about the relationship between lived life and told story, but this problem is amplified in a generational study where people are interviewed at different ages and with different degrees of distance to the issues they talk about. Memories are always reconstructions in the present of what happened in the past, and the narratives will therefore be characterised by selections, linking of memories, interpretations and chosen perspectives (Josselson and Lieblich 1993; Bruner 2003; Rosenthal 2004). Evidently, the stories of the informants' childhood, youth and family life are seen through discourses or 'lenses' that belong to different historical moments, some of them of more recent date than the time they are telling us about. For the eldest generation, such later lenses providing narrative perspectives are the increased standards of living, the possibilities for education and changed norms of morality. In particular, the men emphasise the moral decay in society, whereas the women are more occupied with the increased openness about sex and bodily functions, and the diminished social differences among people. Hardly any of the lenses of the older generation are present in the stories of the middle generation; instead, their narrative perspective highlights the increased enlightenment, the psychological approach and the norm of gender equality. Several of the women in the middle generation tell stories of 'coming out' as feminists, with somewhat ironic depictions of themselves as young girls. They often describe themselves as caricatures of teenage girls, very different from the oldest women who may talk about their youth with humour, joy or sorrow, but never with irony. The self-caricature may also be due to the fact that the women in the middle generation describe themselves much more as members of a specific generation—and their recollections of their own youth, as well as the interviewer's response to them, seem to merge with the media images of their generation as young people. In comparison, the older informants had neither this youth generational identity nor such a strong discourse about the historical period. 'The hard times' in the early 1930s seem to have a much more limited generational reference than the all-inclusive concept of 'the 1950s'.

Time also marks the interviews through specific narrative styles. Across generations there are different 'genres' at work in the ways in which the informants talk about the world and their selves. The oldest generation tends to construct their stories in a rather deterministic 'structuralist' way. As they often say: 'that was the way it was back then'. Many of them are good storytellers. They offer broad and generalised pictures of their family life, their activities and the community they grew up in, but also include many vivid details that almost evoke a feeling of standing in front of a naturalistic landscape painting:

> I must say that I grew up in a good home. I must say I did. And father was a carpenter, so we always had skies and ski sticks. I had an awfully long way to school, so in winter we went on our skies, if the snow was good. And we had sleighs, too. We lived close to the railway station, so when we went to school, we had to go all the way down into the valley, and across the river—I think we had a 6 km-long walk to school. (Ingrid, b. 1910)

It is the outer things that are made central: what one did, what happened, what one had and what one ate, often illustrated through concrete episodes and events. Much more often than the following generations, they talk in terms of a collective 'we'. The descriptive and non-individualist perspective is also seen in their evaluations, where nuances and reservations are seldom conveyed: things were either good or bad—and criticism of parents and homes are very rare. To say that you are discontented seems to go against deeply rooted norms of modesty; only war, death and illnesses can be openly lamented. This also reveals a clear distance from modern reflexivity and psychological discourse. When asked whether they ever experienced adolescence as a difficult time, the (rural) women would typically respond: 'We did not have so many problems in those times' or 'I can't remember that we had like puberty and all that stuff. I can't say I had that'. The old men talk in much of the same genre, but seem a bit more reticent than the old women. Their stories are abbreviated to their absolute essentials. However, the men more often tend to start their tale with the generation before their own—as if they need to place themselves within a larger ancestral network.

The non-individualist and emotionally low-key style of the oldest generation is echoed by the working-class men in the middle generation, who seem quite embarrassed at the request to describe themselves. However, most of the men in this generation rather willingly produce more self-focused narratives. Psychological concepts have become everyday discursive tools, and psychological models are brought in to interpret their lives and feelings:

> I was in rebellion from I was in fourth to fifth grade, so I was a rebel. Against everything, actually. First parents, and that was as it usually is at that age. So then you had few things to hold on to otherwise. I think I was quite a vulnerable child, and I have it today, too, an understanding of how people are, and can detect it very quickly … It may be a bit sentimental, but the image of dandelions growing through the asphalt. Like, always the chance to get through as long as you don't stop. But I've also seen myself in the image of being someone who climbs up a hill made out of quicksand. (Per, b. 1947)

The self-presentation here refers more to a psychological discourse, always problematising one's own motives, seeking the answers in childhood experiences as well as reflecting upon one's own reconstruction of memories. Whereas the men often use this discourse to depict their own personalities, the women instead tend to provide us with lengthy descriptions of family relationships and dynamics. Their recollections of activities and events often slide into interpretations and evaluations. This also seems to imply the removal of a taboo against talking negatively about others—which often involves blaming their parents, especially their mothers. Such statements can now be understood within a legitimate field of analytic and interpretative activity, not as final assertions about how somebody 'really' is. Such a distinction does not seem to carry much meaning for the older generation.

The women in the youngest generation still make use of this psychological discourse, but it is often at the same time ironically negated (belonging not only to their mother's generation, but also to a trend of confessional intimacy in the media, which some of them find ridiculous). Instead of a 'story' of their upbringing, the youngest generation give us bits and pieces, held together more by the underlying emotional tone than by the actual information or a storyline. A reason for this is that what they describe is something they are still in, compared to the temporal distance to the childhood/youth of the older generations, but this does not exclude it from being told in a characteristic generational narrative genre:

> Well, mostly we eat at home, but not dinners really. We just have a sandwich system. We make dinners when we feel like it and have sandwiches when we don't feel like it. My mom got quite frustrated. Like every time she had made something I said: 'Ugh, are we having *that* for dinner?!' [laughs] 'Ugh, I don't want *that*. Phew!' If it looked kind of boring. (Eva, b. 1972, 18 years old)

In some ways this is a much less personalised genre than their mothers' descriptions of family dynamics, but still with a relational focus. Among the middle-class boys, the psychological perspective is more prominent than among girls from the same social background. But the young men also tend—just like their fathers—to use the psychological discourse to enhance their own uniqueness by underlining an explicit outsider status in a constant need to prove themselves as 'unique' and 'different'.

Evidently, these generation-specific genres stem from varied sources. One could be the specific life phase of the informants: it is different to talk about your childhood and youth when you are in the midst of it, when you have children who are in the midst of it or when both you and your children survived it. It may be harder to talk negatively about dead parents than about those who are still around. Another source of the different generational genres could be the relationship in the interview situation: to the oldest generation, we as interviewers slide into the position of the respectful daughter (grandmother/grandfather tell stories about their childhood long ago), to the middle generation, the position of a female friend (intimate confessions), and to the young generation, which is on the threshold of entering university, the position of an admirable researcher (eagerly providing us with information about contemporary youth cultures) or, especially with the young men, a motherly caring figure to whom they can open their heart. Such positionings probably also colour our interpretation and analysis of the interviews as researchers: more curiosity and respect towards the oldest generation, more recognition and (self-)critique towards the middle generation, and more affection and hope when we analyse the informants who are the same age as our own children. There was yet another twist of time in the second round of interviewing where the young informants had become adults. At 30, both men and women now used mainly the psychological and relational genre, also employing it in their often-lengthy tales about jobs and careers. At 40, the focus was rather on how to manage the stressful work-life balance. At this point they were almost the same age as we as researchers had been at the first interview. It is difficult to say exactly how these things influenced the interviews, but it indicates the importance of awareness towards the age of the informants and the relationship between the interviewer and the interviewee as co-producing the narratives and the perspectives chosen.

The different perspectives and narrative genres may also tell us something about historical shifts and how people come to understand themselves in different historical contexts. Viewed strictly as historical sources, all the interviews are remnants from 1991. But the fact that people from the same generations so clearly tend to pick similar discourses when constructing their memoirs of childhood and youth also makes it feasible to view these discourses as 'small pockets of history', preserved in the individuals. The rise of modern reflexivity, for instance, is evident in the narratives across the three generations. The concentration on the outer world among the oldest generation seems easy to understand in light of the scarcity in their childhood; the relational interest in the middle generation could be interpreted as a result of new possibilities of leisure and self-realisation; and, finally, the observing, ironic style of the youngest generation would be hard to imagine without their extensive access to the media, just as their fragmented stories might be an expression of the actual relational havoc surrounding them. The generational stories with many of the same concrete recollections indicate that there are indeed experiences to be interpreted, not only inventions of the present. As Jerome Bruner, and many others, have stated, understanding the self relies on selective remembering to 'adjust the past to the demands of the present and the anticipated future' (Bruner 2003: 213).

Still, the intertwinement of discursive perspectives and memories of the past evidently presents a challenge when it comes to *comparing* the life situations of the different generations. For example, the older women give much more elaborated accounts than their daughters of the social hierarchies in their local community and also of political disagreements, for instance, right-wing fathers and left-wing uncles yelling at each other at family reunions. Does this exclusion of a political world have to do with the obsession with psychology in the middle generation? Or rather with the fact that their childhood coincided with a period in Norwegian history (the 1950s and 1960s) when the construction of the welfare state really took off and was based on important political compromises both between political parties and in the labour market? Due both to this and to the rapidly increasing standards of living, income differences between people actually decreased.

On a purely theoretical level, problems like these may point to the futility of asking what the informants are 'really' talking about. However, if one poses the question on the textual level, it is often possible to get an idea of what belongs to social practices and discourses of the past, and what belongs to later discourses or the present of the interview situation. A close textual reading can, for instance, detect discrete messages about discontent that underlie the old women's assurance that one did not have any problems in those days, or the vulnerability and seriousness that infuse the funny stories of the youngest generation. Sometimes the informants themselves highlight the difference between how they saw it then and how they see it now. As Gabrielle Rosenthal says, narratives of experienced events refer both to the current life and to past experiences. The point is to understand the course of action of the experienced events both when they happened and when they are told. What was the meaning of the event then and what is the meaning now (Rosenthal 2004: 49–50)?

Reading Feelings

A last methodological issue to be considered is how it is possible to read 'feelings' out of research interviews. This question is especially pertinent when the theoretical perspective on feelings draws on psychoanalytic theory, which is developed for and validated in a clinical setting. An in-depth study of emotional meanings is admittedly hard to accomplish in empirical research outside of clinical practice. This has been a target of much debate in the field of psychosocial studies, where some argue that it is not only a possible but also a vital resource for social researchers to make use of transference/countertransference processes in the reading of the informants' unconscious processes, while others have been critical to this (for the discussion on this, see, for instance, Walkerdine 1997; Hollway and Jefferson 2000; Bornat 2004; Frosh and Emerson 2005; Roseneil 2006; Frosh and Baraitser 2008; Hollway 2015; Woodward 2015). My position on this is that using psychoanalytic perspectives in social research does not imply that the researcher should relate to their informants as psychoanalysts to their patients. One issue to consider is that even though qualitative interviews as compared to surveys, experiments and tests may be seen as rich materials and 'thick descriptions', they are indeed very 'meagre', as Chodorow (1999) puts it, when compared to clinical data that stems from often many years of clinical encounters between the patient and the analyst. Another issue is that most social researchers lack proper training in handling and interpreting what goes on in the transference in the interview situation, so the danger of 'wild analysis' cannot be excluded. A third issue is that the analyses of interview transcripts are not (and in my opinion should not be) validated in an interpersonal space that includes the informant. What social researchers basically work with are texts, and texts are not persons (and definitely not when analysing interviews that are 25 years old).

However, when psychosocial methods are implied in social research, it is not primarily the psychobiographical specificity of individual stories but the social patterns to which they speak that is the target (Roseneil 2006: 848). In my case, the whole-sample analysis does not work on the level of individual psychobiographies, but on the level of shared psychological patterns. It is not the defended subjects I am aiming at, but rather the patterns of defence across individual cases, no matter how varied the individual trajectories to this pattern were. Furthermore, the concept of the unconscious I work with is not only or even primarily understood with reference to the dynamically repressed, but rather as a part of the self that organises experience and informs creativity and agency on an emotional level (see Chap. 2). For this reason I relate to my interview transcripts not as persons, but as texts. I regard the interviews as a corpus of text in which I try to find the emotional meaning as an integrated part of what is said, directly or indirectly. Just as narrative perspectives open up 'outwards' to social change, they also open up 'inwards' through conveying the emotional meanings attached to such change (Rudberg and Nielsen 2011).

It is possible to work with a psychoanalytic ontology (Hollway and Jefferson 2000; Roseneil 2006) and to employ a context-sensitive textual analysis and a psychologically sensitive reading that acknowledge that an emotional meaning is always present in what is said, without analysing individual unconscious conflicts. From the way the informants talk and the words they use, it is possible to learn something about their personal images of parents and thus to gain some insight into how also emotional aspects of meanings of gender are part of a person's biography. I have found the psychoanalytic concepts of identification, disidentification, projection, disavowal, idealisation and ambivalence (see Chap. 2) useful as ways to interpret what the informants say about their relationships with others and their own bodies. They may work as 'small pockets of feelings' in the text. What people say about their feelings is sometimes relatively straightforward, while at other times it may be more hidden or ambiguous. The relation between utterance and textual context is an important cue here. If an informant says 'I had a good relationship with my mother' and then proceeds to describe her relationship with her father with much more enthusiasm and detail, then this textual context lends significance to the claim. Another informant could utter exactly the same phrase, but the context of the interview could give it a different meaning compared to the first case. In addition, non-verbal cues like voice, tearfulness, pauses, humorous comments, slips of the tongue or simply the intensity of the tone can be important contextual cues, which are preserved in transcripts (Nielsen 2003). Feelings may also reveal themselves from the textual organisation: what are the contradictions or difficult points in the stories, when do they not make sense? What model of the world and of self–other relationships makes itself known in the way in which the informants talk? In looking at interviews as textual structures with conscious and unconscious layers of meaning, I follow the insight of Ricouer that both meaning (content as structure) and significance (content as reference to the world) are vital parts of the interpretation of texts. Life, Paul Ricoeur says, can be seen as 'an activity and a passion in search of a narrative' (Ricoeur 1991b: 29). When we construct a narrative of our life, we produce a textual structure that 'underscore(s) the mixture of acting and suffering which constitutes the very fabric of life. It is this mixture which the narrative attempts to imitate in a creative way' (Ricoeur 1991b: 28). When we tell a story of our lives, the point is not only to make our lives more intelligible, but also more bearable. We can make ourselves heroes of our own story— however, we cannot actually become the author of our own life. Thus, even though a narrative strives towards homogeneity, it will always be a synthesis of the heterogeneous—a structure of 'discordant concordance' (Ricoeur 1991b: 31).

Valerie Walkerdine (1997) and others have argued that there are also processes of transference in reading texts and that the employment of the researcher's subjectivity in the process of interpretation is indispensable and should not be seen as a source of error. This concurs with Paul Ricouer's view that the indecisiveness of textual meaning first turns into social communication (the significance of the text) when it meets its reader (Ricoeur 1991a: 63). However, in research it is problematic if the significance that emerges says more about the reader than about the text (see also Bornat 2004). It is therefore important to be able to document the interpretation on the textual level: interpreting the emotional layers of the text is not reading 'between the lines', but a broader interpretation of what is 'in the lines' than just reading the words in a very literal way. The German psychoanalyst Alfred Lorenzer and his colleagues, working in the field of cultural studies in the tradition of the late Frankfurt

School, have developed a method for 'deep-hermeneutic cultural inter-pretation' of texts (Lorenzer 1986). The point here is not to analyse the person behind the text, but to understand how the unconscious structures in the text reflect the world we live in. Lorenzer does not reduce the manifest meaning of a text to a latent meaning. While the latent meaning of a dream will often require additional information from the dreamer, the latent meaning of a written text has to be in the text, otherwise it makes little sense. The connecting point between the conscious and the unconscious is found in the symbolic accounts themselves. According to Lorenzer, in order to find the unconscious structure in a text, we have to read the text as openly as an analyst should listen to the talk of a patient. We look at the spots where it 'irritates' (Prokop 1996)—where some-thing 'does not fit' or seems to be missing, where the text becomes con-tradictory or maybe too coherent, or where the rhetoric is experienced as ambiguous, touching or untrustworthy. It may have to do with content, but more often with form—selection, ordering, rhetorical figures and textual images. My focus of the generational patterns in feelings may actually have more in common with the way in which Lorenzer analy-ses the conscious and an unconscious structure of meaning in cultural texts than with psychoanalysis of individuals. According to Lorenzer, the purpose of drawing attention to the unconscious structures in symbolic forms is not to understand the specific biography of the narrator, as it would be in therapy, but to understand how unconscious desires and cultural activity are intertwined. While the psychoanalytic interpreta-tion in therapy aims at changing the analysand, the deep hermeneutic cultural interpretation, by drawing attention to hidden 'life sketches', aims at changing the analyst (or the readers). Lorenzer calls this the dis-tinction between 'analysing the production' and 'analysing the effects' of the text (Lorenzer 1986: 68). Through an autobiographical text, we may gain insight into how a narrator can contribute to the change of culture through the impact his or her symbolic behaviour—stories told or prac-tices engaged in—has on others. In my case, looking for the feelings of gender has exactly this aim: to see how feelings of gender have been used as a creative potential of change.

Reading Generations

It is challenging not only to analyse generational material, but also to read it. I have given the informants names according to their gender, generation and class,[8] and have used the same initials in the names of the same chain (see the Appendix for a survey of the names and social mobility of the 34 chains). Each generation has been given its own empirical chapter, but the names should make it possible to see family links between the chapters. For different reasons, not all interviews were equally useful—and that is the reason that a chain sometimes 'disappears' in later chapters. For the youngest generation, it can also be due to a missing second round of interviews in some cases. In larger quotes from the two older generations, the name of the informant is tagged with the year of birth, whereas for the youngest generation it is the age at the interview (18, 30 or 40) that is marked. Quotes from the informants are in italics whether they appear as block quotes or are integrated in the running text. Most of the informants in the older generation have kept traces of the regional dialects of their childhood. In the translation into English, this class and time colouring was not possible to preserve.

All informants are presented with their class background the first time they are mentioned, both as children and adults. In relation to class division I have used a combination of education, character of work, position at work and economic capital in the family to make a simple system that works reasonably well with the different generations. It distinguishes between housewives (only women), farmers/fishermen families, working class, lower middle class, middle class, upper middle class and families who are self-employed (see the Appendix for definitions and more details). Sometimes, when it makes sense, I also characterise found patterns in terms of a rougher contrast of working class (including lower middle class) versus middle class (including upper middle class) where education or economic capital is the dividing line, but it is important to be aware

[8] In this the databases of Statistics Norway have been very useful. They give information about the frequency of different names in Norway since 1880 (https://www.ssb.no/a/navn/historisk-utvikling-av-jentenavn/ and https://www.ssb.no/a/navn/historisk-utvikling-av-guttenavn/). I am aware that non-Norwegians will probably not be able to appreciate this element of time colouring. However, I have avoided using names with the specific Scandinavian letters æ, ø and å.

that not all informants are covered by these binary pairs. Another issue is that social class can (and in this sample most often does) change from the childhood family to the adult family. I have used age categories to specify this; thus, being a 'working-class boy' means that this informant grew up working class, whereas being a 'middle-class woman' indicates the class in which this informant ended up as an adult. The quotes have been selected to make visible relevant class differences, but they are not in all cases balanced in relation to gender. The reason for privileging quotes from men in some sections is that less is known about men's experiences when it comes to issues like family, care work and bodies/sexuality, and therefore we wanted to pay special attention to this.

Several things should be kept in mind while reading the analyses. Unless something else is mentioned, 'the women' and 'the men' will refer to women and men in our sample, not the general population of women and men in these generations. Another thing that is important to remember is that the men and women in the same generations come from different families. Especially in the section about how the different generations organised work and care in their families as adults, it is important to steer clear of misunderstandings. For instance, when we write what the men or the women thought about their partners' contribution to the household, it is essential to remember that the men and women from the same generation in the sample are *not* couples.

4

Changing Historical, Cultural and Political Contexts

Feelings of gender originate from many other sources besides family relationships and experiences of body and sexuality, which will be the focus in my analysis in this book. Experiences stemming from educational institutions, peer culture and peer relations, and popular culture and media are all important, in addition to the general impact of demographic, economic, political and cultural trends. The different sources cannot be strictly empirically separated. As David Morgan puts it: 'family life is never simply family life … it is always continuous with other areas of existence' (Morgan 1999: 13). Such areas of existence will also float into my analysis when they appear through the lens I direct towards the family and bodily experiences. By describing them separately at first, they may be easier to discover when they make their presence felt in the lived lives of the three generations. Some of the societal conditions I highlight will be particular to Scandinavia or Norway; others will be conditions that are similar in other Western countries. However, the focus will be on the Scandinavian/Norwegian context with an emphasis on the twentieth century.

Family Forms: Equality, Difference and Individual Rights

Processes of modernisation have changed gender relations in all European countries, but the north-western part of Europe had an historical advantage due to a specific pre-industrial family and household formation that gave married women a relatively strong position. The north-western European marriage pattern was characterised by a high marriage age for both men and women, marriage by choice and independent housing for the married couple and their children (Sandvik 1999, also based on the British historian John Hajnal's studies). In this family form, the married couple and the nuclear family constituted the centre, in contrast to the patriarchal control in extended households that were dominant in other agrarian societies. A consequence of the high marriage age and the many who remained single was that many young people, including young women, would work in other households to earn their living before marriage. This gave access to a period of youth outside the direct control of their parents. Hence, the life conditions for young women and men were not so different, and when they married, they had both become adults and brought property and productive resources into the family (Solheim 2012). However, it is also important to note that the types of work that were seen as specifically feminine had lower status than the masculine ones. Married woman did not have any legal capacity (in Norway not until 1888); it was the husband who legally represented the household and who had the right both to economic disposition of the joint property and to keep discipline in his family. The north-western European family model was definitely not an egalitarian one, it was based on both gender differentiation and gender hierarchy, but married woman had economic responsibility and could, depending on the circumstances, have a strong position and authority in the household.

The development of industrial capitalism during the nineteenth century led to a change in the bourgeois family that split private and public domains and redefined the family as a sphere of intimacy instead of production (Hagemann 1999). This 'modern gender revolution' (Solheim 2012: 45) laid the foundation for the two-sphere model implying radical sex differences with regard to both tasks and assumed personal traits and capacities. It represented a gradual change from economic partnership to a complementary gender order, where women lost influence regarding the family's property. However, the old family model maintained a strong position in Norway, which in the nineteenth century only had a very limited and not very wealthy upper class. In spite of the gradual restructuring of the economy during the nineteenth century, the vast majority of people still lived off farming, fishing and forestry, and they continued to do so into the twentieth century. In this rural population—from where many of our informants in the oldest generation came—the traditional family model based on economic cooperation between the spouses continued without interruption (Melby 1999; Crompton et al. 2007). Small-scale farming was often combined with fishing and forestry, which meant that the men had to leave for longer or shorter periods. This also kept up the necessity and importance of women's work and their co-responsibility for the family. Quite a substantial number of women were directly involved in economic activities by the end of the nineteenth century, especially those in the working classes, but also to an increasing extent in the growing middle classes where unmarried daughters often had to seek paid work, for instance, as teachers. Due to the many widowed women and huge emigration mainly of men to the USA before and after 1900, there were a high number of unmarried women. These women either stayed in their families helping out or worked to earn their own living.[1] In addition, many married women took part in the enterprises of their husbands in addition to taking care of the home. In most bourgeois families it was also necessary that the wives took responsibility for the household, although they were assisted by domestic servants. Generally, then, Norwegian women continued to work in or outside of the family, including after the bourgeois gender revolution (Hagemann 1999).

Norway's route to modernisation has some special traits. The country was part of Denmark until the end of the Napoleonic Wars and was then in a union with Sweden until 1905. This delayed industrialisation compared to Denmark and Sweden. Norway did not become a modern

[1] In 1900 20 per cent of men and 30 per cent of women between 30 and 49 years of age were unmarried or widowed (Hagemann 1999).

industrial society until after independence in 1905. By 1945 half of the population lived in the cities, whereas a third still worked in agriculture and fishing. At the same time it is also the case that Norway ratified its first constitution in 1814, which was one of the most radical, liberal and democratic in Europe at that time. Among other things, it established freedom of the press, the separation of legislative, juridical and executive power, and abolished the nobility in the country. During the nineteenth century's union with Sweden, which mainly concerned foreign policy and defence, Norway gradually developed as a nation state. This meant that the emergence of the Norwegian state apparatus and the process of modernisation took place under fairly democratic conditions, at a time where most of the population could read and write, and under the impact of a blooming economy during most of the nineteenth century. In addition to a fairly homogenous population in terms of religion and ethnicity where a majority were independent farmers and fishers, and the lack of both royal power, nobility and a large or rich bourgeoisie, these traits laid a solid foundation for an egalitarian culture. This is also seen in the influential role of popular and social movements, agrarian enlightenment and an increase in the level of general education in the second half of the nineteenth and the first half of the twentieth centuries (Melby et al. 2008: 5). As a result, egalitarian values, self-determination and emphasis on social inclusion rather than differentiation along the boundaries of public and private became part of the Norwegian national culture. The same traits are, with minor differences, seen in all the other Nordic countries. As the Nordic historians Melby, Ravn and Wetterberg describe it: 'The Nordic model is distinguished by individualism combined with state responsibility for the common welfare through social reform and intervention … a political culture in which it was a state responsibility to reform society, relying on the active participation of the citizens' (Melby et al. 2008: 5).

The relatively egalitarian character of the Nordic societies and family structure, and the interaction between the state and civil society, may explain why the Nordic countries became engaged in policies of gender equality earlier than other European countries:[2] 'The democratic

[2] Women gained the right to vote in 1906 in Finland, in 1913 in Norway, in 1915 in Denmark and Iceland, and in 1919 in Sweden.

integration of women in civil society was a hallmark of the Nordic political culture, as much as women's agency is one among several factors that explain this culture' (Melby et al. 2008: 5). New marriage laws were adopted in all the Nordic countries during the first decades of the new century. Unlike legislation in the rest of Europe at this time, these laws recognised married women as individuals in their own right by granting them the right to take up gainful work without the consent of their husbands and by establishing economic equality in marriage. Husband and wife were made jointly responsible for family provision and were also established as independent, formally equal owners of their respective property. Melby et al. (2008: 8) argue that this could actually be seen as an early 'modified dual breadwinner model'. However, it was also a model based on unquestioned ideas of gender differentiation, as women's unpaid work in the family was equated in principle with men's maintenance by money. In this way the law bridged the economic partnership of the old family model and the new male earner/female carer family, based on the bourgeois family model. Tax legislation clearly encouraged the latter model and continued to do so in Norway until 1959. However, one might say that the emphasis was more on the principle of gender differentiation than on a belief in gender difference (Melby et al. 2008: 1). What united the old and new family models was the focus on family functions more than on gender identities or naturalised gender norms. This again contributed to tension with the principle of equal rights.

The economic decline in the 1920s and 1930s and the difficult conditions in the labour market that followed gave an advantage to the principle of gender differentiation. The numbers of housewives increased in the inter-war period. The farmer women became fewer, more working-class women could afford to quit their job and middle-class women lost their domestic servants. In addition, women married at a younger age than before and had fewer children.[3] Since there was still a high number

[3] Between 1900 and 1930, statistics show that 40 per cent of married women in Norway were registered as housewives. After 1930 it increased rapidly and in 1950 it was 53 per cent. The year 1960 saw this figure peak before it started to decrease. These numbers also include farmer women and women who worked in family enterprises. Only 4–5 per cent of the married women were registered as having paid work in 1900 and in 1950. However, the statistics did not include part-time work before 1920 (Melby 1999: 234, 270). Occasional small and informal jobs, which many women took to improve the family economy, are not registered either.

of unmarried women until the 1930s, there were also many women in paid work. But the absolute majority of married women were housewives and could now spend more time on housework, which in this period was professionalised through research and information campaigns (Melby 1999; Hagemann 2010). During the Second World War, Norway was occupied for five years by Germany. This meant that there was no general draft in those years and thus no need for women to step in for the men in factories and other workplaces as was the case in many other countries. The male earner/female carer family policy was continued in the first decades after the war where the Scandinavian countries saw almost two decades of social democratic majority governments. Due to the economic boom and the need for women's labour outside the family, family policy in the late 1950s became engaged with the idea of 'women's two roles' as mothers and workers, but from the 1960s this changed into an equality-oriented discourse about women's right to 'freedom of choice' (Melby et al. 2008: 11). Thus, regarding the old tension between gender differentiation and individual rights, the latter now gained ground. Melby argues that the historically short period of the 'housewife era' mainly functioned as a makeshift to curb the increasing conflict between the old values of collective moral and work and the new values of individualism, which by itself triggered further modernisation and individualisation—including undermining the gender order itself (Melby 1999: 230).

These features of the Nordic countries have fostered a specific blend of equality norms and individually based rights in contrast to family rights that have had a stronger position in other welfare states in Europe. The longstanding aim has been to make every individual, including married women, economically independent, something that has contributed to weaken both patriarchal and parental authority. The orientation towards egalitarianism and individual rights is seen with regard to children as well. Norms of child-centred upbringing and a view of the child as a self-contained individual came earlier in Scandinavia than anywhere else (Therborn 1993). Corporal physical punishment, for instance, was banned in Norwegian schools in 1936 and in the family in 1972, and state-provided sex education was introduced early (de Coninck-Smith 2003). The Nordic countries were also the first to adopt individual legal rights for children (Therborn 1993; de Coninck-Smith 2003).[4] Generally speaking, Scandinavian children enjoyed a relatively anti-authoritarian upbringing from the early 1950s, a free and relatively child-centred school system and less gender-stereotyped discourses than was the case in other European countries and the USA (see, for instance, Breines 1992; Jamieson 1998; Lawler 2000; Brannen et al. 2004).

Improved Living Standards, Social Security, Class and Education

As sons and daughters of workers, small farmers and fishers, often with many siblings in cramped quarters, almost all of our informants in the oldest generation described a childhood with material standards very far from what their grandchildren had come to consider an ordinary standard of living. They emphasised that they did not starve, but in their detailed memories—kept through more than half a century—of what they ate at the different meals of the day and often also the exact prices for everyday groceries, we can see a reflection of life circumstances where food and clothing and the money to buy them were not taken for granted. For this generation of working-class and rural children, sufficient food and clothing and parents striving to provide this equalled a good childhood. Mothers who became widows had to manage both household and work for money outside, as there was no social security at that point other than the socially degrading poor relief fund. Class differences were prominent, both economically and culturally. However, belonging to the middle class did not necessarily entail much economic security either. In cases where the father died early, the mother often had to take unskilled paid work out of pure necessity.

The twentieth century saw a rapid increase in living standards. During the first decades of the new century in Norway, the threat of mass poverty was replaced by a basic social security (Kjeldstadli 1994: 96). The

[4] In Norway children born out of wedlock gained the right to inherit from the father and carry his name from 1915. The state also supplied economic support if the father of the child did not pay (Melby et al. 2008: 10).

improved living conditions led to better public health. The height and weight of children went up, and class differences in children and young people's physical growth and development gradually disappeared. Yet, income differences between the social classes increased until the Second World War. Norway was neutral during the First World War and was occupied during the Second World War.

Compared to what children in many other countries experienced, relatively few Scandinavian children had absent fathers because of the wars or saw them injured or killed.[5] The deep sense of loss and separation found in other countries in this generation of children (Chodorow 2000; Brannen 2015) is not present in the narratives of those of our informants who grew up during the war. More of the men than the women in our study took part in the resistance movement or remember dramatic episodes. The women mention their fear of German soldiers and especially the Gestapo, that things were closed down or taken over by the Nazis, that it was a boring time to be young and that there was a severe lack of food and clothing. During the German occupation, the development of the new welfare state that had started in the mid-1930s came to a halt. After the war all social institutions had to be rebuilt and many commodities were rationed into the 1950s.

As in the rest of Europe, there was a rapid increase in living standards from the 1950s, which was in the beginning still within norms of modesty and savings in daily life. From 1950 to 1970, private consumption tripled and differences in income among various groups of people were greatly reduced (Lange 1998). The informants in the middle generation do not talk about the question of whether they had enough food when they describe the living conditions of their childhood, but remember the fashionable clothes they yearned for that could only be granted on special occasions like birthdays or Christmas. Tight economy is, however, not remembered as a permanent state. In this generation, everybody, except children of single or divorced mothers, recalls how much better off their family became during the 1960s and they have vivid recollections of how

[5] About 0.3 per cent of the Norwegian population lost their lives due to the Second World War. (www.arkivverket.no/arkivverket). This includes 738 of the 772 Norwegian Jews (adults and children) who were deported—with the assistance of the Norwegian state administration—to German extermination camps during the war. Only 34 returned alive.

new consumer goods continuously arrived in the family: electric cookers, washing machines, refrigerators, transistor radios, tape-recorders, TVs and finally even a car for dad! The stories are filled with details about when their families got these commodities compared with other families, but the later they are born, the less they talk about this. It had become the normal state of affairs.

Not only did private consumption go up as the middle generation came of age, but so too did state-provided public services like health care, education and care services for children, the ill, the disabled and the elderly. The Nordic welfare states were gradually developed from the mid-1930s. In Norway the first laws about unemployment benefits, paid sick leave and retirement benefits were introduced in the 1930s, in addition to work hour regulation, paid holiday and laws about worker protection. After the war, in the 1940s, came the child benefit for all families, the educational loan fund for students and cheap housing loans to buy apartments in the new suburbs; in the 1950s full retirement schemes for all; and in the 1960s support for single mothers and disability benefits. The whole system of national security was fully established by 1970. Along with a progressive taxation system, this led to less poverty and social inequality in the Nordic societies than in other countries (Korpi 2000). This is also some of the background for class journeys of this period being experienced as less dramatic than in countries with larger class and income differences. The period from 1935 to 1970 has been described as a period dominated by social consensus in Norway, as a period of integration and gathering around common goals (Lange 1998). As one of our informants, born in 1947, said: '*it was a period of economic boom, nobody was unemployed. It was just available, and everything just progressed*'.

The new laws of social security and work security reshaped the frames for the oldest generation's lives as adults, but it was the expanding educational system that became decisive for their children. Whereas many in the older generation had to quit school early or give up the further education they wanted for economic reasons or due to family obligations, access to schools became easier for the middle generation. Before 1936, children only had to attend school when they were between seven and 12 years of age (although most stayed until their confirmation at 14), and children from rural areas only attended school every second day. From

1936, seven years of ordinary school became mandatory and in 1969 this was extended to nine years. High schools were built in rural areas too, and the state provided educational loans in combination with free access to universities and colleges with the aim of making it economically possible for students from poor families to also enter higher education. There was a strong political incentive for encouraging young people to get higher education, regardless of class and gender, as education was seen as the main tool to increase equality and justice and reduce class differences in the population. The number who graduated from high school in Norway increased from three per cent of the age cohort in 1930 to ten per cent in 1960 and 36 per cent in 1990 (academic track). Girls surpassed boys in frequency of high school graduation in 1975, and during the 1980s they also became the majority in higher education (Statistics Norway http://www.ssb.no/a/english/histstat/). Social reproduction through education was somewhat reduced, but did not disappear. New intersections between gender and class were established: taking the educational track to social mobility became more common and successful for working-class girls than for working-class boys in the post-war generations. Before the 1960s, marriage was the most prevalent path to social mobility for all women, but with the expansion of the educational system and with girls on average achieving better in school than boys, this changed. The opportunities for girls in the educational system may partly be explained by the system's degree of formalisation: if you do well on one level, you are invited to enter the next (Frønes 2001). This has not least been the case in the Nordic countries, where there have been few private schools or elite schools, and where higher education has been, and still is, free.

The encouragement of girls' education also led to a new intersection between gender and generation in the post-war years: the Norwegian economist Kari Skrede (1999) writes that this period had one policy for the daughters and another for the mothers. The policy for the mothers was based firmly on the gendered provider/carer family model, while the policy for the daughters had as its goal the breaking down of all kinds of class and gender barriers through the system of education. This 'policy for the daughters' is also seen in the early reduction of the gender gap in higher education in the Nordic countries. Compared to other European countries, the gender gaps in education among those born in the 1940 are small (Korpi 2000: 137).

The youngest generation was born at a time when the national security system had just been fully established. Continuing education after compulsory school has over the three generations changed from being a privilege of the few to being a matter of course and, finally, a necessity for young people who want to create a competitive CV. The youngest generation was born in the year when Norway voted against membership in the EU (1972), but their childhood and youth still coincided with increasing internationalisation, mediatisation and new communication technologies. However, when we interviewed them in 1991, the Internet and the GSM net for mobile phones had not yet been launched.

The youngest generation grew up with self-evident affluence. Even though there were different economic standards in different families, nobody mentions not getting the clothes they want because of a lack of money. However, some did have parents who were critical towards brand-label clothing. For this generation as young persons, class differences seem to be perceived mainly as incidental differences in taste of music, clothes and lifestyle. Instead of talking about poor people, this generation talks about 'losers'. One middle-class informant from our sample described girls coming from the eastern suburbs of Oslo not as less privileged than herself, but as '*very common, a lot of make-up, quit school after junior high*'. But in the period when this generation came of age, income differences actually started to increase again in Norway. Trends of deregulation put pressure on the organisation of welfare state provisions, and the labour market became less stable and predictable. A recession took place in the late 1970s and marked the end of the stable political climate led by the social democratic party. Around the time we did our interviews in 1991, unemployment was relatively high, especially among young people.[6]

Norway found oil in 1969 and the state-owned oil industry made the country into one of the world's richest during the following decades. This

[6] In 1992 there was about six per cent unemployment in total and about 13 per cent for 15–24-year-olds (Statistics Norway). This led to an expansion of higher education, which encouraged more people in our youngest generation to choose this option.

contributed to reducing the insecurity and inequality-promoting effects of the era of deregulation and economic crises, but not at the same pace as the growing social differences. Increasing competition in getting into the higher education, jobs, promotions and individualised salaries made life more stressful for young people compared with the previous decades. But in spite of increasing deregulations, privatisation and the population becoming more heterogeneous due to increased migration, so far the national security system has not been seriously affected (Korpi 2000; Ellingsæter and Widerberg 2012).

Gender Equality: Policy and Practice

In 1979 the law of gender equality was ratified in Norway. In the following two decades gender equality policies had high public priority. The increasing numbers of working mothers gave rise to new social challenges that needed a political solution. In addition, women's low degree of participation in political life, their absence from high professional and managerial positions, and problems of equal pay and discrimination became increasingly visible and were perceived as incompatible with the new norms of gender equality that were supposed to prevail in all spheres of society. An important cultural and political push in the struggle for gender equality came from the Women's Movement, which mobilised in Norway from the early 1970s as in the rest of the Western world, but also continued on from older and less radical women's organisations. The Norwegian social scientist Helga Hernes has described the process as a result of 'state feminism', a combination of 'feminism from below' (the movements and organisations in civil society) and 'feminism from above' (the legislation facilitated by feminist bureaucrats and politicians) (Hernes 1987). What especially came to distinguish the Nordic 'caring state' from other Western countries was that care for children, disabled people and the elderly from early on was seen as a public responsibility and was given a universal form (Leira 2012). From the 1980s, women's economic chances were supported by the implementation of gender quotas and other anti-discrimination legislation with regard to education and work, and the expansion of parental leaves and public daycare with regard to families. From the 1990s onwards, the political model of the universal breadwinner was extended to the idea of the universal carer (Fraser 1997). Men's rights as fathers received increasing attention (Korsvik 2011), and a special and mandatory father's quota of the parental leave was implemented in 1993.[7] This has created a unique situation for Norwegian fathers when it comes to care, which today they only share with fathers in Sweden, Iceland and Germany. Quotas for men were also introduced in education and jobs related to care for and teaching of children. All this indicates that the Nordic gender equality model not only led to 'defamilisation' with its emphasis on women's economic independence, but also entails elements of 'refamilisation' through generous systems of parental leave for both parents, paid absence from work to take care of sick children, and a special cash-for-care allowance introduced in 1998[8] (Ellingsæter and Leira 2006; Ellingsæter 2012).

Norway represents an interesting case in the Nordic context because it demonstrates more clearly than the other countries the tension between gender differentiation and gender equality that goes back to the beginning of the twentieth century. This can partly be explained by conflicts between different class fractions of women (Sainsbury 2001) and

[7] The quota earmarked four weeks of the by then 42-week-long parental leave for the father. Six weeks (plus three weeks before birth) were earmarked the mother, so 29 weeks were left to be decided by the parents themselves. The father quota was expanded after 1993, almost in parallel with the expansion of the total parental leave. In 2011 the father quota was 12 weeks (and the total parental leave 47 weeks). In 2013 the social democratic government decided to expand it to 14 weeks, but the following year a new right-wing government reduced it to 10 weeks. Before the father quota was introduced in 1993, very few fathers took out any of the joint parental leave. After it was introduced, a very large majority of fathers took out their quota, but only a few took out more than their earmarked weeks. It is the fathers with the highest and the lowest income who take the shortest leave (Ellingsæter 2012).

[8] This reform gave a cash-for-care allowance for families with children under the age of three who did not attend publicly subsidised daycare, which was by then still in demand. It was introduced by a centre-right government, headed by the Christian Democratic Party, and the declared aim was to give families the choice of deciding the best care for their children and to contribute to more equal state remittances for childcare regardless of the chosen form of care. The proposal was held in strictly gender-neutral terms, but the effect of the reform was gendered since almost no fathers took out the allowance. The number of women in paid work was not reduced by the cash-for-care reform (the allowance was small), but the increase stopped for a few years until more public daycare had become available. Working-class and immigrant families are overrepresented among those who use the cash-for-care benefit today. But as more of the non-immigrant mothers than the immigrant mothers combine the allowance with paid work, the reform has to an increasing degree been seen as a problem for the integration of immigrant women and their children (Ellingsæter 2012).

partly by the stronger hold of religion in some regions of Norway and its continuing influence in politics (Korpi 2000; Melby et al. 2008). In 1960 Norway was among the countries in the Western world with the lowest rates of women in paid work, and women's entry into the labour market came a decade later than in the other Nordic countries. The development of daycare also came very slowly, and even today the number of Norwegian women working part-time is higher than in the other Nordic countries (Kitterød and Rønsen 2012). On the basis of these observations, researchers have described Norway as a more family-oriented and maternalist culture than the other Nordic countries (Knudsen and Wærness 2001; Sainsbury 2001; Borchorst 2008). It is probably more accurate to say that political disagreements have contributed to a dualistic family model (Ellingsæter 2012). However, the Norwegian tension between different family models, in combination with the cross-political agreement to prioritise care, may also be seen as having facilitated the track towards a universal caregiver model which may potentially transgress the equality/difference dilemma (Fraser 1997). The long parental leave, the father quota and other generous schemes to improve the care for children can be seen as a recognition of the importance of parental care, including the fact that it does not have to be gender-differentiated.

The middle generation in our sample became parents in around 1970, so when the Women's Movement and the other radical movements of the 1970s took off, they were already established with families of their own. They are just ahead of what has been called a change of gear in family formation in the mid-1970s where the practice of cohabitation increased and the age for marriage and the birth of the first child went up (Noack and Hovde 2012; Pedersen 2012). Some of the women in our sample participated in marches on March 8 and demonstrations in favour of free abortion, and read the journals from the Women's Movement, and some of the men remember that their wives became radicalised. The impact of the Women's Movement is also seen as a frame of reference in the interviews when our informants talk about quarrels of housework and of divorces.

The 1970s was the decade where Norwegian women entered the labour market in large numbers, and during the 1980s this also came to include women with young children.[9] During the childhood of our youngest generation—from 1972 to 1990—the percentage of married or cohabiting women with children under 15 years of age in paid work increased from 43 per cent to 77 per cent[10] (Kitterød and Rønsen 2012: 163). However, what also characterised this period was that the development of daycare was far from following the number of working mothers (Leira 2002). Thus, the women of our middle generation belong to the specific cohorts of young mothers who took up paid work before the state provisions to cater to this was developed: in 1970 the maternity leave was 12 weeks and the daycare coverage was three per cent.[11] In the same period (1970–1990) women on average reduced the time they spent on care and housework considerably more than men increased their contribution. The father's participation in housework depends on how many hours the mother works and how high her income is (Kjeldstad and Lappegård 2010; Brannen 2015).[12] Private help in the house has until recently been

[9] In the UK mothers with small children entered the labour market a decade later, in the 1990s. In 2000 full-time employment among women with children in the UK was still much lower than in the Scandinavian countries (Fagani 2007; Brannen et al. 2004). Nordic women have on average the highest labour force participation in Europe and also when part-time is taken into consideration (den Dulk and Doorne-Huiskes 2007).

[10] During this period, however, half of the women worked part-time, and the differentiation between part-time/full-time followed levels of education: the longer the education, the more full-time work (Skrede 1986; Kitterød and Rønsen 2012). In 2010 the number of mothers in paid work had increased to 87 per cent. The numbers also include women on parental leave, and as the leave was considerably prolonged in the same period of time (from 12 weeks in 1970 to 28 weeks in 1990, and to 46 weeks in 2010), the numbers are not directly comparable (Kitterød and Rønsen 2012; Ellingsæter 2012).

[11] In 1990 the daycare coverage had increased to 35 per cent, which was still far behind the number of working mothers with young children. In particular, the coverage for children under three years was a problem until the beginning of the 2000s. The coverage in Oslo was much higher than the average in the entire country (Myhre 1994). There was also a social differentiation as middle-class children more often attended public daycare than children from working-class families (Ellingsæter 2012). Only in 2009 did public daycare become a right for children from the age of 12 months. The public daycare coverage in the Nordic countries is much higher and much cheaper than in most other European countries. For instance, in 2005, childcare costs represented 12 per cent of a family's net income in Norway and 27 per cent in the UK (den Dulk and Doorne-Huiskes 2007).

[12] In 1971 (the year our youngest generation was born) women spent 29 hours a week on average on housework, while men spent four hours (maintenance work, care work and shopping not included). In 1990 (the time we conducted our interviews) for number of hours for women had reduced to 16, while for men it increased to five hours. In 2010 (when we did the last interviews with the youngest generation) for number of hours for women had reduced to 12 hours, while for men it increased to seven hours. In the same timeframe, men doubled the time spent on care,

very rare in Norway outside of high-status families and was at the time when we did our interviews associated more with household income than with employment of the woman in the family (Kitterød 2009).

It has been argued that the Nordic gender equality policies have been more attuned to the life form of families where both parents have full-time and attractive jobs and where the women can benefit from schemes to promote women's careers in work and politics. Support of gender equality both in attitude and practice are related to education and job status, especially for women (Crompton et al. 2007; Kjeldstad and Lappegård 2010). This tendency is also reflected in the middle generation in our sample, where most of the middle-class women had full-time jobs, or close to full-time, and most had stayed home only during periods of parental leave, whereas some of the working-class women worked part-time and had stayed at home for some years when their children were small. Working-class women and women from certain ethnic groups tend to be sceptical of middle-class women's career orientation and prefer to spend more time with their family, and some may also prefer more distinct gender roles in the home and regarding childcare. However, the majority of them support the idea of gender equality and especially political measures for equal pay and statutory rights against sexualised violence (Walby 1997; Skilbrei 2005; Melby et al. 2008; Andersen and Aarseth 2012). Discrepancies between attitudes to gender equality and the practised gender equality, especially with regard to housework, are also within all social groups, but in different forms. Generally, for women practice is less equal than their attitudes to gender equality, whereas for men it is the other way round (Kjeldstad and Lappegård 2010). It is also the case for all groups that structural forces may increase the dissonance between attitudes and practices: in working-class and immigrant families, who in general are more in favour of a traditional division of work, economic and practical conditions often make their actual practices more gender-equal. In middle-class families, especially those where the husband has a high salary, structural conditions make it possible for the women to

---

whereas the hours were the same for women (Kitterød and Rønsen 2012). Still, Nordic families share the domestic work more equally than is the case in other European countries (den Dulk and Doorne-Huiskes 2007).

work less. Thus, somewhat paradoxically, a positive attitude to gender equality may still be drawn towards a more gender-traditional practice. A contributing factor here is also the increasing demand of long work hours in high-status professional jobs, especially in the private sector (Andersen and Aarseth 2012; Kavli 2012; Brannen 2015). This picture is reflected by the fact that the men who use the father quota the least are those with either very high or very low incomes (Ellingsæter 2012).

Gender equality as a norm and value has a high degree of support across the Norwegian population. Today 70 per cent of the Norwegian population has a positive attitude to the family model where both breadwinning and domestic work are shared between the spouses (NOU 15 2012). However, there is also a rising critique of the pressured lives of families with small children and double careers, and younger people have voiced their opinions about more freedom of choice and individual solutions (Melby et al. 2008; Andersen and Aarseth 2012). Still, the political discussions of gender equality are mainly limited to questions like 'how far' gender equality should go, to what degree it should also focus on men's situations or include other dimensions of discrimination, and to what degree gender equality in the family and in private enterprises should be a private choice or a target of state intervention. Arguments for a return to the old gender contract with distinct roles for women and men or even to the housewife model of the 1950s are rarely seen outside the contexts of extreme political or religious groups.[13]

Youth, Gender and Modernity

A last contextual framing important to the study is the way the period of youth and sexual norms changed during the twentieth century. Especially in the post-war years the educational policy encouraged individuality in girls from early on, both in the family and in school, and the earlier pro-

[13] In recent years, the changing gender contract has provoked some very negative and even violent reactions in Europe and the USA among people belonging to the extreme political right or religious groups who see modernisation as a threat to 'God-given' values. One of the worst incidents took place in Norway in 2011, where a right-wing terrorist killed 69 people and legitimised it as a war against modern gender relations *and* Muslim immigration.

vision of sex education in schools may also have been significant. The social processes that had an impact on the family in the twentieth century had far-reaching effects on what it meant to be a young person: individualisation, increasing affluence, extended education, social and geographical mobility and increased consumption. Modernisation processes gradually led to a demarcation of youth as a separate life phase all over the Western world, and the need for what Erik H. Erikson has coined a psychosocial moratorium (Erikson 1968: 156). Increased reflexivity, choice and reorientation become urgent issues when new generations cannot simply take over their parents' way of life, but have to find their own way. For many it involved a prolonged period of education and/or increased geographical mobility. The concept of moratorium has been criticised for generalising the life trajectory of middle-class youth. A relatively free and experimental period of life between childhood and adult life was indeed first a privilege of young men from the bourgeoisie, and later to some degree also the young women from the middle classes who got higher education. However, as we have seen earlier, the agrarian family model of north-western European often allowed for a period free of parents' control between childhood and marriage. To call it a moratorium would stretch the concept too far, both because it was a period of hard work, little pay and being under the authority of the new household, and because the young person after this period of work often returned to his or her local community and largely continued the way of life of his or her parents' generation. However, with industrialisation and urbanisation, more young people from rural areas and the working class took up work in the cities as industrial workers, apprentices, office workers or maids. This meant both more formally regulated work hours than working in a rural household had done, and gradually also better pay, which gave a historically new possibility for young people to spend money. Freedom, consumption and leisure became closely intertwined, especially for young working-class girls (Thorsen 1993a, b; Drotner 1999): theirs was a strong urge 'to become modern' (Søland 2000; Ekerwald 2002). While girls from rural areas found themselves more confined by family obligations and middle-class girls of the cities experienced more control by their parents, including demands in relation to education, working-class girls in the big cities who were often outside the reach of their parents' control got access to free time and a little money of their own (Thorsen 1993a, b). One of our informants in the oldest generation illustrates this. Borghild, born into a rural working-class family in 1911, remembers having a long row with her parents before she was finally allowed to take up a post as a housemaid for a well-off family in Oslo in 1928. The first thing she did when she was out of the sight of her mother was to cut off her braids and get a perm. She received a relatively good salary and this allowed her to buy make-up and fashionable clothes. A series of retouched portraits show her and a girlfriend in Oslo in the late 1920s with wavy hair, fur collars, pearl necklaces and 'diva gazes'. Since she was in the lucky situation that she did not have to send money back home to her family, she could also invest in things for her future, for instance, a full dinner set that cost her half a month's salary. When we interviewed her more than half a century later, the dinner set still sparkled in the vitrine cabinet in her rural home.

To relax, to enjoy yourself, to have fun has constituted the central agenda of the twentieth century's emerging youth cultures. The rising standards of living made an increasing number of young people reach for more than the thrift and toil of their parents' lives, and it also opened up new horizons of individual freedom from family demands and moral obligations. This profound change in moral orientation in modern society was closely intertwined with the rise of mass culture and consumption. In the 1920s and 1930s youthful fun became connected to fashion, music, films, smoking, drinking, dating and romance—all of which required money, material goods and special arenas for young people, and made the older generation panic (Frykmann 1988; Modell 1989; Wennhall 1994; Drotner 1999; Søland 2000; Illouz 2007). Photos of Norwegian high-school classes from the first decade of the twentieth century show young women in long dresses and topknots, whereas in school photos only two decades later, all the female students had short hair and fashionable clothes (Krohg 1996). Modern technologies like radio, phonographs, film and magazines led to the breakthrough of an international youth style in the 1920s. The impact was strongest in the cities, even if young women from our sample who grew up in remote rural areas in Norway also followed the new times closely through radio, touring films and fashion journals. In the 1930s and 1940s youth culture became more separated from the adult world. With the arrival of jazz, swing and hot, young people started to pursue their own taste in music and ways of dancing, and young female bodies were now exposed in shorts and two-piece bathing suits. The 'swingpjatters' from the early 1940s released a regular moral panic among adults in the Scandinavian countries when they danced to swing, jazz and foxtrot in their shocking outfits (Frykmann 1988; Wennhall 1994). The arrival of the sound film in the early 1930s led to an indulging in film stars and glamour. The romantic melodrama became the grand genre of popular culture of the inter-war period, especially addressing young women. The Danish youth and media researcher Kirsten Drotner (1999) argues that the mixture of moral dilemmas and emotional intensities especially appealed to young women as it could be understood as a symbolic staging of the increasing tension between autonomy and dependency that young women felt culturally and psychologically at this time.

Mediasation, commercialisation and generational protest increased in the youth cultures of the post-war period, represented by the middle generation in our sample. Music and clothes styles for young people were now separated out in marketing and sales (Cook and Kaiser 2004) based on the rapidly increasing levels of consumption. The 'teenager' was conceived by the marketing sector in the US in the 1940s and was used for the first time in print in Norway in 1951. 'Must-have' fashion items and wonders like one's own private transistor radio or battery-operated record player became epidemics in this generation of baby boomers in the 1950s and 1960s. Young people now identified as a special age group through the youth cultural sign systems, including the new youth magazines that became available at this time featuring youth fashion, beauty tips, music and film material. Rock and beat music became the cultural hallmark of this generation. An intense cultivation of music bands, film actors and idols takes over for the romantic melodrama of the inter-war years (Bjurström 1980). The idea that you can change your own personality through a new style is introduced (Johnson 1993). A girl in our middle generation, born in 1948, moved for two years to another city with her family. She still recalls her dream of how she, on her return, would have changed personality to become an outgoing and popular girl in new smart outfits and how this would change her position among her peers. In the late 1960s and 1970s the generational protest assumed more political forms, including a critical stand towards commercialisation and fashion. Long hair, hippie style and jeans took over from high heels and teased hairdos. None of our informants were directly active in political movements, but those who received higher education remember it as a period where they developed more radical political views and participated in demonstrations.

Around 1990, the youth period of the youngest generation in our sample, fashionable clothes had become brand-label clothing, and the youth style and music had become more differentiated and divided into a plethora of subcultures that signalled not only youth, but also what kind of youth (Bjurström 1997; Lynne 2000). Modern cafés had reached Oslo and were frequented by our middle-class informants, whereas our working-class informants preferred to meet at discos. The VCR and CD player had arrived, and this generation spent much time watching films and TV series together (Drotner 1991). Issues of conformity and uniqueness were at stake in new ways. To follow mainstream fashion or fads uncritically or to not be choosy in music was, at least for middle-class youth, a sign of immaturity (Christensen 1994; Jensen 2001). One of our informants, for instance, said the following about binge drinking parties: '*Okay, fine, but you're over it by the time you get to high school, like [laughs], at least I was … You're supposed to have, to show that you're in control, because that is simply a teenybopper thing.*' Everybody should be in control and 'be themselves', but the ubiquitous commercial youth cultural sign systems seemed to overtake even the most original. Counter cultures like Punk, Goth, Hip Hop and Rave are associated with the 1980s and 1990s (Bjurström 1997), but except for the music, few of our informants identified strongly with these youth cultures. We do not find anything like the generational protest and student revolt of the 1970s in this generation, but many young people, especially young women, became engaged in political activism relating to environment protection, anti-racist work, EU-protest and squatting (Christensen 1994). Compared to our two older generations as young people, the political engagement is actually much more pronounced in our youngest generation.

Of special interest in the context of this book are the ways these youth cultures contributed to changing the meaning of gender and sexuality.

The twentieth century saw huge changes in sexual morals and conduct (Segal 1994; Brumberg 1997; Jamieson 1998). The sexual revolution entailed sexual debuts at a younger age for both women and men, starting in the 1950s, and from 1970 women began having sex at a younger age than men (Pedersen 2005). Sex education for young people was gradually introduced in the second half of the century (de Coninck-Smith 2003) and gay and lesbian rights became a political issue (Plummer 1995; Kristiansen 2008). From the 1980s there was a marked increase in the commercial sexualisation of public space and also easier access to pornography through new media (Sørensen 2002; Knudsen and Sørensen 2006). A focus on HIV/AIDS, rape, sexual violence and harassment is characteristic of the period when we did our interviews (Plummer 1995). Young people, especially young women, are often seen as victims of this increasing sexualisation (Brumberg 1997; Wolf 1997). However, seen from a generational perspective, they have also been agents in the formation of more liberal sexual norms. Whereas adult women in various historical periods have challenged gender structures in work, the economy and politics, young women have rather worked 'through' gender (Nielsen 2004). By gradually changing the norms for how gender, the body and sexuality can be represented, by reframing sexuality and morality in public spaces as well as privately, young women across these three generations have simultaneously carved out spaces for female agency in relation to the body and sexuality. Young men have to a lesser degree been seen as either social agents or loci of changing sexual mores. Ken Corbett (2009) claims that the understanding of men's bodies and desires has not been seen as refigured or reconceptualised like women's bodies and desire have been, but rather have been hampered by traditional Freudian formulations. Corbett finds that men's bodies and desire 'are as disavowed as once women's bodies were' before the advent of feminism (2009: 218). Willy Pedersen (2005) also argues that whereas young women's sexual activities are seen as modern and progressive today, young men's sexual activities are seen as old-fashioned and reactionary, even when women and men engage in the same kind of sexual activities (for instance, watching pornography or purchasing sex toys). Our interviews will illuminate some of the changes that have also taken place in men's bodies and desires, but when it comes to contextual framing, the available sources offer the story seen from the perspective of the young women.

The shift in normative ideals that the young girls in these three generations identify can be described as a move from the 'nice girl' of the inter-war period to the 'popular girl' of the post-war period and to the 'autonomous girl' by the end of the century (Nielsen 2004; Nielsen and Rudberg 2007). The Danish-American historian Birgitte Søland has in a study of young Danish women in the 1920s (Søland 2000) observed that the concept of 'nice girls' appears exactly at the historical moment in the 1920s when young girls started to go out on their own with their friends, something that made them vulnerable to sexual assaults and bad reputations. Public space in the city was an especially ambiguous territory, a zone of individual freedom without the family bonds that were still intact in the countryside. Søland describes a battle from bastion to bastion with regard to young women's bodies: short dresses, short hair, sleeveless tops, bathing suits and so on—everything modern was associated with being cheap. One critique of the time was that the girls' presence in the public space blurred the lines between respectable and non-respectable women. In this normative vacuum, Søland says, it was felt as necessary to construct a dividing line between 'nice' and 'cheap' girls. By identifying themselves as nice girls, only out to have some fun, the young women could defend their right to be in a public space without losing their reputation. Female friends gained importance both as 'partners in crime' and as providing a space to discuss what the limits should be in relation to behaviour and self-presentation. The changing limits for respectable femininity are also seen in the new ideal of the young woman at this time: the lively and energetic girl with an appealing mixture of sweetness and charm replaced the shy and modest Victorian girl (Thorsen 1997; Telste 2002). The line between nice and cheap girls was indeed sharp and dangerous in the inter-war period. In particular, young working-class women were at risk of being coded as the sexual and deviant 'other' against which nice femininity was defined (see also Skeggs 1997).

The 'nice girl' disappeared during the war. The sight of young girls on their own in public space no longer shocked or provoked; thus, young women had gained more freedom and did not have to legitimise their presence by being nice. The nice girl had by now rather become a boring girl, but the 'cheap girl' was still around. This presented the young women in this generation with the difficulty of avoiding the stigma as 'cheap', while still having no clear-cut guidelines for what a girl was actually allowed to do. The American sociologist Winnie Breines (1992) writes about the contradiction in the USA in the 1950s and early 1960s between a rising glorification and commercialisation of sex in the public space conveyed by ads, music and movies, and traditional sexual morals with its demand for virginity. Virginity was not so explicitly celebrated as an ideal in the Scandinavian context, but girls could easily be stigmatised as 'cheap' if they were together with more than one boy. Breines describes how the new freedom and individuality of the 1950s and 1960s also implied a new form of exposure for young women. They were more present in the public space and they were evaluated by other young people on the basis of their individual qualities. This is probably one reason why looks, social charms and popularity with the boys were so overwhelmingly important for the young women of this generation, paradoxically enough at a time where they had more opportunities for education than ever before. Being popular and being clever in school often stood in irreconcilable opposition to each other in this generation (Breines 1992; Brumberg 1997). Relationships among girls were extended from being the 'partners in crime' of the oldest generation to including a more brutal rivalry for boys and popularity, as the free market seldom allows for sentimentality. The disappearance of the 'nice girls' in this generation, especially under the influence of the sexual revolution from the late 1960s, the increased knowledge about sexuality and the arrival of the pill,[14] may have encouraged more experimental behaviour in relation to drinking and smoking, as well as more provocative dressing and use of make-up, all causing a heightened level of conflict with parents. But the absence of a clear line between nice girls and cheap girls also meant that sexual morality was on its way to becoming a personal matter and responsibility, not just something to adapt to (Ravesloot et al. 1999).[15] Thus, freedom in the public

[14] The pill came in 1967 but was not generally in use in Norway until the 1970s. Free abortion was implemented in 1978. Thus, the women of our middle generation could not take advantage of these new possibilities before they were married and had had children.

[15] Ravesloot et al. (1999) conclude this from a study of courtship and sexuality of young people in the 1950s and 1990s from the Netherlands, where they find a change from prohibition morality to

space carved out by the inter-war generation under the banner of being nice girls was further elaborated by the post-war generation in a curious blend of increased individualised morality and responsibility on the one hand and a strengthening of the heterosexual script on the other.

If the nice girl had disappeared for the post-war generation, the contour of the 'cheap' girl became blurry towards the end of the twentieth century. Young women were now allowed to experience both desire and ambition as gender-syntonic. Double standards for girls and boys are still at work, but the dominant view is now that it is a purely personal matter when and with whom to have sex—as long as one is cautious about using contraception (McRobbie and Garber 1975; Pedersen 2005). It is now rather the fear of *not* being self-reliant and independent enough that interferes with both friendships and sexual relations. The popular and boy-crazy girl now lingers on the edge of conformity, neither true to herself nor to her female friends. The danger is no longer that of being 'a fallen women', but rather of being 'a fallen subject' (Nielsen and Rudberg 2007). The ideal of the 'autonomous' girl may be finishing off the 'cheap' girl, but in turn produces another anti-type: the weak and dependent girl who cannot stand up for herself. Such girls are no longer seen as 'cheap', but rather as 'exposed', as girls vulnerable to sexual assaults. This discourse has become widespread in social and medical research on youth sexuality, where early sexual experiences have been consistently associated with poor resources and early general behaviour problems, especially among young girls. Thus, the class position of the 'exposed' girl is unchanged compared to the 'cheap' girl in the two oldest generations (see Pedersen et al. (2003) for a review). In all generations we find a specially designed category for young girls who have too much sex or sex in the wrong way, and this category has almost inextricably been connected to working-class girls.

For the middle-class girls in this generation, the gender-related problem is not so much sexuality as their bodies, which have now become the most ultimate expression of the self. The demands of exercise and health as well as the widespread panic regarding 'epidemics of fat' (Bordo 1999:

situational ethics (Ravesloot et al. 1999). In our study we find the same direction of change, but taking place already in the middle generation (the 1960s) (see Chap. 8).

69) had become a dominating cultural discourse when we interviewed the youngest generation as 18-year-olds. According to the North American historian Joan Brumberg (1997), this represents a historical trend in the last century, where society changed focus from inner qualities to outer looks, which in turn were ever-more commercialised and uniformly presented. The body appears to be a central battlefield between new subjectivities and old gender discourses both outside and inside young women today. This tension was exactly the point of frustration that exploded in the Scandinavian countries in around 2000 in a number of debate books by young feminists of the same age as our youngest generation (for instance, Skugge et al. 1999). The young middle-class women behind these books did not have any problems in making their voices heard, getting good marks and good jobs; the problem was that they were still caught in gender stereotypes, especially when it came to the body project. As body and style have become the central points of modern self-construction, the young women seem to be caught in a dilemma: it is deeply offending to girls who see themselves as subjects to be reduced to body and gender. The books by the young feminists circled this topic: their problem was not that they were not pretty enough, but that they still *cared about* being pretty enough. Shame is connected to having failed as a self-contained individual. This context of shifting youth cultures, and especially the cultural meanings surrounding the young female body, is an important context in which to understand the feelings of gender that these three generations have experienced in connection to their own and other bodies in their youth.

5

Gender Complementarity in People born between 1900 and 1920

Men's Work and Women's Work

We didn't have many earthly possessions. But we did have our own house and enough food … We had a good and happy childhood, at the same time as we had to work. And we have taken care of each other … During the summer, when my father worked at the docks—when all the coal boats came in—he earnt 1200 kr. And then we bought flour and coffee and sugar, margarine, potatoes and such for winter, in bulk so that we'd more or less get through the winter. He also had a boat he sometimes used to go fishing for dinner, when the weather allowed it … And mother always cooked, she was good at cooking. They bought pig's trotters that she pickled herself. We could eat that instead of bread, so that was in order to save bread … Quite amazing how she made the money go round … She also used to clean people's houses when they needed it, she did that too … My father helped at home as much as he could. And then he was a cobbler. We never had to stay home because we didn't have shoes. Never! (Martha, b. 1913)

Martha's account of her childhood in a working-class family in a small fishing town in northern Norway gives us a glimpse of how it could be to grow up in the early part of the twentieth century. The key words are industriousness, thrift and solidarity. It was a poor childhood of simple living conditions and hard work for the majority of children, but not descending into starvation (Danielsen 1990; Kjeldstadli 1994; Nielsen 2006). The vast majority of our 21 interviewees from the eldest generation, born between 1899 and 1927, grew up, like Martha, with many siblings in families of smallholders, farmers and fishermen. They were working-class, lower middle-class or small self-employed families where money was scarce and the income insecure. As mentioned in Chap. 4, such were the living conditions of most people in Norway before the introduction of the first public policies on social security from the mid-1930s onwards.

A gendered division of work was part of the struggle to survive. Yet it took on different forms according to the rural/urban divide, which was of huge importance at a time when the majority lived in rural areas. Economic and cultural class differences crossed this main divide in a variety of ways. Borghild, a rural girl born in 1911, characterised her family as '*a family of fighters with the women inside and the men outside*'. In farmer families women would assist in men's outdoor work when they were needed, or they would do all of the work if the husband for some reason was absent. In city families, if the father had a small enterprise, the mother would assist him in different ways. In one case a mother opened her own shop, but named it after her husband. There was less flexibility the other way round, but on rare occasions men assisted in household work, for instance, in periods of male unemployment or on special occasions like the annual slaughter or at Christmas. In rural families the father generally handled the money, but the mother could occasionally make some of her own money by taking in washing and sewing jobs for people or by selling eggs and vegetables from the farm. Conversely, in the cities the father usually handed over his salary to the mother so that she could make sure that it was used in the most economical way (see also Åström 1986; Thorsen 1993a). Most people in this generation say that their fathers made the major decisions, while their mothers made decisions concerning the household and child rearing.

What is worth noticing in these descriptions of the gender divisions of their childhood is that both parents' contributions are seen as *work.* Fathers provided money through their work on the farm or outside the family, but the mothers' contribution to the family's survival is considered just as essential. Like Martha, the other informants describe how their mothers' superior skills at household work and needlework meant being able to stretch funds to provide enough food and clothing. The women in this generation give detailed accounts of their mothers' work, while the men mainly remember the food she served. Einar, who grew up at a smallholding, still remembers this with fondness and in great detail nearly 50 years later:

> *Mother made something she called chopped potatoes. It was a bit of fried pork and some chopped-up potatoes from the day before. And I thought that was delicious. And then there was a lot of oats, raw oats with milk. We had good milk since we got it from the farm. And then mother fried roe and waffles, and she made the best of what she had. I'd say that. And mother's meatballs! I've never tasted meatballs like these ever again [laughs]!* (Einar, b. 1923)

Children, especially those growing up in rural families, were introduced to this gendered division of work early on: girls were supposed to help their mothers inside the house, while sons helped their fathers outside the house. Children from urban working-class families also helped out, but here the practical circumstances sometimes led to less gendered divisions of work. Martha describes how she and her nine siblings were given their share of the work according to age, not gender: when they were five or six years old, the job was to take out the goats and sheep to pasture; when they were older, they delivered coal to customers in the mornings before school, in a wheelbarrow during summer and on a sledge during winter. If there had been a storm, they would collect driftwood underneath the piers. Later again they worked folding newspapers, or they delivered the newspaper or bills to people. All the money they earned was handed over to their mother. Martha still remembers that they got 2 kr. for folding 3000 papers—'*and that was actually a barrel of coal*'. Martha's father died when she was 17, making her the main breadwinner in her family until she married at 25. She recalls, clearly moved, how her older brother came back from sea and gave her a gold watch as a sign of appreciation. Most of the children who helped out in their families emphasise that it gave them a feeling of belonging. The work could be strenuous, but it is never described as negative, as the long and cold walk to school and back was, for instance. Johanna (b. 1910), who grew up at a small farm and worked as hard as Martha throughout her childhood and youth, explains why she did not mind helping out: '*I wanted terribly to be part of what was happening*'.

There was generally greater flexibility in women's work both for the rural and urban children: girls would often assist their fathers as well as helping their mothers, whereas very few boys assisted their mothers with work inside the house. Both girls and boys remember it as positive to help their fathers outside. The only boy who reports that he and his brothers (he had no sisters) helped their mother in the kitchen on a more regular basis resented it and much preferred helping their father. He remembers with disgust that he and his brothers were called their mother's 'little servants' (Martin, from a smallholder family, b. 1905). Brothers also got more free time and their education was given priority over that of their sisters. As boys they were expected to earn their living outside of the family, unless they were due to inherit the family farm. For girls, the responsibility for their families extended into their adult lives, and in the cases where they stayed at home to help out, this meant having to ask their parents for money for all necessities (see Thorsen 1993a). But neither girls nor boys from rural families got much education at all at this time. For economic reasons, it was necessary that they started work early, within or outside the family. The men are brief when they talk about school—they didn't belong there, writing was difficult, they didn't do well: '*well, yes, school didn't go so well for me, I guess you could say … we moved too much … it became too much of a mess*' (Anton, from a smallholder family, b. 1900). Work counted more than school where they grew up and it was a relief when they could start apprenticeships as 15-year-olds. The women generally have more happy memories of school—often remembering themselves as clever—but the rural girls also saw it as pretty irrelevant even if was enjoyable. Johanna, who is otherwise rather reserved, becomes quite ecstatic when she remembers how much she liked maths:

> *And I really wanted to do math, I really wanted to do math, I really wanted to do math, and I was, and I was, can't explain how much I wanted to do math all the time . . . and you know what, I want to do math still, yes, I do.* (Johanna, b. 1910)

What came after compulsory school was less clear for the girls than for the boys. Most of the rural girls stayed home helping their mothers or took jobs as domestic servants in other families until they married. Johanna did both: first she stayed at home to help out because her sister had already left—'*I just couldn't imagine leaving father and mother and put them out, no, I just couldn't*', she says—and later took up a post as a dairymaid at another farm. Finally she stayed half a year in a school for domestic science to learn the theory behind what her mother had taught her in practice. This turned out to be a perfect route of preparation for marrying a wealthy farmer, which she did when she was 23. For urban girls, there were more chances to continue on to middle school because there were more schools in the cities and their families did not need them in the same way. The urban girls in our sample recall that their mothers played an important role in letting them continue in school, often against the wishes of their more traditional fathers who thought education was not necessary for girls who were going to marry anyway. Clara (lower middle class, b. 1912), for example, had a mother who prioritised the education of her daughters because her sons could become sailors after compulsory school and thus had a career mapped out for them. In Martha's poor family all the siblings completed middle school thanks to an ambitious mother who herself had problems with reading and writing. Because of her good grades, Martha got into the telegraph school, and it was with this qualification that she could provide for her family when her father died in 1930. Some of the rural girls eventually saw a chance to get away from home by taking jobs as domestic servants for urban families. These families often took gross advantage of their proficiency in household work and acceptance of hard work.[1] The smallholder daughter Karen remembers with pride her first job as servant girl in Oslo:

---

[1] In 1930 40 per cent of all women with gainful work were domestic servants. In 1950 it was 25 per cent, but at this time the majority of them were employed in farm work, not in the cities (Melby 1999).

> *I was used to working and then, oh, I got so much praise, oh, I got so much praise … I remember Mrs Herman Andersen, he was a wholesaler, they lived on the ground floor, then she came and was like, 'Look at Karen, oh, how nice she has made it.' And you know, I cleaned and really went at it, because I thought … Everything was so easy, you know, compared to what I had at home, so I thought it was really fun, and you were paid for it!* (Karen, b. 1924)

What has been labelled in cultural history as 'the mentality of work' (Le Goff 1978, as cited in Thorsen 1993a) or the moral imperative of 'being of use' (Gullestad 1996) was thus installed particularly among the women in the eldest generation during early childhood. For those who did not enter into social mobility, it was kept as a strong and guiding moral value throughout their life.

Growing up urban middle class during this time did not automatically imply better material conditions or increased security than for the working class. Even if it did, the basic moral of diligence and frugality was similar. Some of the middle-class women of this generation in our sample also experienced having to leave school and start working to help the family to survive economically when the father died. However, with regard to family culture, values and life expectations, these poorer middle-class girls still share some traits with the very few informants from this generation who belonged to relatively well-off families. Harald (born 1899) and Dagny (born 1911) for example, who both grew up upper middle class, also describe a gendered division of work, albeit in quite a different version. The idea of work is here usually limited to describe the fathers' activities outside the family. However, the fathers' work is mostly implied by the fact that they needed to rest when they came home. Harald had a father who taught at the city's best upper secondary school:

> *Father always had a nap. In the afternoons he laid on a chaise longue, I guess you could call it a divan. Then we had no business in the room next to the dining room. We had to keep away. He was to be completely undisturbed and he needed that because he … and when he was done napping, he drank coffee. And then he marked papers, you know. And he had private pupils. So he had enough to do. He also worked in the handicrafts association, when he was a secretary there.* (Harald, b. 1899)

Well-off urban families had maids to do the harder household chores and Harald's mother's most important responsibility was rearing and educating the children. The father did not interfere, not even with the homework of the children, but he was present as a silent authority behind the mother. His word was the 'law'. When the children came of age, including Harald's two sisters, their father participated more actively in their future educational choices. Dagny also received higher education, backed up by both her parents (see Lorentzen (2012) about the bourgeois father's presence in the family in the early twentieth century).

Both Harald and Dagny did some work at home. Harald chopped wood and Dagny learnt to wash her own clothes when she came of age—the latter much to the dismay of the elderly maid who had been with the family since before Dagny was born. Other middle-class girls talk about doing the dishes, but nobody even comes close to the amount of work we heard about in the more ordinary childhoods. In the middle class during this time period, upbringing is not done through work, but separated off as a specific task of its own: children had to learn to behave, to bow and make curtsy, to dance, be polite to their elders, to develop good table manners, to speak properly, to do well in school and to not be greedy or egotistic. Assisting the mother's charity work, however, could be seen as educational work since it taught the children compassion with the poor. Dagny was a single child, adored and spoiled by her father, who was a wealthy bank manager in their small town. Her mother was a good pianist and dedicated much of her time to charity work, where Dagny had to assist:

> *You should've seen the amazing Christmas care packages mother made for people in the hard 1930s, when people were really struggling. Yes. And they weren't paupers' gifts either, far from it! They had those bazaars for Christmas and the money they made off of them went to the city's needy, as we said back then ... All the tasks mother gave me! I was supposed to sing, then do this, then do that, you know, then do the flowers ... There was no mercy, it was like that to have an active mum. Get ready to work!* (Dagny, b. 1911)

Thus, the distinction between work and care, which in the less privileged families was depicted as a continuum of gendered work and the provision of food, is in the upper-class families separated into the father's *work* and the mother's educational *care and compassion*.

Idealisation and Ambivalence

What feelings of gender did this division of work leave in the children who grew up with it? And is it possible to see social patterns in such feelings related to gender and social class? Both women and men have most to say about the skill sets and activities of same-sex adults, but in the relationship with their own same-sex parent, this is not without emotional ambivalence. They also share an idealisation of the opposite-sex parent, but the sons' idealisations of their mothers are less intense than the daughters' idealisation of their fathers. Ambivalent or not, the fathers represented a world outside the family that the sons knew they would become part of, whereas the daughters knew that their main access to the outside world went through marriage.

Sons: Respected Fathers and Invisible Mothers

Across social class, most of the men in the eldest generation talk extensively and with great pride about their fathers, the respect they had for him, how clever or how sociable a person he was and the positions he held in the community. Fathers are perceived as persons with authority: Knut, from a smallholder family, says:

> *I had a lot of respect for my father. Maybe not as much for my mother, because she was quieter and calmer. But it was my father who could discipline us a bit, you could say. But we weren't scared of him.* (Knut, b. 1925)

It is not primarily, or hardly at all, the stern and punishing father who emerges in the stories of the male informants. The father—and men in general—are depicted much more as the social gender, and as those who were creative and adventurous (see also Rudberg 1983). Several of the sons use the expression 'jack-of-all-trades' when they characterise fathers, grandfathers and uncles, and in this image they seem to condense a feeling of a special combination of skills, creativity and pleasure associated with masculinity. Only Anton describes his father as more socially withdrawn, and here the son–father identification seems to be weaker. The main pattern is that fathers are seen as impressive people having things (a car, a beard, friends), doing things (making tools, repairing things, singing, playing instruments) and enjoying a good time (drinking and smoking, playing cards, talking, telling jokes). Gunnar offers this vivid image of his father sitting cross-legged on his tailor's table, while other men dropped by for a chat and a drink:

> *You know that the joker in the deck sits in that position, because it was one of those long, old-fashioned tailor tables. And he tended to use snuff while he worked, because he couldn't smoke then. And then he smoked a pipe whenever someone came by ... But he knew how to sew, because there was a lot of crafting skill going into his seams. Then he'd just sit on the table, talking excitedly. He kept going like that until he was almost 70 years old.* (Gunnar, b. 1926)

The contrast is huge compared to how he describes his kind but invisible mother, who actually did much of the precision work in the father's tailor shop:

> *It was totally like, 'sorry I'm alive' ... And, well, I actually remember less about her, because she always made herself so invisible, to put it like that. Couldn't make time for anything, you know. Anything called leisure time—I never saw her sit down.*

Gunnar's mother died when he was only 13, so that might partially explain the faint image he has of her, but we find the same pattern in other men's stories. Compared to the vivid and detailed depictions of their fathers, they have surprisingly little to say about their mothers. The mothers are mostly described briefly as extraordinarily kind and hardworking, but at the same time as rather anonymous. Mothers emerge mainly as persons to feel sorry for. '*Mother was the kindest creature in the world*', Knut says. '*Mother always did her best*', Anton says. When asked directly, the men may remember that she was the one who both comforted them when they were miserable and who punished them when they did something wrong. But her services—the sweet as well as the sour—are taken for granted. One could interpret this as a defence against having to admit to their dependency on her, which may also be a reason for the need to exaggerate her weakness or her harmless kindness. They do remember their mothers' hard work, but imply that she worked *too* hard for a woman.

Even though women's work is seen as proper work in this generation, it stays within the borders of gendered work. Some mothers had to perform what the sons understand as men's work, and this calls for their compassion and may even trigger some critical remarks towards the otherwise admired fathers. In these cases the mothers emerge as stronger objects of positive identification. Einar describes his mother in very positive terms: she was strong and tough, but also a person who could allow herself a drink and a dance. Thus, she embodies both the strength and some of the fun normally attributed to men. But he thinks she had to do too much of the hard work on the small farm and says ironically about his father that '*he was afraid of getting dirt on his fingers*'. The compassion and identification with the mother here override the fact that the father worked most of the week as a road worker, which evidently also makes your fingers dirty. The working-class boy John, whose father died early, describes with a mixture of admiration and compassion his mother who 'worked like a man'. She was 'her own boss' and became unusually strong:

> *I could see mother was strong. We lived on the fourth floor and there were no washing machines back then. The washboard was the washing machine. Making a fire in the washhouse and everything. And a hand-driven mangle, and large and small wringers that thundered on. Mother picked up that tub like it was a basket of feathers and carried it up to the attic and hung the laundry. She was strong. But she must've made herself strong. You see that a woman can be strong too.* (John, b. 1919)

Because she was such a kind person in life, the chapel was crowded at her funeral in spite of her having been just '*a regular, simple person*'. She is described through her generosity and hard work, yet John offers a much more colourful and enthusiastic description of his father who died from a venereal disease when John was only five. His father had been very clever in everything he did, and even bought a car! In the accounts of Einar and John the mother emerges as a visible person because the gender order went wrong in one way or another. But no matter how strong women may be, they are still seen as victims of circumstance. Only the upper middle-class boy Harald depicts his mother in her own right without making her into a person to feel sorry for. She is described as an intelligent and educated woman who taught him to read and write, and who also maintained strict discipline among the children, sometimes with corporal punishment. However, in keeping with the other men in his generation, Harald is still much more elaborate in his descriptions of his father and his public positions.

Most of the men say they resemble their fathers, but the identification is rarely without some ambivalence. Questions of authority and competition seep into their stories: how well did they do in their own lives, compared to their fathers, uncles or brothers? Masculine competition appears to be an important underlying issue here. For some of them, the ambivalence is connected to an unfinished settlement with authority: Knut, who says that he admired and respected his father, also stresses that he himself is a less controlling person and a better craftsman than his father. He sees more similarities between himself and his paternal grandfather, who, he says, was kinder and better with his hands. On several occasions during the interview, he emphasises his own independence and support of equality. He has '*never grovelled for the boss*' and unjust treatment makes him extremely angry. This energy has made him very active in the union.

Hence, we may discern a class-related pattern of feelings of gender among the men in eldest generation where the mothers' strength is reinterpreted as weakness and disowned as feminine. Skilfulness, work and fun, but also issues of authority and competition are emotionally connected to masculinity, and they identify with this masculine world. The emotional meaning of femininity is associated with being a victim of hard social conditions or is idealised as a faint and abstract goodness, except when connected with enjoyable memories of food. It calls for their compassion because they are fond of their kind mothers, but not for engagement and positive identification, unless the mother also embodies some of the masculine values. The general pattern is that the identification with the mothers is split off, and they try to be like their fathers—including the ambivalences that this identification entails.

Daughters: Strict Mothers, Kind Fathers

Quite a different image of mothers emerges in the interviews with the women of this generation. The women do not see their mothers as weak; quite the opposite, as they see them as very capable and hardworking people. Mothers were the first to rise and the last to go to bed. In most cases, mothers are described as competent, strong and healthy, often stronger than the many fathers who fell ill or died of exhaustion. Johanna, who grew up at a small farm, says that her mother did much of the '*men's work*' and that the mother tried to conceal this from her husband, who suffered from weak health. Her mother's proficiency in household work and Johanna's participation in this are described in detail, almost as bodily memories, and with considerable enthusiasm:

> *Mother had a great knack for all kinds of work, apart from using the axe; she didn't know how to do that, no, no. But with food and cooking, and I really liked to be close to her when she was dealing with food, and know what she added here and there, and learn it all, also how to bake bread. I really liked being with her, because I had the impression that she knew what she was doing, her housework, and I got to learn it. She sewed shirts too, we didn't buy them at that time, she made working shirts for the men. She weaved often, and then she sewed, and then I learnt how to sew, and that was the best of all!* (Johanna, b. 1910)

Especially for the farmer girls, but also, as we have seen, for an urban working-class girl like Martha, femininity is positively associated with an ability to work, something that is also seen in the female informants' depiction of strong, clever and nice grandmothers and aunts. These were in fact nicer than their own mothers, who are often described as rather strict and short-tempered. The mothers are the ones who smack them, and they seem to be the primary agents who convey the mentality of work and frugality to their daughters. So even if the relationships between mothers and daughters are close in practice, and the daughters identify positively with the skill sets they gain from their mothers, we also find some relational ambivalence towards these powerful, competent and often quick-tempered mothers. In cases where the mother insisted that the young adult daughter should stay home and help out against her will, we find traces of bitterness that are quickly disowned as soon as they surface in their stories. However, bitterness is expressed with less reservation against 'selfish sisters' who just went away and left it to their younger sisters to stay and help the parents. This was the case for Ingrid (b. 1910), whose mother owned the shop carrying the father's name. Her mother needed a helping hand in the shop and the daughter stayed on from she was 14 and until she married at 25, working from 8 am to 8 pm with very little pay. Her sisters '*just left, leaving me behind, and then I had to stay*', she says, still resentful.

Compared to these strong and strict, clever and hardworking mothers, the father emerges as the kinder person in their memories of childhood and youth, calmer in his temper and often associated with fun and pleasure. He took time to talk with them and made toys for them. Ingrid remembers her father making skis and sledges for her and her sisters, and she describes her father as a calm and balanced man, who was never angry. He was also seriously engaged in moral questions and in the society around him. As with the sons, the daughters take pride in the fathers' positions in the local community; however, they offer more elaborate descriptions of the father as a person. Most of the women say they felt closer to their fathers than to their mothers, resembling their fathers more in terms of their mindset. Johanna, who we just heard enthusiastically describe how much she learnt from her mother, says with pride that her father always preferred her to help him with the work outside because she was so strong and persevering. While they worked side by side, her father told her many things about politics and about his travels around the world as a young man—'*he was quite an encyclopaedia*', she says. They never disagreed on anything: '*I felt very much … on the same wavelength.*' However, she also understood that the political world was reserved for men. Girls could accompany their mothers to religious meetings or meetings in the farmer women's union, but not their fathers to political meetings.[2] Even if the women in this generation felt attachment to and identification with their fathers, they do not consider their fathers' skill sets as models for themselves. Thus, their idealisation of him may be an expression of aspirations they had to abandon. The farmer's daughter Helga (b. 1918) conveys this indirectly when describing how she experienced the deaths of her parents: '*It was terrible when mother died, of course, but it was even worse when father died.*'

The relational ambivalence towards the mother never makes the farmer girls question their mothers' proficiency, and we do not find the competitive drive that is present among the men. On the contrary, the farmer girls stress that they themselves as adults never even came close to their mothers' level of proficiency and diligence. Among the rural working-class girls we find a more ambivalent evaluation of the mothers' work and a sadder tone in the descriptions of their admired, but often more distant and tired, fathers (see Lucey et al. 2016). Here the mother's proficiency is more often associated with perfectionism and exaggerated frugality than with the relatively high status of female work in the farming culture. Gerd, who grew up in a poor rural working-class family, mentions her mother's neglect of the children because she was so intensely occupied with housework:

> *She was good at it [housework], she sort of had, she pottered around and sort of made the housework last the rest of the day [laughs], I have to say that. Because I'm the type that has to be done with it quickly and then sit down to do something else. But she pottered around, ironed everything she didn't have to iron, ironed no-iron sheets and duvet covers, and all the undershirts. It was always ironed, she ironed at night, and it wasn't necessary, because you see, if you iron these things, they stretch. If you didn't iron them, they'd fit better. I've never done that, ironed like that… They never knew what we were up to, oh no, we were by the lake, we lay by the lake all summer, and my youngest sister, she almost drowned. I don't understand that mum dared this, I wouldn't have dared.* (Gerd, b. 1927)

[2] Martha is an exception here. Political Labour had a strong history and position in the town where she grew up. Her father was active both in the union and the party and her mother joined Labour Day marches and meetings about legalising abortions. Martha herself joined Labour's youth organisation.

In this case Gerd comes close to a disidentification with her mother. She explains her own choice of having only one child with reference to this: she wanted to have time for the child. She also mentions her own mastery of fine needlework, one of the few things that her clever mother was not good at. In contrast to this ambivalent description of her mother, she describes her father with tenderness and compassion, but also portrays him as a weaker figure who died early of the hard work. '*Father was too good to live*', she says, still sorrowful after so many years. She has fond memories of how she sat on his lap as a little girl when her mother was away and that he had sweets in his pocket. When she came of age, their relationship became more distant, but she still treasures one memory from her youth when her father took her in a cab to the nearest town to buy her clothes for the upcoming confirmation: '*you can decide for yourself, he said, yes, both shoes and a hat and gloves, and I … yes, he gave me that*'.

What we see in the stories of all these women are variations of a tension between an ambivalent identification with the strong mothers' world, to which they belong, and a positive but socially impossible identification with the idealised fathers, who live in a bigger world that is inaccessible and sometimes even unthinkable for them as girls to strive towards. This psychological tension may have been intensified in this generation of youth through the signs of a new and bigger world brought to the most remote farming communities in this historical period by budding communication technologies: radio, films, magazines and the first traces of youth culture and youth fashion. The rural working-class girls, who were not to the same degree protected by the high status of female work that characterised the traditional farming culture, seem to have been attracted to this modern world quite early on. Thus, they dethrone their mothers in a way that we will see became the general pattern in the next generation. Another sign of an emerging bigger world at this time was the increased geographical mobility. Many of the women talk about aunts and sisters who made it to the city or even to America. They may criticise and envy these women, especially if they were their sisters, but also criticise themselves for not being bold enough to do the same. For some it was because of external restrictions, while for others it was their own fear or ambivalences that kept them back. Johanna says that listening to her father's adventures had made her want to get out there, maybe get a job, see how other people lived, '*but no further than I could get back home*'.

The least degree of ambivalence towards mothers and the least idealisation of fathers are found among the middle-class girls. They also see their mothers as strong and competent, but rather than focusing on her skills to run the household, their emphasis is on her persona as intelligent, educated, mild, caring and loving. '*There are no weak women in our family*', Dagny claims with pride. Dagny also adored her father and she was often allowed to visit him in the bank nearby, where he worked. In other middle-class families where the fathers were not much at home, the fathers are depicted by their daughters as rather vague figures, living in a different world. They may be described as good-looking and charming men and thus as attractive 'others', but seldom present enough to compete with mothers as objects of identification. This seems to represent less of a problem when the mother, as in these cases, is seen as both strong and caring and also associated with a broader repertoire of skills than merely household work. However, as we shall see later, these self-confident girls were partly out of sync with the social possibilities of the time: even for them, there were few routes out of their families other than through marriage.

The emotional relationships with the parents expressed by the women and the men in this generation display both complementarity and asymmetry. Both women and men identify positively with the knowledge and skill sets of the same-sex parent. However, the ambivalence that often comes with this identification appears to be of a different kind. For the men, it is connected to competition between men, the question of whether they managed to become the equals of their fathers. Their identification with their mothers is split off, maybe because it represents their own weakness and dependency on them, except in their legitimate need for food. For the women, the skill sets of the same-sex parent are inflected by the mother's strictness and sometimes her perfectionism, which stand as contrasts to the father's kindness and calmness. They belong to their mother's world, but there is also a world outside that may hold more attractions and that has a much stronger contour and presence in their narrative about their fathers than the men's muted depictions of their mothers' world. Thus, the ambivalence towards the same-sex parent and the idealisations of the opposite-sex parent appear to have different psychological dynamics. For the women, the question is not whether they became their mothers' equals, but was being like her actually anything to strive for? Was mother clever or was she a too hardworking, nagging and overachieving perfectionist? In the case of the women, the identification with the gender order is thus undertaken with some emotional reservation that we do not see among the men.

(Female) Bodies and (Male) Sexuality

The gender complementarity experienced by the eldest generation is also found in the way they talk—or do not talk—about bodies and sexuality, including the gender specific emotional ambivalences we just heard of. Bodies, and especially the generative and problematic aspects of bodies, are more or less associated with women, whereas sexuality is construed as an exclusively male urge to be lived out or kept in check.

According to the Norwegian social anthropologist Marianne Gullestad (1996), women in general tend to talk more about the body compared to men—both its pleasures and problems. This is not quite borne out in our study, where the men also often inform us about injuries and diseases, both due to the war and their old age. However, these stories are still associated with male strength and outward activity, since they are usually told in order to underline the importance of enduring and overcoming personal bodily suffering. Thus, the experiences of their own bodies reflect their general mentality of work and their feelings about masculinity. The contempt for weaklings who lack the stamina to overcome such troubles is often brutally clear, and the taboo against complaining is evident. It is not unreasonable to interpret this as a defence against the fear of losing masculinity. Knut also says in the interview that, in his eyes, a man who is occupied with his appearance is not a man.

The fact that a male body, ailing or not, is obliged to take responsibility for himself and others is strikingly formulated by Einar, who was injured in the war. He reports numerous surgeries, bleeding wounds and continuous pains. This has evidently ruled his whole life and has made everyday activities into almost insurmountable challenges. Yet being a man who stakes his honour on providing for his family, he expects to endure this. The self-evident masculinity personified in the strong, working body is central when it comes to providing for a family. It is also important as part of a competitive comparison between men, often in connection with size and strength. Harald describes his own bodily assets with great satisfaction: when he was 15, most people thought he was 18, in contrast to his tiny and frail brother. He thinks that the brother's later grudge against him is due to this difference in size and strength. At the same time as size/strength are important factors, they should come 'naturally' (meaning through work) and the body itself is not yet objectified or dwelled upon unless it fails as an instrument. The interest in bodies per se is felt as feminine, and biological, age-related changes ('puberty' is not yet a term common in this generation) are associated with girls, not boys. For Knut the happenings in the world around clearly overshadowed his own experience of the bodily transition from child to man:

> *How it is with girls, I don't know. But right now I'll only talk about myself. I felt like I never had a problem when I was 14, going on 15, 16, 17. Because you could say that I came right into the outbreak of this war. There was a lot of excitement around that. You wondered how it was going. You saw that the Germans were advancing on and on. And then they were suddenly retreating, and others came in. I don't think you had a lot of time to think about yourself, for there was so much excitement around what was happening in the world … So that bodily change and that you changed from being a child to becoming an adult—I think girls notice that much more than boys do.* (Knut, b. 1925)

In many ways the women confirm the men's conception of the body as a particularly female sphere of interest. Although some working-class and farmer girls deny having had any time to 'sit and mope' over their own bodies, there is no taboo on talking about the sick or suffering body. In fact, it seems that it is only when the generative body can be understood as a sick body (and not as a sexual body) that it can be talked about at all (Thorsen 1993a). It is not hard to get the women to talk about their menstruations. Mundane activities like knitting and washing sanitary towels, then hanging them out to dry in public make the generative body a constant presence in their lives. But only the upper-middle class girl

Dagny had a mother who told her about menstruation before it happened. For most of the other women, menstruation forms a narrative of being scared almost to death as a totally unknowing young girl, then silence about what had happened, excruciating pain and more work (sewing and washing sanitary towels), as well as unbearable public embarrassment when they sometimes experienced bleeding through their clothes in the classroom. Some of the women talk about the relief they felt when they finally reached menopause. The discourse is quite straightforward: this is the 'women's curse', literally revealing the shame associated with one's own bodily impurity. The body gains more positive connotations when it comes to appearance. A nice figure and thick or curly hair was a good resource on the marriage market, as was being good at household work. If you did not possess any of these bodily advantages, there was not much to do about it. Nobody remembers dieting, but they put some effort into getting their hair done. Only among the middle-class girls do we hear about more specific worries like an ugly nose, short legs or pimples, but there was not much they could do about those either.

Seen from a psychosocial perspective, the self-evident male body in this generation seems to be part of the strong same-sex identification among the men, emotionally invested in the ideal image of the father, but also involving an undercurrent of possible humiliation and competitive loss both in comparison with other men and with regard to the fear of female weakness. For the women, the inherent ambivalence in the same-sex identification with the mother, who is both competent and yet not quite what one wants to emulate, might be reflected in the way they relate to their own generative body as more of a burden than a source of pleasure.

If the body is understood as 'female' immanence by both men and women in this generation, sexuality is as clearly and unanimously understood as 'male'. However, some of the gender similarities in *practice* are surprising: the norm of abstaining from sex at least until formally engaged was quite strong for both the women and the men. Martin says that he never kissed a girl before he met his wife when he was 29 years old. Later he wondered about the reasons for this and thinks that it might be because he did not want to hurt the girl:

> *No, and I thought about that later. Why didn't I do it—I was afraid that I would make her sad if I wasn't sure about it. That was what lay behind it. It wasn't that I didn't want it, I don't even need to tell you that. It wasn't ... But I thought that ... I didn't have relations with my wife before we were married.*
>
> *Q: So you waited?*
>
> *Yes, we did. You could say, we were engaged to be married when I came home, which we weren't the first time. But I know that mother had made up one bed for us. We were going to sleep in the same bed.*
>
> *Q: When you were engaged. So your mother did that.*
>
> *Yes, I thought it was strange. I told my mother, no ... And I asked her quietly to ...* (Martin, b. 1905)

Martin shows not only a great amount of self-control; he is also a moral guardian compared to his own religious mother. Some of the men are quite vague about sexual activities, but indicate both feelings of guilt and the necessity of self-discipline. Harald asks rhetorically: '*What is the problem with a little masturbation? That doesn't hurt anyone.*' At the other extreme, Gunnar talks about his wild youth, involving a lot of female liaisons and detailed prescriptions for seduction. The consequence of all this activity was that he got a venereal disease, which he presents as yet another hilarious story from his youth. But even such sexual excesses are socially regulated: starting a family acts as a sharp boundary between wild, irresponsible youth and grown-up masculinity. Gunnar assures us that after marriage he was never unfaithful again. Today, he claims that a real man is a man who does *not* carry on the way he did when he was young:

> *Maybe I'm not the right person to, I have admitted to my childhood and wild periods. But if we say that a man gets to the age when he stands at the threshold of starting his own family and does so. And then doesn't give a shit about it and says 'as long as I get my desires satisfied' by purchasing them, and it affects the family. I don't consider that a man. Those people ought to shoot themselves.* (Gunnar, b. 1926)

In the case of these two young men—the sexually restrained one and the sexually 'wild' one respectively—we may discern different feelings of gender: Martin, who is afraid of hurting women, is one of the men who felt close to his own brave mother, while Gunnar idealises his socially extrovert father and depicts his mother as quite anonymous. Although the psychological and motivational points of departure are different, the results will in both cases be a strong emotional investment in gender difference, and in the moral order that sustains such differences, including the complementarity that is seen as necessary to bridge the gap.

Although male sexuality has to be kept in check, even harsher rules apply to women: while men can be wild for a certain period and then develop into responsible adults, women do not enjoy the same freedoms. To be sexually wild will destroy their quality as potential mothers and wives. To the men, the possibility of female sexuality seems to go against nature, and the few who have experienced being approached by women find it almost monstrous. They cannot relate female sexuality to their emotional experiences of femininity, and sometimes their unconscious fears about it are activated. The women themselves also stick to the distinction between 'cheap' and 'nice' girls, although most of them did have sex with their future husbands after being formally engaged. There seems to be less feelings of guilt involved in this for the women than for the men, possibly because the initiative came from their fiancés. According to all the women in the eldest generation, the positive aspect of the strict norms was the lack of pressure on a girl to have sex before she was engaged. If a girl was pressured (and many tell us about hot and impatient suitors), she had the unquestionable right to say no. Unlike the men, none of the women say that following those rules was in conflict with their own sexual needs.

The women are even less willing than the men to talk about their own sexual experiences in the interviews. One says straight out that she does not want to talk about this, and in other cases this unwillingness is so strongly implied that the interviewer simply skips the questions related to sexuality. Those who do say something about their own sexuality are very brief. Ellen, a middle-class woman born in 1923 who waited to have sex until after her wedding, says briefly that she experienced it as a natural thing when it happened and that she had just followed her own feelings and instincts. But apart from Ellen those who say anything at all refer to sex as something they did mainly because their male partner wanted it. To be disinterested in sex is here seen as a fact of life, a part of female nature, maybe even inherited from their mother, as Borghild explains:

> *I was the type who didn't really care for sex, you know, not everyone does, and I think I inherited that from my mother, because I think she was like that too. I understood it, saw that she didn't really want to go to bed, no, many probably felt like that, and many I've spoken to said that they didn't think it was such a big deal…*
>
> *Q: That the boys were more interested?*
>
> *Yes, that, that is difficult, when you get married, because you think that … You have to do it whether you want to or not, satisfy your husband, but I had a kind husband, yes. I've been sick a lot and various things, I often had bronchitis and that affected my stomach badly, so I guess it was, yes, he was very kind. I told the doctor once that I have such an extraordinary husband. So yes, he understood, and he was scared to ruin me that way … Well, but we still had four kids, so it was all right [laughs].* (Borghild, b. 1911)

Although sex is depicted as something one engaged in primarily for one's husband's sake, there are also stories of youthful attractions to rather 'wild' and dangerous young men who were good-looking and good at dancing. Sometimes they could even be foreign soldiers during the Second World War, but the women who admit to this quickly assure us that they never acted on it.[3] Middle-class girls who were more confined by parental control indulged in romantic ideas rather than actions. Some of these women describe themselves as '*butterflies*' flying from one infatuation to the next. Dagny recalls that she '*fell for all boys—anything in trousers … I was constantly in love*'. However, for all the women, regardless of class, there were strict limits to observe. The female informants have little empathy with girls who became pregnant out of wedlock, thereby imposing great social shame on their parents.

[3] And if they did, this is probably not something that can be talked about in this kind of interview. In one case we learned only in the second interview with the woman's granddaughter (when the granddaughter was approaching 30) that the grandmother had in fact become pregnant by a German soldier and that the granddaughter's mother had been the result of that pregnancy. The only thing we registered during the first round of interviews with the three women was that they told incompatible stories about their grandmother's marriages and divorces.

For many of the women, especially those who grew up in rural areas, deliberations when it came to marriage followed a different logic than their youthful infatuations: the exciting dancers were rejected in favour of men who had the potential of becoming solid providers in marriages based on complementary gender roles, although they were not necessarily much fun or good at dancing. Helga, a farmer girl whose husband became a successful building contractor in the city, says the following when asked about why she married him:

> *It had to be his calm, sober way of being … A properly solid guy … Kind and … but … He could've been a bit more … fun, in a way, but that's … Then it's the matter of his work being his interest.* (Helga, b. 1918)

Helga met her future husband when she was in her mid-twenties and she remembers how anxious she had been before that about never getting married. This would have meant ending up as an old unmarried aunt at the farm.[4] It is not difficult to understand that accepting a decent marriage proposal in this generation could be a result of pragmatic considerations. But by silencing their own youthful attraction to the wild and dangerous men, they also split the relationship with the husband off from the image of the playful, fascinating father. The men, on the other hand, could in many ways safeguard the image of the 'good' mother in the shape of their wives, including their feelings of guilt towards this kind angel. They had to overcome their own wild, youthful masculinity in order to become responsible. When it comes to marriage, the women in this generation seem to have a more pragmatic view than the men, who often express a more romantic or even sentimental approach to companionship. They talk more about love in connection with their marriages than the women do, but also indicate that love deepens when the wife does a good job in the family. In this way both parties cooperate to establish the complementary gender order of nice women and responsible men. For the women, however, the emotional investment in this

---

[4] As mentioned in Chap. 4, from 1860 to 1930 there was a surplus of women in the population due both to higher mortality rates among men and to immigration. This meant that many women stayed unmarried all their life in this historical period. Thus, Helga's fear of not getting married and ending up at the family farm was based on real-life experience (Hagemann 1999; Melby 1999).

gender difference does not seem attached to their feelings of gender in the same way as for the men. If he could be said to be marrying an image of his good mother, she is clearly not marrying her fun father. The different and gender-specific emotional investment in the complementary gender order will, as we will see later, represent an unsolved tension in this generation's marriages.

Asymmetries or Irregularities in the Gender Order?

Variations in feelings of gender difference emerge once more when women and men reflect more explicitly on gender. For most of them, across gender and social class, gender complementarity is so self-evident that they do not have much to say *about* gender. Answers to questions about this most often boil down to the observation that there are natural differences between man and woman, and that these differences are expressed in the division of work. However, as we have seen, the interviews also convey the informants' knowledge of irregularities, asymmetries and inherent hierarchies in this assumed natural gender order: irregularities like women who had to work like men or men who got ill from doing men's work and even died from it; asymmetries in men's and women's, girls' and boys' work, duties and rights in rural families; hierarchies of what was seen as more or less important or exiting, or who held which privileges. In farmer families the dimension of inside/outside and the access to money and leisure time in particular contain messages regarding the hierarchy implicit in the acclaimed gender complementarity with regard to work.

When asked directly, both genders say that girls and boys were brought up in the same way, but in the women's narratives this statement is contradicted by the practices described and their ironic or even bitter comments made in relation to these. Rural girls talk about how boys got away more easily because they only helped outside rather than having to do stable work in the mornings and evenings and housework around the clock, like the girls. This meant that boys got more leisure time. '*Oh, the poor boys!*', says Gerd and laughs bitterly when she compares the workload put on the sisters versus the brothers in her family. Karen says about his brother: '*he had the rights to take over the farm and I did not, but that was how it was back then*'. Still, she had to help out much more than him with cleaning and milking: '*he did not care much about those things, no, boys could get out of it, you know, girls had to be there*'. Urban girls also remark on this, albeit with more emphasis on their parents' preferences. Lilly, one of eight siblings and with a self-employed father, says:

> *I felt like the boys were allowed to do more than the girls were, really. I felt that they had more freedom. And mother really valued her two sons, you know, so … Many of us felt like we girls weren't worth much. In some way or other. Because it was they who were … Well, they were boys, you know. It was such a big deal. Oh, goodness! But they were nice boys.* (Lilly, b. 1922)

The women clearly recognise differential treatment, but this recognition is quickly taken back when the interviewer asks about it from a modern perspective of gender discrimination—the women both know and don't know. Agnes (b. 1912) was the daughter of a wealthy grocer in Oslo and was among the few in this generation who received higher education. She recalls how she encountered gender discriminatory attitudes from adult men, including her own father, with regard to her educational trajectory. But at that time, she says, you were so used to boys and men having privileges that you did not really think much about it. The combination of acceptance and discontent with the gender order may also explain why sibling rivalry is more clearly expressed as anger towards lazy and selfish sisters who took advantages that were perceived to be outside their scope as girls.

In spite of the almost preconscious form of this knowledge, the women of this generation are clearly more aware of structures of gender inequality than the men. What the women sense as power-related *asymmetries* inherent in the gender order, the men rather tend to see as incidental *irregularities* to be mended. The men who had seen their mothers and other poor women of their childhood striving understand this as a gender order gone astray. For a man to leave men's work to his wife is interpreted as a lack of love. Einar, who criticised his father for being afraid of getting dirt on his fingers, says:

> *I would say that if it were me, then I would've done it instead of my wife. I think that's more of a man's job, to do those things … What I find strange is that people who had so much, who depended on each other as much as they did, that they didn't show more signs of affection and courtesy … But I guess it was like that back then.* (Einar, b. 1923)

Whereas the women implicitly perceive the gender order as unjust, the men's perspective is instead to fight the irregularities and restore the order. Or perhaps they want to refine the order so that they can make space for more love and recognition than they had seen between their parents? The men are not making a plea for their own privileges as men, but argue for a system of mutual respect, dependency and contribution. Through this effort of restoration, we see a reformulation of the gendered division of men's and women's work of their childhood to a more idealised and complementary notion of *male work* and *female care*. It is seen in their reflections on gender where they refer to men's physical strength and role as natural providers, and women's special ability to care and give love (see Walkerdine & Jimenez 2012). More often than not, their gender ideals are exemplified by their own caring wives and by the indirect descriptions of themselves as responsible adult men. In this model of complementarity, women are strongly idealised, but only in the roles of mothers and caring wives. Compared to the muted idealisation of their own invisible mothers, this restored gender order values and renders visible female care. Martin expresses it in this way:

> *Then I would say that the woman, she is equal to the man. In all circumstances. Nothing to separate. I almost value her more since I think she has such an important and rich task in life. And she is more caring than we men are. When I think about all the way from birth and the entire … I would say I respect her more than I respect men. Absolutely. I absolutely value her more highly. And even more because she has more tenderness and is more loving. Soft.* (Martin, b. 1905)

For most of the men in this generation, divorce becomes the ultimate betrayal of the gender complementarity model. It makes a mockery of the mutual dependency and shared destiny between a man and a woman, and is devastating for the children. They become rather upset when they talk about how women and men today go out alone with their respective friends instead of going out as a couple—they would never go anywhere without their wives! They criticise marital infidelity and the decreased work ethic, but most of all they lament the modern divorce rates. They take pride in the fact that they have been married to their wives for more than half a century. The moral decay embodied by divorce is seen in John's evasive formulations on the topic, the only man in this generation who says that he at some point contemplated divorce:

> *It went smoothly to begin with … It was later, yes. But, and then you had to get yourself together because you started to get old, you know, and there was nothing to move out for.*
>
> *Q: What did you think about then?*
>
> *Oh, I had a lot of strange thoughts. But, it went away.* (John, b. 1919)

In this way, the crumbling gender order of the present becomes the quintessence of the general moral decay for the men in the eldest generation.

We see no traces of such an enthusiastic recommendation to restore the order of gender complementarity among the women, which makes sense in light of their double identifications and their more pragmatic approach to the choice of marriage partner. While pronounced in the interviews with the men, attention to modern divorce rates is more or less absent in the women's interviews. The women's understanding of men's and women's toil in their childhood is different from the men's. Some of them rather question the strict rural work division of their childhood and say that work could have been more of a joint venture between husband and wife. Refining gender complementarity does not seem to be an obvious solution here. But as young women they were also so embedded in the gender order of their times that they did not offer any alternative to the men's project. And compared with the lives of their hardworking mothers, the cultural reformulation of male work and female care also had its temptations. One of them says:

> *I guess there was something implicit, that you didn't have to struggle so much, because you weren't going to support anyone … Back then it was the man who was responsible for the support … It was alright to be a girl.* (Agnes, b. 1912)

The emotional upgrading of femininity by the men from invisible mothers to caring wives seems to run opposite to the women's emotional downgrading of masculinity from fun fathers to boring providers.

Refining Gender Complementarity

As young couples and parents in the years after the Second World War, this generation chose to organise their lives through a gendered division of work into providers and housewives. This may be seen as a *life project* of this generation, especially for the men. Most of the men came from smallholder families and became urban working class themselves. Having their wives stay at home was something they *wanted* in order to spare them the hard toil that their mothers had had to endure, and to secure their children the best possible childhood. They describe it as a deliberate choice and talk about it with pride. It may be seen as a project where their feelings of gender and their reflections on experiences from their own childhood matched the new demands of the labour market, the rise in living standards, family policies and childcare regimes of the post-war welfare state, and the possibility for most families to survive on one income (see Chap. 4). Thus, we may see this as an historical moment where a biographically formed subjectivity, including a specific way to feel about gender, and the economic, structural and political conditions reinforced each other to create a social change in gender relations. But as the women's feelings of gender did not run parallel to the men's and as the new model also had a price tag for men themselves, tensions and unrest are built into the new life project from the very beginning. A blind spot in the new gender arrangement is the implication of the move from a rural to an urban context, which was crucial in this generation. The idea of refining gender complementarity had for many been conceived of in a rural context where women's work did not confine them to the house, but worked less well when put into practice within an urban setting where housewives were expected to do their work within the home. We see these different tensions and problems in the ways in which men and women talk about their married life and their relationships with their children.

All the men we interviewed in this generation became the sole or main providers for their families, and none were divorced. In some cases their wives took part-time jobs—always adjusted to the needs of the families—but this is not an elaborated topic of discussion in the interviews. A few men acknowledge that it did help with the family's economy, but they stress her contribution within the family much more. The men were prepared to work hard as providers to enable their wives to stay at home, and in this process of refining gender complementarity, women's work was transformed into care and service. Knut gives this depiction of his own family life:

> *Well, we got up in the morning, she got up with me. She made my work lunch. I went to work, and when I came home, what was the first thing I did? Sniff, sniff, what is for dinner today? Because that was exciting. I didn't know, because she was the one who did all that.* (Knut, b. 1925)

He also stresses the emotional services in form of the soothing effects his wife has on his own more aggressive temper:

> *Oh yes, I can be a hothead and get it out. But then I have someone who has such a soothing effect on me that she calms me down pretty fast. She is my exact opposite, you see, because she is calm. She steadies me if I feel some kind of injustice. Then she manages to quiet me down.*

Given the clear identification with their own fathers, it is not surprising that it never occurs to the men that it was an option *not* to work outside the family. But the accentuation of gender division in the family itself gave the men a strong work identity. In spite of being retired at the time of the interview, they talked extensively about the places where they had worked, how rarely they were absent from work and how well they did: '*Yes, I put my job above everything else*', says the working-class man Anton. But this dedication to their work also meant that they did not have much time to spend at home, either to do household work or to spend time with their children. As the Norwegian gender researcher Jørgen Lorentzen has argued, this was a period where the father's importance *to* the family was strengthened, at the same time as his importance *in* the family was weakened (Lorentzen 2012: 83). Most of the men express gratitude to and admiration for their wives' contributions to the household, including their proficiency as child carers and child rearers. Einar says:

> *We had three children and it went really well, she was very capable. She was a very clever girl. And there was no flippancy, she was quite grown-up, I must say. Very responsible and such a wonderful mother. I never had to think about the kids. I could work and so on. Never needed to worry ... Could trust her one hundred per cent. She took care of the kids ... Food and shelter and always well kept. And she didn't have a job outside the house. I wanted her to be home with the kids.* (Einar, b. 1923)

However, Einar also worked hard to make ends meet. He worked long hours in his shop as a shoemaker to provide for his family, which was not easy since he was suffering from severe health issues following his war injury:

> *I managed. Had to go to work. I had dependants and had brought children into the world and one had a responsibility. A huge responsibility. Bringing children into the world, that's an enormous responsibility. And you can't give up. You just have to keep going. Even if it hurts a bit sometimes. You get so much joy from it too. You have the joy of coming home. And then it doesn't hurt as much as it does when you leave in the morning. Then the children come home from school and then there is life and joy.* (Einar, b. 1923)

Even if the provider/housewife arrangement seemed to have had the strongest supporters among the men in this generation, it would be wrong to interpret it only as a model privileging men, as has often been the case in feminist analyses of housework (Hartman 1981; Haavind 1982; Oakley 1990). However, the opposite view that men were 'relegated' and 'displaced' from the family in 'the golden age of the housewife' (Lorentzen 2012: 79ff.) make them too much into passive victims of the ideology of the time. From the perspective of the men themselves, especially those who stayed or became working class in the cities, providing for their families and letting their wives stay home was also a gift of love they wanted to give. And it was a way to prove oneself as a grown-up and responsible man. Many of the men convey indirectly the sacrifices this ideal gender order put on them as well, and the losses that came with it. Some of them regret and apologise at the time of the interview that they did not take enough part in their children's lives, for instance, in their sons' sports activities, but they basically accept that the consequence of the natural order of things was that the children had a closer relationship with their mothers. As fathers their role was to provide the money and to be the authority, while the mother should give the children love and care. But the price they paid—and were willing to pay—emerges in the striking contrast between the proud descriptions of their accomplishments at work and their replies when asked what have been the most important things in their lives. Einar describes having a family as the high point of his life, and in different versions we find the same feeling expressed by almost all the men of this generation:

> *Q: what has made you most happy in your life?*
> *It must have been when I became a father, I have to say. That has been my everything. I have to explain: when you have children and when you get that responsibility and have a home and so on. Having my own home, that was great. I thought that was lovely.* (Einar, b. 1923)

As young men, creating their own family and home was an important part of their dreams. This appraisal of the family and emotional bonds may also have been strengthened further in this generation of men because of the experiences of the Second World War, as is clearly the case with Einar.

It is remarkable, though, how often feelings of guilt pop up in connection with gender among the men in this generation. There are traces of guilt in their compassion with their mothers, with regard to sexuality, in their absence from their children's lives and even when it comes to work. John, who held blue-collar jobs all his life, says: '*I have worked my entire life. If I was idle for two to three minutes, I felt bad.*' Furthermore, the strong idealisations of their wives and their sentimental depictions of 'good' femininity sometimes bear traces of guilt. Altogether, this indicates that the gender complementarity model also created problems within masculinity.

An indication of this possible connection between gender complementarity and masculine guilt is the fact that we find the least of these tensions among the few men who spent more time with their children, even if they also had wives who stayed at home. An example is the working-class man Gunnar, the son of the sociable tailor who lost his wife early and had to manage his ten children with the help of his eldest daughter. Gunnar is the only man of this generation in our sample who says he took part in the care of his children from early on. He says he had a special '*knack for nursing children*'. He pushed the pram and changed nappies and helped wash them, remembering this as very unusual for the times. He also took a lot of photos. Gunnar's love of his father encompassed more than the father's social position, as he also depicts him a unique and mild man who loved cats and people, and was generous to everybody without expecting anything in return. Thus, it may be that this father came to represent care, but without jeopardising his position among other men.

Martin and Harald, who are among the oldest men in the sample, could also spend time with their children as they continued a rural gender order by having their jobs close to the home. Martin was educated as a gardener and eventually became the manager of a nursery, which included a house for the family to live in. His wife was in charge of the home and the children, but he could drop by during the day and, for instance, help the children with their homework. Harald took an unusual route for an upper middle-class boy and became a farmer, with his father's help and consent. He emphasises how lucky he was in the choice of his loyal and hardworking wife:

> *Well, I have said that they mostly have their mother to thank for their upbringing, since I had the farm work. And in addition to that I got quite a few positions of trust by and by. The main thing was that we worked for ten hours a day back then, from 6 am or 6.30 am. Then we went inside for food and out again afterwards. And if you had meetings at night, there wasn't much time left for the children. So it was my wife who took care of that.* (Harald, b. 1899)

However, as a farmer he had the opportunity to spend more time with his children than the working-class fathers did, especially with his sons as they started to help out on the farm when they came of age. It is noteworthy that both Martin and Harald saw their mothers as strong and capable and thus do not associate gender complementarity with female weakness.

Compared to the idealisation of female care and the gratitude expressed by the men towards their wives, the silence on these matters from the women we have interviewed is more than striking. They seem to share the view that they, as women, had the main responsibility for home and family, and with no public childcare available, they did not have much choice in the matter. They tried to be more caring mothers to their children than their own hardworking mothers had been, for instance, by having fewer children, more time for them and being less strict. In this way they are clearly complicit in creating the new family model, but they definitely do not describe it as 'a golden age' Lorentzen (2012: 79) like the men do. They idealise neither their own nor their husbands' contributions. Hardly any of the women express the kind of admiration for men's efforts as providers or their own husbands' personal qualifications as the men do towards their wives. If the refined gender complementarity was given as a gift of love from the men in this generation, it does not appear to have been received as that. The idealisation of gender complementarity belongs to the men; the women made the best they could out of it. Maybe the women's small critical remarks of the asymmetries in the gender complementarity model gradually fizzled out? The times were definitely on the men's side in a period where it was both ideologically and economically arranged for married women to stay at home. The women adjusted to realities and also complied through their sensible choice of marriage partners and because of the benefits they gained. For many women of this generation, marriage and establishing your own home was the main route to freedom and independence from their parents. Ingrid, who spent her youth working in her mother's shop, felt that she finally was set free when she married: '*No chance, back then you got married, and then you had a man to take care of you.*' Helga, the farmer girl who married a hardworking and successful contractor and who helped out with the company's accounting at the kitchen table, says as she looks back: '*At least I have tried to be loyal and kind … I feel like I have stood by him all these years.*'

The lack of enthusiasm is understandable in the light of their double and more ambivalent gender identifications, including the split between boring husbands and fun fathers. It may also be seen in light of women's double burden of work that gradually found its way into the gender complementarity model. The vast majority of the women remained housewives after they married, but most of them kept occasional part-time jobs outside the family if it was necessary or compatible with their responsibility for the family, and if they had their husbands' consent. A few of the women we interviewed had worked outside the family most of their lives. Agnes, who worked as a doctor, could hire nannies and housemaids to make things go around, but this came to an end when she divorced and drastically had to reduce her spending. Another example was the working-class woman Karen, who kept her paid work after she married because she liked it and because the family needed the extra money. Only in Karen's family do we find a husband mentioned for taking part in the household work, for instance, by making dinner on the days Karen did the 'mommy shift' (evening/night work). But she made sure she neglected nothing just because she had chosen to keep her job. The minute she was home from work, the potatoes were on the stove and the wash bucket was at the ready.

Even though they agreed to become and stay housewives, the women are much more critical in retrospect of this way of organising life than the men. It is hard to imagine that their husbands would not have been aware of this discontent, but the men in our sample never mention it. This may indicate that the men's idealisation of their wives could also be a retrospective account where idealisation works as a defence against accepting the problems their life projects ran into.

It is the women who grew up middle-class and those who received or had wanted to receive higher education who most openly express their discontent in the interviews. Some of them felt overqualified and frustrated. '*I was of no use at anything*', says Dagny, who was not able to use her law degree in the small town where her husband got a job. Ellen, who had to postpone her strong dream of an education first when her father died when she was 16 and then because the school was taken over by the Nazis during the war, finally gave in when she married: '*then it was natural to quit, and to be at home—that was as it should be*'. But in hindsight she thinks it would have been better for her to get out more:

> *You use yourself differently than when you're at home, you know … Yes, a little shut in. I don't know if my children really benefited that much or understood why*

> *I was at home. All these years, I was always at home when they came home, and so on. I don't think that.... , if I had been out, I think they would've been just fine. I think I've done a lot more for them, really, than I had needed to do. And that I don't ... I don't think they have noticed or appreciated it.* (Ellen, b. 1923)

Clara, who became a nurse and divorced before her child was born, is clear on the advantages this difficult choice of divorce gave her: it was a challenge to be a single mother in the 1950s, but it also meant that she had to learn a lot of the things that a husband would otherwise have done. She believes this has made her very independent, as well as allowing her to travel as much as she wanted—'*and I hadn't done that if I had been in a marriage*'. Many of the women from farmer or working-class families, who had less education or educational aspirations, also say that they would have liked to experience the world a bit more or to have learnt more. Some say that their husbands worked too much and were at home too little. Some reproach themselves that they were not curious or courageous enough, or that they were too frugal all their lives. There are some unsettled matters here, but it is important to be aware of the retrospective perspective: at the time of the interview, they knew how radically women's lives had changed in their daughters' generation. In the end, the vast majority of them conclude that they have been very lucky in life and have no reason to complain. They used the skill sets they had learnt from their mothers and became effective housewives—although some of them felt that there was little to do in a small apartment in town compared with the bigger rural households that their mothers had been in charge of.

Justice versus Equity

Asking about attitudes to 'gender equality' is evidently anachronistic for the two eldest generations. The modern discourse about gender equality did not take off in Norway until the 1970s. However, the concept seemed to make retrospective sense for the older generation by activating either earlier experiences of differential treatment and injustice or, instead, a defence of the gender order as they knew it from their childhood or adult life. Their reflections on equality and justice are connected to class rather than to gender, but when asked directly about gender equality, they tend to frame it as an appraisal of the positive and negative sides of the old gender order compared with today's gender order. For the men, modern gender equality is fundamentally at odds with their own life project as it makes their own form of masculinity—and the sacrifices that came with it—worthless. It also makes their idealised stay-at-home wives the targets of critique. They are occupied with the crumbling moral order in many areas and trace this decay back to the material greed of modern times, where people expect to get everything in their lap without having to work for it. As we have seen, their critique of modern times is epitomised by their worry about the increasing prevalence of divorces.

However, these old men are also aware that things *have* changed since they established their own families. Some of them help their wives more in the household now after they have they retired, and think this is fair but not easy to learn at such a late age.[5] Their investment in the gender complementary model is much stronger than the women's and they strive to reconcile this with the new times. Behind their worry for young mothers today we discern compassion with their own hardworking mothers, whereas the discontent of the women of their own generation seems to have gone more or less unnoticed. Martin, who idealised the female homemaker in his own marriage, says:

> *Now it's more even. Man and wife are more on the same footing. Often they both work. My daughter-in-law—and then he has to help with various things at home. Before they got married too. Inside as well, when she is at work and comes home at 16.30. And they have two children. So it's much more even now. It wasn't like that back then. The wife didn't work, outside the home. There's probably more of that today, but it could result in the wife being more overworked when she both has a salaried job and has to keep the home.*
>
> *Q: Yes, because she is still responsible for the home?*
>
> *Yes, you never get away from that, that equality that the husband does the same things, looking after the children or those things. And we are probably not*

[5] Statistics from 1988 onwards indicate a clear rise in positive attitudes to equal sharing of housework and childcare in all cohorts. For instance, the percentage of the cohort born 1931–1934 who thought housework should be shared equally rose from 38 per cent in 1988 to 52 per cent in 2008 (Hansen and Slagsvold 2012: Table 6.2).

> *fit for the task. It becomes a chore for us, without the joy it is for the wife. It can't be, because we are differently wired. Quite differently wired.* (Martin, b. 1905)

Martin defends the complementary gender order by invoking psychological differences, but is also at pains to make clear that this order does *not* represent a value hierarchy, but quite the opposite. Others refer to biological differences in strength. Harald is fiercely against the gender-neutral law regarding taking over the farm that was passed in 1974: '*It doesn't fit a girl to be a farmer*', he says, it is too much hard work. But even in situations where the woman is strong, it feels 'against nature' to mess with the gender categories. John, who talked about his mother's strength when she carried the laundry basket up to the attic, laughingly cites a former Labour politician who once said in response to a question about his view on gender equality: '*In our house there are two different genders, that's all he said.*' However, John also feels it necessary to assure the interviewer: '*But I would never step on a woman*' and he adds that violence against women is '*the absolute bottom*'. The gender complementarity order also presupposes a decent and protective man. Some of the men support the idea of gender equality in the workplace. These are working-class men who have been active in their unions and who extend their resistance against class inequalities to embrace gender equality. Gunnar, the son of the sociable tailor, has even been a pioneer in hiring women in his workplace. But even these more gender-progressive old men find it a bit exaggerated if women *have* to be better than men all the time, and privately prefer women to stay home as long as there are children to care for. They defend the mild and kind motherliness of the feminine carer against new ideas of women becoming like men.

Even though none of the women in the oldest generation would call themselves feminists, their attitude to gender equality is markedly more positive than the men's. Like the men of their generation, the women criticise both the class differences from their childhood and the material greed of today. They worry about their stressed daughters who have to take care of both family and outside work, but they also think that the daughters have managed this situation rather well and admire them for it. Thus, for the women, the belief in gender complementarity is not so emotionally hard-wired as it is for the men. We only hear one explicit defence of the gender complementarity model among the eldest generation of women. It comes from Borghild, who stayed rural working class all her life, and she emphasises the joint responsibility and the value of women's work in the agrarian family economy:

> *So far my opinion has been that a woman, she belongs to the house, and a man should go to work … in the old days, they started out with two empty hands, the man struggled outside and she struggled inside, maybe with a lot of kids, and they got by then, and I think they would've gotten by today too if they hadn't started with that gender equality. But that's of course because they have so much education today that if they marry, they want to continue with whatever they were educated to do, and there's something to be said for that too. But then I think it's all too easy that the woman may think 'I can just leave it all, because I have my education and I can get another job', and then it'll affect the kids and they'll get the same attitude.* (Borghild, b. 1911)

Other women with agrarian roots instead connect the question of gender equality to the asymmetries and injustices in the gender order of their childhood. Johanna, who married a farmer, says quietly that she thinks that too much hard work fell on women and that there should have been more cooperation between husband and wife. Had she been younger, she would have liked to have a job of her own outside the family.

The strongest support for gender equality is found among the women who received a higher education or had wanted one. The combination of strong and kind mothers and distant fathers in the middle-class families seems to have produced fertile soil for supporting gender equality, even if they were not able to put it into practice in their own lives. Their focus is on the equal capabilities of women and men and on women's right to freedom of choice. Clara grew up in a community where most men were at sea and the women took care of things at home. She connects her positive attitude to gender equality today to her experience of strong women and an encouraging mother, but it was not a relevant issue when she was young:

> *We were girls after all, and I thought I had quite a strong position as a young girl in my circles. So I didn't really think that it, I wasn't so concerned with*

> *that. I did feel that, well, I have always been pretty self-reliant, really. And I've done what I wanted … and with a wonderful mother who listened to what you said. Was never … she thought it was great that you were independent and did what you thought, that you did your own thing. I have always made the conditions of my own life. I have never asked anyone what I should become or anything like that.* (Clara, b. 1912)

Agnes, also born in 1912, had a more subdued mother, but still understood her message: '*Mother was a little … she thought women should be forward. That's for sure, without her saying anything, then … she liked it.*' When she was finally allowed by her father to attend university in 1932, she experienced being part of the first cohort of medical students where there were '*lots and lots of girls. There were seven out of 50, and that is a lot*'. However, even the women with higher education were first and foremost obliged to be wives and mothers, unless they divorced. Whereas the men in this generation are loyal to their belief in gender complementarity, at least within the family and with regard to personal capabilities, the women are stuck in the tension between beliefs in justice, equality and freedom on the one hand, and the strong social norm of gender complementarity and gender hierarchy on the other.

6

Gender Equality and the Struggles of People born in 1940s

Monica Rudberg

Men's Work and Women's Service

> *Well, he earnt the money and she spent it [laughs]. Because she never worked, she stayed at home. Most did, back then. But she was the one who took care of everything. She paid the bills and did the shopping. I guess that was pretty common at the time. Especially that one person was at home and the other was at work from early morning till the late afternoon.*
>
> *Q: Did she have the most say in how to bring up the children?*
>
> *I guess so. I can't really say, because she was at home and we went to school and came home again, and she was there when we came home and he had already gone when we left; when we got up, he had already gone. And he came home after we did. So automatically it's the one staying at home who took care of that, yes.*
>
> *Q: Did you have a relationship with your father or was he a little distant?*
>
> *Not distant, I'd say, pretty normal. Not that we've had any sort of, what do you call it, affectionate relationship.* (Arne, b. 1930)

Arne, born in 1930, grew up urban working class. He is the son of Anton, who dedicated himself fully to his work in order to provide for his wife and children. Anton himself grew up at a smallholding and moved to the city, where he started working as a carpenter shortly after the First World War. From Arne and the others of the middle generation in our sample, we learn how they as children experienced the refined gender complementarity model promoted by their fathers and ambiguously adapted to by their mothers, and what traces it left in their own conceptions and feelings of gender. The main bulk of the 33 women and men we interviewed from this generation are born between 1940 and 1953; seven are born before the Second World War. Most of them grew up in working-class or lower middle-class families in cities, while some came from the upper middle class. A few grew up at farms or smallholdings and describe much of the same rural work patterns between men and women as the eldest generation did. But even in these cases the division urban/rural holds much less significance in this generation than it did in the previous one.

In the cities, the provider/carer model led to more absent fathers and more present mothers, as in Arne's case. Most of the informants describe the division of work and care in terms of fathers who worked long hours and then fell asleep on the couch with the newspaper over their heads. Some fathers left in the morning before the children were awake, or left after dinner to tend to a second job or to help friends and family with construction work. Social class does not add much variation to this general picture. Dagny's daughter Drude (b. 1940) remembers that the whole family tiptoed around when her organist father rehearsed. They knew he needed peace and concentration to work. In this case the father worked from home a good deal, but he never took part in any kind of housework or carework and was often served his breakfast in bed. The children of this generation remember their fathers mainly from holidays and weekends when they took them camping, went on walks in the forest or took them to sporting events. This is more fondly remembered by the women than by the men. The women remember how joyful these occasions were compared to their mothers' preoccupation with her tedious housework. The men stress that these events, nice as they might have been, did not make the fathers sufficiently present in their lives.

In the implementation of the provider/carer model, the work, toil and economic contributions of women—which were stressed by the eldest generation when talking about the families they grew up in—are transformed to female *service and consumption*, whereas *work and money* belong to the male world. The distinction between men's work outside the family and women's responsibilities at home may resemble what we heard from the upper middle-class families in the previous generation (with fathers sleeping on the couch after dinner and mothers in charge of the children's upbringing). Supported by the improved conditions of living and the family politics of the welfare state in the post-war period, this family model also became the normal one in Norway from the mid-twentieth century in working-class and lower middle-class families (see Chap. 4). However, the stay-at-home mother figure who emerges in the narratives of the middle generation is rarely the educated middle-class mother of the older generation who had maids to help her with the household tasks, but rather is a busy housewife with a limited horizon. As we have already seen in the previous chapter, only a few of the mothers *were* actually exclusively housewives all their lives, yet most of them are described by their children mainly in this capacity. The provider/carer model seems to have led to such a strongly male-connotated concept of 'work' that women's work became invisible, even when it was done outside the home and paid. Most of the informants say that their fathers did not do anything in the household, some laugh at the very thought that he should, and others remember with some resentment that he never lifted a finger at home and even had to do less than the children. Some of the informants from working-class families with full-time working mothers briefly mention that their fathers helped out a bit, but what they did in the household is not described further. Kirsten (b. 1953), a working-class woman and the daughter of Karen who took the 'mommy-shifts' (evening/night work), does not mention in her interview that her father cooked dinner as her mother did, but rather recalls how her working mother prioritised and spent too much time on the housework. Gunnar, the only man in the eldest generation who said he took part in the childcare, is described by his son Geir as a father who worked around the clock, but Geir also admits that due to his father's special personality, he was always like '*a magnet on children*'. Thus, to some extent it may have been the case that the father's care was also made invisible within this strict frame of male work and female care.

In the provider/carer family the work of children disappears too, not only symbolically as with women's work and with men's care, but also in reality. Children helping out is irrelevant to a father who works outside home and is to a large extent unnecessary for a mother who has all day to do her housework in a small dwelling in the city. Also in rural areas child labour lost legitimacy during the period of the middle generation. Those who grew up on a farm still see the parents' work as an expression of skill, but we hear much less enthusiastic reports about helping out and learning from parents than was the case in the previous generation (see also Slettan 1984; Thorsen 1993a). The work of children disappears both for material, political and educational reasons (cf. Chap. 4), and as an effect of the provider/carer organisation of the family that became dominant.

This disappearance creates a *generational paradox* in the transmittance of the gender order: even though the gendered division of work in the family was much stronger in the childhood of this generation compared to the previous one, they are not themselves as children brought into it as their own parents were when they grew up. As children, most of the girls, but to some degree also the boys, often did some simple chores like setting the table, peeling the potatoes, washing up or taking out the rubbish. Most of the women remember this with resentment, while a few of the men are in retrospect more appreciative because it gave them better qualifications in housework than their fathers had. Children of full-time working mothers or single mothers had to do more, but it did not represent or resemble the transference of skills that the previous generation experienced and talked about with pride for them either. Thus, there is a rift in the social bond between fathers and sons, and mothers and daughters. Children are not part of their same-sex parent's world as they were in the previous generation. This means less gendering and more individualisation. The obligation in the previous generation, especially for daughters, to put the needs of their families first also disappears with the generation born after 1940. Seen from a generational perspective, the gendered division of work and care in the family by itself contributed to processes of individualisation that undermined the very same gender order. Most of the urban girls and boys attended gender-segregated classes in primary school, but this practice was discontinued in around 1960. So, in spite of still-existing gender-discriminatory practices (more housework for girls, for instance), the housewife-mothers, as well as the teachers of this time, increasingly did not see boys and girls, but children. The focus was redirected to child development and away from conveying norms for behaviour (Rudberg 1983; Myhre 1994; Nielsen 1998).

Education in this generation went from being a privilege of the few to becoming more of a matter of course, as shown by the fact that half of both the men and women in our sample continued to middle school. But there are also visible class and gender differences with regard to prosperity in school and the choice of further education. In general, the women in our sample did better in school and were less dependent on their social background for educational success than the men. Few of the women, however, had any clear goals and direction when they finished school, but since the educational system was there at hand, extended and free, and their parents urged them to get more education, they drifted into further education in a highly gender-conventional way. Ellen from the eldest generation, who had to give up her intense wish of an education, has a daughter, Elsa, a middle-class girl born in 1948, who drifted into library school by using '*the elimination method in the occupational handbook*'. She had hardly been to a library, but thought the subject looked OK and then it only took three years. Martha's daughter[1] dropped out of high school and never got an education; however, as an adult she worked her way up to a very good career. Johanna, who loved doing maths so strongly but never considered it possible to pursue an education, had a daughter, Jorun, born in 1943 at the farm, whose main motivation to finish high school was that it meant that she could move away from the village: '*it was all about going to school, then you could get away*'. When she later chose to become a teacher, it was '*completely unconscious and without consciousness*'. Most of the women in the middle generation describe their choice of education as more or less accidental, and for many of them the most important consideration was to find a school in the same town as where their fiancé

[1] Martha's daughter was not interviewed, but Martha's granddaughter Mari was. Information about Martha's daughter is thus gleaned from the interviews with her mother and her daughter respectively.

went to school. The vast majority of the women in our sample became teachers, nurses, librarians or secretaries, mostly because these jobs were easy to combine with family obligations: '*I don't think I dreamt of anything but getting married and having children, and to be a teacher*', Helga's daughter Hanne (b. 1947) says. Turid, a working-class girl, also born in 1947, recalls: '*It was important to get through your education first, and then you thought, you really wanted a family.*' A few of the women experienced serious life crises connected to illness when they were young, and these women talk about a more serious and reflected choice of education.

The men did less well in school, but in contrast to their fathers, they do not deem school irrelevant. They give interpersonal and psychological explanations for their failures in forms of insensitive teachers and bullying, or blame themselves for being too lazy. Nevertheless, since the possibilities in the job market were many in the 1960s, most of the men made satisfying careers through climbing the ladder in the companies they worked for. Their choices of trade were no less gender-conventional than the women's educational choices, as all of them, except two, went into technical jobs or sales/business. This kind of career, made possible in a context where theoretical qualifications were seen as increasingly important but still attainable through practice due to an expanding job market and new industries (for instance, the developing IT industry), seems to have encouraged the emergence of a new narrative about masculinity and schooling, 'the myth of effortless achievement' (Epstein 1998). They made their way anyway and often better than those swots who had better grades in school (female as well as male nerds). They redefine the detours they had to take because of bad grades as strengths and a more creative and non-conformist way to success. Thus, in the educational trajectories of this generation we see a mixture of new individualism and old gender scripts, which also characterised their childhoods.

Anger, Distance and Closeness

The rift in the social bond between fathers and sons, and mothers and daughters that came to characterise the childhood of the middle generation is also processed on an emotional level. The harsh critique conveyed in the interviews of their parents' gendered division of work is infused with these feelings. The ambivalences we found in the eldest generation's identification with the same-sex parent, to whose world they saw themselves as belonging, have in the middle generation become more of a disidentification or a negative identification. What emerges is a new generational pattern of feeling closer to or being more like the opposite-sex parent, but the character of these feelings and their consequences is different for women and men and reflects the asymmetries in the gender order they grew up in. The shift of identification with the same-sex to the opposite-sex parent is stronger and involves much more emotional conflict and temperature for the women than the men.

Sons: Distant Fathers, Close Mothers

What the majority of men emphasise in the depiction of their parents is the available mother and the distant father. There is a remarkable shift in the perspective from 'who father is for the world', which we found in the previous generation of men's admiration for their fathers, to 'who father is for me', which we find in this generation's more low-key and somewhat disengaged descriptions of their fathers. This may express both an increasing individualisation and an actual lack of knowledge of the father's merits since he is working outside the home. His absence may in itself lead either to doubts about how successful he really is in the world or to more abstract fantasies of what it entails to be a man (see also Chodorow 1978).

Evidently, the fathers' masculinity is seen as quite outdated in the eyes of their sons, whether it is the fathers' public positions, work ethics or class identities. Knut, who held his own father in high esteem, has a son, Kjell, a working-class boy born in 1946, who says sarcastically: '*Father was and still is the last worker in the country, I think.*' Kjell finds his father's proficiency as a handyman convenient, but it does not make his father an object of admiration, as in the previous generation. This may also reflect the social mobility in the middle generation: just to be an honest worker is nothing to strive for. The relationship with the father is described as more bland than explicitly conflictual. Einar—the man who was injured in the war and made huge sacrifices in order to provide for his family so well that his wife could stay at home with the children—is described by his son Egil in this way:

> *I guess he has never been the type to be very ... He has done his job differently when it comes to kids and childrearing. He made sure we had a place to live and money for food and clothes. It hasn't been very ... He hasn't been the type to have a lot of bodily contact or to express much emotion. Very firm, you could say ... There haven't been any particularly serious conflicts between us. But not a very close relationship either, at least not in many, many years. But I have a lot of respect for him. He is a very sort of strait-laced person and honest and sincere and dutiful. And he has done quite a few things that command respect, I think.* (Egil, b. 1949)

What is wrong with fathers is not their authoritarian style, but their lack of communicative skills, emotional presence and openness. Kjell compares his father's emotional closure with his much warmer and kinder maternal grandfather, who represented '*everything father wasn't ... attentive and caring*'. John's son Jan, a working-class boy born in 1947, characterises his father as a '*fairly bad psychologist ... there was nothing directly bad in him, but he is an egoist ... selfish and takes himself pretty seriously*'. Among the middle-class sons there is more identification with fathers based on admiration for their knowledge and activities, but also they agree that their fathers' strong side was not psychological insight. Helge, born in 1938 at the farm his father Harald bought, talks with pride about his father's political activities and vast consumption of books, but adds that '*I don't think he has read any psychological novels*'.[2] It is remarkable that the only men in this generation—Geir, Magne and Helge—who say that they admire and resemble their fathers are the sons of the three men who for different reasons spent more time with their children: Gunnar,

[2] Holter and Aarseth (1993), who interviewed 23 Norwegian men between the age of 25 and 45 at the same time as we did our interviews (1991–1992), find much of the same: two-thirds of the men had negative or bland descriptions of their fathers—and their critique is not directed towards the father's authority but towards his absence and distance to the children. A Swedish study (Bengtsson 2001) of men born in the mid-1960s indicates an increasing identification with mothers, compared to men born in the mid-1930s who only identify with their fathers.

Martin and Harald.[3] Geir stresses his father's way with children and also sees himself as a sociable person, just like his father and grandfather (the tailor). '*A lot of silliness in our bodies*', he says about the playfulness of all the men in the family. At the same time, the sons also report a positive relationship with their mothers and say that they resemble them too.

The majority of the men say that they are unlike their fathers and that they had a closer relationship with their mothers.[4] She was the one they went to and confided in when they had problems or felt miserable. The description of the mother is often characterised by a tone of tenderness. They acknowledge with gratitude the comfort and service she provided. What mothers actually *do* becomes much more visible here than in the previous generation of men's often muted depiction of their mothers' work. The men in this middle generation are also more aware of the potential fate of invisibility of their mothers' services, like in Egil's account of his mother:

> *Yes, she was very caring at home, afraid that we wouldn't have everything we needed and was there for us in all possible ways, but perhaps too kind, she didn't demand enough from us. She fixed everything. It was like that, she cooked for us, made our packed lunches. Organised our clothes, tidied our rooms too. And kept an eye out and … She didn't maybe get a lot in return. What can I say, she might have, since we have had such a good relationship all these years and we never had any big conflicts, so I think she was happy with how we turned out. But in everyday life she got very little attention and praise for the work she did.* (Egil, b. 1949)

There are still traces of the mother as the kind victim, but Egil knows much more about what his mother actually does and he emphasises the reward in terms of relationships his mother gained. In the wake left after the absent fathers, the mother and the kind of things she does have become more visible. The close relationships between mothers and sons appear to have contributed to an identification with care and the emo-

[3] Holter and Aarseth (1993: 66) find the same: fathers whose work permitted closer contact with their sons are perceived as 'good fathers'.

[4] Two men, both upper middle class, describe psychologically labile mothers and a relation of distance. These two men connect this to specific circumstances in their families and as something uncommon for the time.

tional aspects of life. Willy, a working-class boy (b. 1925), says: '*I could almost read my mother's feelings.*' It may also lead to an incipient understanding that not only cooking but also care in general may represent a piece of decent work and a job to be done (see also Holter and Aarseth 1993). This does not, however, entail an identification with the housework she does or her position as a housewife. Whereas the men in the eldest generation felt empathy with their mothers who had to work too much, the men in the middle generation feel sorry for the potential lost in their mothers who were restricted as housewives with too little to do. Kjell puts it this way:

> *It's a shame … I would describe my mother as, well, how should I put it, I nearly said that she hasn't been able to use her abilities. I actually think she has far superior abilities to my father when it comes to … well, maybe not the practical things, but more intelligence-wise. My mother is more intelligent than my father. But she has never, until recently she has never had the chance to exert herself outside of the house. She was always at home. And I think she maybe should have had the chance to work outside the house earlier than she did. I think she would have enjoyed it, I don't doubt that for a second.* (Kjell, b. 1946)

The sons in this generation do not show the same contempt for the mother's weak position and the emptiness of her life that will become so prevalent among the daughters. There seems to be a new possibility for sons to identify with the mother's emotional care work in this generation, without necessarily giving up the strength or autonomy usually associated with masculinity. Even when the mother is described as an energetic housewife with 'dust on her brain', she is seen as a powerful figure. The tone is humorous and the descriptions respectful, like in this account from the otherwise quite father-identified Geir:

> *Very thorough and dust on the brain, cleaning herself to death. Vacuuming and cleaning and when she does something, it's not bloody half-arsed. Then she does it 100 per cent. I don't think you can find people like that today, when it comes to cleaning and tidying and order … But maybe she likes to be in charge. What can I say, the boss, but I don't mean the boss in the strict sense of the word. But if she has said something, it's smart to do what she has said.*

> *Q: Did she have most of the power at home?*
> *Yes, she has been the chief [laughs]. Absolutely, she has been the chief.* (Geir, b. 1948)

Daughters: Weak Mothers, Rational Fathers

The warm emotional tone in this working-class boy's description of his chief-housewife-mother stands in striking contrast to the chilly tone of the following account from Inger, a working-class girl born in 1950. She is the daughter of Ingrid, who had to help out in her mother's shop until she was 25 and then married and became a housewife. Inger says about her mother:

> *A very skilled housewife, perfect, you know … newly polished silver and … all that, and homemade bread on Saturdays … and that type of thing … She is kind of living a lie, she hasn't done anything sensible with her life other than being a stay-at-home wife.* (Inger, b. 1950)

The mothers that emerge in the accounts from sons and daughters in this generation are very different indeed. Also among the female informants, the critique of the outdated mentality of work is directed mainly towards their same-sex parent, but as girls they were much more exposed to their mothers than the boys were to their fathers. Jorun grew up on a farm, just like her mother Johanna, but we find nothing of Johanna's enthralled description of how much she learnt from her mother when Jorun speaks about her mother:

> *The only thing that counted was working, working all the time. And she didn't work at a normal pace, she had to work furiously. I don't think I remember how old I was when I decided that I would never become like that … and that I was waiting to get out of there … I'm not sure she needed to do that, to do everything 110 per cent, 100 would have been enough … She even monogrammed my father's handkerchiefs.* (Jorun, b. 1944)

This is a pattern of which we saw traces among rural working-class/lower middle-class women in the previous generation, but in the middle generation the contempt really explodes. The mother's skill sets are hardly seen as important at all and she is rejected as a model for the daughter's life. Even the mothers' advice to their daughters about getting an education, not marrying too early and becoming economically independent is remembered by many of the women as yet another example of the mothers' occupation with control and facade: '*She always went on about getting an education … we were better than others, et cetera, and that was complete horseshit*', says Jorun. They rarely connect the advice from their mothers to their own successful educational trajectories, and thus tend to make this intergenerational link invisible. The tone of the daughters is often angry or contemptuous and it has a considerably higher temperature than the men's bland critique and disappointment in their fathers. More than half of the women report negative or clearly ambivalent relationships with their mothers and very few mention her as the parent they felt closest to. Few think they resemble her—and if they do, they do not see it as something to their advantage. Some of them admit that the mother had a potential for doing something else, getting an education or a career, but, in contrast to the men, they often blame the mother herself for not having done anything with her life. The open negative identification with the mother is also supported by a more liberal tone in ideas of child rearing and a more psychological orientation. The daughters talk through the modern psychological discourse when they criticise the mother's emotional closure, mixed signals and endless occupation with keeping up a neat and proper facade. In this we can see a parallel to the men's critique of their fathers' emotional indolence, but with more emphasis on the mothers' emotional messiness.

Some of the farmer girls in this generation still acknowledge their mothers' strength and proficiency, and some of the middle-class girls see their mothers as kind and cultured, and may also remember with gratitude their mothers' interest in their education. For a few of them, identification rises from compassion with the weak mother. The upper middle-class girl Olaug says that she became a feminist when she was seven years old by seeing her mother struggle with the laundry in the basement: '*she was standing in a black hole, doing laundry*'. Olaug is one of the few daughters in this generation who helped out at home:

> *I felt that she had a lot to do, and I felt that I ought to help her from I was very little, because I felt sorry for her ... Yes, I was there for her, I was, all the time. My sister wasn't and my brother wasn't. They didn't understand. They didn't see what it was like for her—and I'm still the one who understands.* (Olaug, b. 1946)

But not even these good daughters take their mothers as role models anymore. The farmer girls do not want to stay in the rural areas and the middle-class girls tend to identify more strongly with their fathers, whether emotionally or as models for their own lives. This is also the case in families where the mothers worked full-time. The mothers have lost authority both culturally and psychologically. Those who had mothers who stayed at home felt surveilled; those who had working mothers complain about having been overloaded with responsibilities. In the eyes of the girls in this generation, mothers just couldn't get it right.

The father is the admired parent for almost all the girls in this generation.[5] Only in cases where the father was violent or very moody did the daughter resort to the mother, who was then seen as a victim in need of the daughter's protection. The overwhelming pattern is that fathers are idealised as either very rational and modern (compared to the mothers' intolerance and manipulative ways), or calm and generous (compared to the mothers' stinginess and perfectionism), or sensitive and creative (compared to the mothers' superficial sociability or boring rationality), or as knowledgeable and oriented towards a bigger world (compared to the mothers who are only occupied with their own house). The daughters share the fathers' interest in the bigger world and want to become like them: '*I'd say I was a Daddy's girl, yes, I was ... Mother was a homebody, she mainly stayed at home [speaks quietly]*', says Solveig (b. 1945), who grew up at a smallholding. There is something at stake here between mothers and daughters that is different from the relationship between fathers and sons, and between mothers and sons. The combination of increasing individualisation and the strong gendered provider/carer model in their

[5] Bengtsson also finds a change from women born in the 1930s who identified with their mothers to a more diverse pattern among those born in the 1950s and 1960s. Like us, she finds that the women who identified with their fathers were daughters of stay-at-home mothers (Bengtsson 2001: 88).

families seems to present the daughters of this generation with a very difficult psychological dynamic with their mothers, and the relationships with the fathers must be understood as part of this. There are several aspects to this.

One is that the provider/carer model positions the mother with less status and power in the family than, for instance, women in the farmer or fishing culture, or in the old middle-class family, where she represented and transmitted the educational and cultured values in the family. As a housewife, the mother becomes more like a servant in the family. This is not only the case in relation to the husband, but also represents a displacement of power between mother and children, especially for the daughters: from being one who assisted her mother, the daughter now may see herself as her mother's only task in life: '*I am the most important thing that happened in her life, that she gave birth to me is kind of her main feat*', says Gerd's daughter Grete, a rural working-class girl born in 1946. This places the daughter in an ambiguous gender position: she is of the same gender as the weak mother, but is at the same time her superior.

Another aspect is that this weak mother's everyday presence in the family also gives her another kind of power—an emotional and psychological power over the children. This is an issue that is much more elaborated upon by daughters than by sons. The women's recollection of their mothers' greater indulgence with their brothers may indicate that the mothers were less controlling and more service-minded towards their sons than towards their daughters. Sons may also to a greater degree have been able to receive the mothers' care without feeling caught in it because their gender safeguarded the psychological separation from her. The two men who described psychologically labile mothers seem to distance themselves more from the relational problems than the daughters do. Compared to this, the daughters' high level of conflict and strong ambivalences between anger and feeling guilty, between the craving of freedom and the longing for endless care and love, indicate that they have struggled more with upholding the boundaries and their own identity as a separate being. This double-sided face of weakness and power is what comes through in the daughters' description of their mothers' manipulative and psychologically labile behaviour and the way in which the mother drew the children into the psychological tensions and conflicts in the family:

> *One couldn't speak of anything, and we mustn't ... nothing could ... see the light of day, and I guess I understood later that this was a big mistake. We should've talked about all those things, gotten things aired out and ... been done with it all.* (Jorun, b. 1943)
>
> *My mother has rather ... in a way disciplined, or has had to stoop much in her life, so that it has become a bit more ... she has found other ways to maybe get back at people, or to survive, right.* (Grete, b. 1946)

The daughters' idealisation of their fathers can be seen in relation to this: they were needed as psychological liberators from the emotionally chaotic relation to mothers and to grow out of the dependency on the mother (Chodorow 1978). The different variations we see in the general pattern of negative/ambivalent relation to mothers and idealisation of fathers, then, will rely, among other things, on the father's ability to fill this role as the liberator from the mother.

A third aspect is that the daughters of this generation are expected, by parents, teachers and politicians, to get higher education and head in a different direction from their mothers (cf. Chap. 4), and their fathers are the only available models for a life outside of the family. We find no mention of weak and ill fathers in this generation: fathers are, almost by definition, strong and secure.

In spite of the strong gendering of work and care in the environment in which the middle generation grew up, the psychological consequences of the very same arrangement seems to have gone in the opposite direction. The disidentification with their same-sex parent triggered complicated processes of cross-gendering and potential degendering. The values of the opposite-sex parent's world became more visible and attractive. For the men, this does not entail a full identification with the mother's work and status, and they do not demarcate themselves from their fathers in the same intense, emotional way that the women do from their mothers. In this sense the men are the ones with double identifications in this generation. For the women, the identification with the father is more unambiguous, but there are emotionally unsettled issues at stake in their relationships with their mothers and in handling the fact that they are of the same gender as her. Considering the life project of their fathers—to refine gender complementarity in order to save their wives the struggles their mothers had endured, and to secure their children a safe and good childhood—and the sacrifices both men and women of this generation made to accomplish this dream—it is painful to see how little acknowledgement and understanding their children had for this project. But this generational drama also created the emotional energy that made it possible to enter the difficult process of transforming the complementary gender order.

Sexualising the Body

Compared with the cross-gender identifications with parents and with the elements of degendering that characterise the childhood of the middle generation, their period of youth is described in surprisingly gendered terms. If the eldest generation could be described as having become gendered within their families, the middle generation instead became gendered among their peers during adolescence. The strengthening of the youthful gender script in this period is closely connected with the new flourishing youth cultures, and young people becoming a new and important consumer group (see Chap. 4). This does not in itself, however, explain what feelings of gender these new practices could possibly connect to. Is there a link between the marked sexualisation of the body in this generation and the ambivalences towards one's own gender in a time when gender was still a strong symbolic and structural reality? For the men, it appears that the same-sex peers became a more important model for masculinity than fathers, who were not only more absent than before, but also too 'old-fashioned' to emulate in these new, dynamic times. For the women, both female friends and heterosexual relations appear to have become important sources of closeness as well as liberation from their mothers. These gendered peer relations were to a large degree mediated through bodily practices.

The men in this generation perceived, as their fathers did, their bodies as unproblematic: '*No, I can't remember that being a problem. It has been fine*' is Helge's immediate response when asked about how he experienced his body when he came of age. The self-evident body is no longer connected with the mentality of work, but rather with sports and physical competitions, which seem to have replaced work as the arena for masculine physical achievements. But the insistence on body strength coming 'naturally' is the same as in the previous generation, implying, for instance, that bodybuilding is scorned as effeminate 'self-indulgence'.

In one respect the body has become a more explicitly male issue in this generation, which is evident in the worry about what their bodies reveal about their masculine sexual identity, and especially whether their genitals were masculine enough. When Knut in the oldest generation was asked about puberty, he started talking about the war instead. When his son Kjell is asked the same question, he relates in detail to his own bodily insecurity:

> *Yes, I remember quite a bit of that ... To go into the shower and see ... I remember well that it was difficult to have a smaller willy than some of the others. Than many, maybe. I didn't have hair down there either, as one should. So I was probably abnormal. I don't know if I was scared, but I was definitely very insecure and unsure whether I was like everybody else. And then we read that this willy was supposed to be hard around the clock. And if it didn't do that then it was definitely no good. You were supposed to be very tough. I wasn't tough and didn't have a hard-on around the clock either. And then one after another started going to bed with girls. If it was true or not, in retrospect ... there were probably lots of lies. I found this hard and I guess I experienced an insecure puberty. I probably did.* (Kjell, b. 1946)

This bodily uncertainty also involves competition among the boys: comparing penis size in the school shower is a dark memory for many. There are also stories of hurtful ignorance and embarrassment, for instance, when it came to buying condoms. Thus, we are able to discern a new vulnerability—and therefore objectification—in contrast to the 'self-evident' body of the men in the eldest generation, but it is also an objectification that puts more emphasis on sexuality.

However, the sexualising of the body is much stronger when the men talk about the female body and in the importance they give to the physical attractiveness of women. For instance, this is seen in the way they formulate their ideals for the woman of their dreams. Whereas their fathers, when asked about such ideals, either went silent or vaguely gestured towards their own wives, the men in this generation readily offered details concerning breasts, figure, hairstyles, hair colour and so on—often with reference to film icons. Sometimes this focus on female bodies is depicted in the interviews as a sort of youthful sin, which later in life becomes disturbing in relation to ideas of gender equality. Kjell tells us that he was body-obsessed as a young man, dreaming about girls with long hair and big breasts. His ideal of a woman has evolved since then, he says, but evidently some of the old dreams are still alive:

> *If I have to pick an ideal, it has to be a woman who … who has courage and audacity … who is highly intelligent … who is engaged, and who is attractive. Not necessarily as beautiful as a film star, but she must have large breasts.*

For the women in the middle generation too, the body is much more in focus than for the women in the eldest generation, and much more problematic than for the men in their own generation. The relation to the generative body is now the least of the problem. Half of the women were informed by their mothers in advance and the rest knew about it from their friends. Puberty is discursively installed as a life phase and questions about 'when did you feel that you were grown-up?' are most often answered with 'my first period', in contrast with the eldest generation, who mentioned their confirmation and end of school when asked the same question. In this generation it is also less problematic to tell the mother about what had happened and get her to help with sanitary belts and pads. The experience of menstruation is more varied than it was among their mothers, who all felt that it was a 'curse'. Most of the daughters are clearly ambivalent—menstruation is a nuisance but also a fact of life.

The sexualisation and gendering of the body become most evident in the women's intense beauty routines. Compared with their mothers' innocent joy of getting new dresses and shoes, the practices of the women in this generation are much more elaborate and detailed. There is quite a lot of pleasure in this kind of beauty work, which was often done together with female friends. Fashion, consumption and a more sexualised youth culture are all involved in this process—and both the lack of same-sex generational bonds and the heightened levels of conflict between daughters and mothers may promote the insistent wish to be different and to preside over their own bodies and looks. However, in the overwhelming number of cases, the project is described as a hopeless affair. Almost all the women remember having very negative feelings about their own bodies as young girls, and their stories circle around the new concept of 'flaws', a word only used by the women in our interviews in this generation. The contrast to the men is striking: the image of the relatively unproblematic bodies, where only penis size and embarrassment when purchasing condoms were issues to worry about, is countered by the women's long list of flaws, complaining about being too big, too fat, too tall, too thin, too flat-chested, having too big a nose or too large a space between the front teeth. '*I got nowhere with my looks*', Dagny's daughter Drude says, even if her mother—like most of the upper middle-class mothers—told her that she was pretty. Even women who show us pictures of themselves as lovely young girls remember how unhappy they were with their appearances. This is also the first generation that mentions dieting and exercising to keep their weight down. Olaug kept a record of her weight and always compared it to 'Miss Norway's', of whom she had a picture on her wall in her bedroom. Some of the women remember weight loss that would have been understood as eating disorders today, but at that time their parents just wondered if they might have some caught some infection that caused them to lose weight.

Youth in this generation coincided with the period of the 'sexual revolution', which obviously had an impact with regard to both discourse and behaviour, but again in quite gender-specific ways. No one in this generation waits to have sex until they are engaged or married, but for the women, their first time is most often with the partner they later marry, whereas for the men it is not. The fear of pregnancy is present for both genders and it appears to have been well founded, since the use of contraceptives is quite haphazard. The dread of pregnancy is in this generation not due to social shame, as it was for the women in the previous generation, but threatened freedom. Pregnancy meant that one 'had to marry', and quite a few of both the men and the women in our sample experienced exactly this.

The looser norms seem to have left this generation in a void concerning what one should and should not do. The sharp line between nice and cheap girls that guided the informants in the eldest generation has become blurred. A new division between 'fun' girls and 'dull' girls arises. The 'fun' girls are the popular ones, the ones attractive to boys and the ones who are always invited to parties. The middle-class girls in our sample mainly chose the safety of 'being smart', resigning themselves to the fact that this also made them bores. Drude kissed a boy she did not know from before on her high school graduation trip to Copenhagen in 1958 and had severe moral qualms afterwards. When she later, at 23 years old, was pondering having sex with her steady boyfriend, she had pangs of doubt. She consulted her mother Dagny, who, as a liberal and educated woman, thought it was quite OK as long as Drude felt it was a serious relationship. But this only added to Drude's ruminations because then she had to think about whether the relation was serious *enough*. The absence of moral standards seems to have promoted reflections on personal morality, which again led to more variation in behaviour. Vigdis, a working-class girl born in 1951, recalls: '*I pondered a lot: what can one do? What can't one do? What do the others do? What can I do?*' Some girls, like Drude, became extremely careful; others took advantage of the liberal norms and went around searching for exciting boys. But that the sexual pressure on girls became much stronger than in the previous generation is beyond doubt. Many of the working-class girls whose sexual respectability was more vulnerable than that of the middle-class girls solved the problem by entering into steady relationships at an early age (see also Skeggs 1997).

Also among the men in this generation, we sense some confusion about what rules the girls followed and how to interpret the signals from them. Quite a few of the men experienced as young boys falling in love with a girl and being rejected for reasons they did not understand. The working-class boy Jan (b. 1947), says that '*infatuations are actually really painful. You become a volcano, violent forces really. Emotions that you think you don't have, right. That enter [laughs]*'. For some of them, this meant giving up intimacy and instead going for all the sex they could get. But the sexual debut could be embarrassing, and the rules of conduct when it comes to sex were not experienced as clear-cut either. The working-class boy Geir describes his sexual debut quite defensively:

> *It wasn't rape, it wasn't. She wanted to, but it wasn't quite 100 per cent OK, I remember that. Struggled a little, but I don't know if that was to, what do you say, play hard to get or something. It never quite dawned on me … We were making out … and you can feel her body underneath the clothes and all that, and you begin to undress her, and, it's fine that there's a limit sooner or later, you knew that because you'd been there before. But when the whole thing, there was no raised finger or verbal protest, nothing like that. It was more like giggling and laughing, and as I said, if it had been rape, I'd have known. But for me … I was sure she was holding back to tease me. That was my experience. But when the clothes were off and stuff, it had to be OK.* (Geir, b.1948)

Confused or not, what clearly has changed in this generation of men is that the feelings of guilt or shame that were so obvious among the eldest generation of men have disappeared, and the fear of hurting the girl also seems to have diminished. Almost all of the men had their first heterosexual intercourse outside a steady relationship. It is often talked about as a fun story about youthful clumsiness, '*finished on the way in*', but also involving excitement and '*violently*' good feelings. Some of the men are rather brutal—they seem to have grabbed whatever was offered them, but afterwards they describe these sexually active women as almost nymphomaniac, and not girlfriend material. Sexuality is clearly anchored in the body—almost what the male body is all about—and yet is also seen as a separate thing, not really a part of the man himself. Helge comments on his own youthful sexuality in this way: '*sex is something the body came up with*'. Their choice of marriage seems to have come as a rather pragmatic decision, not involving a lot of romantic feelings. Some of the men dreaded the idea of losing their freedom, some 'had to marry', while others realised that the time had come. Seen in retrospect the men do not recommend the split between intimacy and sexuality that guided their youth. More than half of them divorced later and stress that it was only in their second marriage that they learned about the value of closeness and intimate relations. This process should probably be seen in the light of the changing discourses of both sexuality and gender relations in the period, but perhaps the psychological roots of the dilemma could also be found in the cross-identifications with their mothers?

Whereas the men occupy the new youth cultural arena with gusto, sexuality is not discussed in terms of female desire and satisfaction at all. Just like the men, the women reject the possibility of female initiative when they were young girls: '*not even thinking about it*', as one of them puts it. Some of the women use the euphemism of being '*swept off their feet*' to describe their infatuations, but we are a far cry from the more or less uncontrollable lust that the men in this generation describe. On the contrary, the heterosexual debut of the women is often depicted as rather indifferent or even hurtful. The most important and almost only legitimate reason for sex among the young women is to be in love, and romance is a much more elaborated theme among the women in this generation than in the previous one, where only some of the middle-class women talked about it. Yet this focus on romantic love often had a somewhat instrumental touch to it: across social class, the young women's relationships with boyfriends often became part of the liberation from parents. That this relatively unprotected journey out into the world is quite risky is not so surprising given the stories we heard from the men. In some of our interviewees' cases the risks involved rape and abortions, with all the humiliation, anxiety and bodily pains that these involved. The route to autonomy could also lead to a *new* asymmetrical relationship where the young woman found herself controlled by her boyfriend instead of her parents. Kirsten describes a psychologically invading mother as well as a controlling father, depicting her own '*restless*' and '*wild*' youth as a way out. At 16 she became involved in a gang where the older boys were attractive, not least because of their access to cars. As a grown-up, her description of this exciting life is still enthusiastic:

> *We drove around, Opel … huge car, it was very exciting, but I was only about seventeen years old myself … down to the centre, of course, people-watching and going to the Main Square, and … in winter we drove to this other place outside the city centre and drifted around there, it was very exciting, it was quite cool because not that many of us were allowed to have a car, and this guy was … nineteen.* (Kirsten, b. 1953)

Alas, Kirsten's wild youth only lasted a year as she became pregnant and the two families—her own and her boyfriend's—arranged for the young couple to get married. This marriage did not last, since the young man proved to be both irresponsible and childish, never taking care of the baby but remaining one of the boys. In retrospect it is hard for her and many of the women in this generation to explain why they chose the men they did, and almost half of the early marriages ended in divorce.

The paradoxical liberation through sexuality on the men's terms seems to have implied stronger gender differentiation and heterosexual normativity among young women in this generation, in spite of their identification with their fathers and disidentification with their mothers. Yet, the lack of clear-cut moral guidelines also resulted in a stronger awareness of their own responsibility and a potential reflexivity with regard to the double standards involved. This may have instigated the frustration that for this generation of women would not remain a subdued irritation in the way it did for their mothers.

Gender as Power or a Fact of Life?

Seen in connection with the bland or negative emotional relationship with the same-sex parent, it may not be surprising that men and women in this generation have much to say about what kind of man/woman they do *not* want to be, whereas their positive alternatives are more vague or seem to develop only through the practices of their adult life. However, the energy to search for new ways of doing and defining gender can also be seen as fuelled by the energy of disidentification and cross-identification from their childhood and youth. The challenge they face is to redefine the meaning of their own gender through an identification with the other. The gender differentiation in their youth period may be seen as a temporary remedy, but they do not stay there and in their further life trajectories, women and men seem to handle the challenge of gender in different ways. Since the meaning of gender changed quite radically during their lives, especially among those who received more education than their parents, their reflections on gender in the interviews are tied more to a reflection on their adult lives. This, however, does not prevent a link also to feelings of gender stemming from their childhood and youth.

The women talk about gender differences solely with reference to differential treatment, inequality and power relations. Two formative experiences are relevant to many of them: the unequal treatment they experienced compared with their brothers and the lack of equality in their marriages, the latter of which led to the many divorces. Nearly all of the women who had brothers remember with resentment that their brothers had to do less housework, were the mother's favourite and, in a few cases, were given better educational possibilities. Yet the differences they report are quite minor compared to what the previous generations experienced with much less resentment. In contrast to their mothers' sibling rivalry, which was most often directed at their own 'league' of sisters, the women's jealousy in this generation is directed towards their brothers. Boys and men have become someone they compare themselves to and any potential relevance of gender differences is banished. It is remarkable that so few of the men talk about sibling rivalry and, if they do, it is connected to competition between brothers. This may reflect their position in the gender hierarchy and their more self-evident right of being.

Many women in this generation describe themselves in gender-neutral or traditionally masculine terms: '*quite strong, quite social, quite creative, to some extent ambitious*', says Nina, a rural working-class girl born in 1944, who received higher education. These qualities are not seen as masculine, but rather as expressions of modern femininity, compared with their mother's old-fashioned domestic femininity. This degendering of modern femininity also reflects the fact that 'masculine' skills were at this time increasingly valued in the course of education and work for those women who became middle class. In spite of the strong cross-gender identification with their fathers, the women construct their identities almost exclusively along the lines of female generational difference, rather than as gender difference. For the women in this generation, the negative relationships with their mothers and positive identification with their fathers seem to block the view to the fathers' part in the creation of the mothers as fussy housewives. Their mothers' personal qualities are described as the negative opposite to what they see as positive in themselves: whereas their mothers were occupied with minor details, lived for others, were dependent and submissive, occupied with facade, perfectionist, manipulative, personally insecure, ignorant and old-fashioned, they see themselves as engaged in society at large, doing things on their own, independent and demanding equality, relaxed, open and honest, standing up for themselves, enlightened and modern. This is clearly a construction of the 1950s housewife from the perspective of the Women's Movement and the modern gender equality norms that came with the 1970s. It is based on an exaggeration of their mothers' identities and practices as housewives, and also seems to feed on their feelings of gender from their childhood.

The negative evaluation of traditional femininity is also seen, especially among the middle-class women, when they talk about girlishness or sexualised femininity. Some of them say that they have never felt comfortable with too much intimate talk or preoccupation with appearances; others remember girls from their childhood who excluded other girls who did not conform to a stereotypical girls' culture. They renounce their own youthful selves as submissive, ignorant and traditional. It was only later and under the influence of education, divorce or the general atmosphere of the Women's Movement that they '*woke up*', they say. In this way, the contrast between the old-fashioned and the modern femininity is also a narrative about personal development and increasing enlightenment: the emphasis is on how they fought their way out of a restricted gender role by themselves and became the self-determined persons they are today. Nina describes it in this way:

> *I don't think I became free until I reached thirty. And then I divorced, and yes, felt like I really made a choice for the first time, that I chose something myself, for real … So in my thirties I felt completely superior in a way … economically independent despite having two small children. And I did my job well, I thought I was a good teacher … a very good period and I was very strong … I felt very much like I was running my own existence.* (Nina, b. 1943)

The men's developmental narratives are almost the opposite. Whereas the women see themselves as having gone from a problematic femininity as young girls to a mature individuality, the men in the same period describe a route from a self-evident masculinity in their youth to an adult masculinity that is more often experienced as 'in crisis'. The issue of gender raises more difficult questions for the men than for the women, as the men tend to define gender more in terms of difference than in terms of generation. Most of them, regardless of class, want to become a different kind of man than their distant and 'bad psychologist' fathers, but instead of neutralising traditional gender traits as the women do, they ponder to what degree this wanted generational difference might make them 'feminine'. Kjell says:

> *I probably have … yes, I have always had an affinity for softer values, well, a little. I guess I'm what I consider a feminine man without being feminine. But I guess I have some, and then I mean positive traits that entail daring to show feelings and daring to cuddle with animals and children. Men often feel insecure about things like that. I guess I am more secure there. And today I must say that the ideal man, that's got to be me.* (Kjell, b. 1946)

A way to secure the gender border is to underline sexual difference and attraction, which most of the men do regardless of their stance on gender issues. They may be critical of the macho behaviour of their youth, but not of their belief in gender differences. As a result of this dilemma between gender and individuality, we find an often quite paradoxical mix of claims of gender equality and claims of gender difference in the stories of almost every male interviewee of this generation, a combination that is much less present among the women.

In different ways the men work to redefine or extend or adjust their masculinity without losing it. For some of them, like Kjell, this project involves a strong critique of traditional masculinity and a concomitant embracement of behaviour that connotes femininity, like emotional openness and adopting 'soft values'. Kjell's account of traditional masculinity bears traces of feminist critiques from the 1970s and 1980s:

> *What do you think they [men] talk about when they're out? Work and money. Status and money. Women can talk about children, they can talk about a lot of things. They can talk about economics and status too. And they talk about environmental issues. While men care about money and status. How much do you make in your current job? What are you working on right now? They can talk about football. And cars. If you start talking about children, what do men do? They glance at their watches and say that they probably have to go soon. They become insecure right away.* (Kjell, b. 1946)

The psychological discourse also finds its way into these men's self-descriptions. They talk about situations where they have felt secure or insecure, or about feelings of '*alienation*', '*inner rage*' or '*the importance of being yourself*'. They describe themselves as a different kind of man than their fathers, with a more developed inner life, softer values and emotional capacities. But having already gendered these capacities (or the absence of them) so strongly, they face the problem of indirectly feminising themselves. This is a brand-new generational pattern—even if it does not apply to the majority of the men in this generation. Some have more classical critical remarks against what they see as the unsympathetic aspects of women's behaviour, especially gossiping, talking behind people's backs and exposing private details about their husbands to others, and they tend to believe that this constitutes expressions of innate or natural gender differences. Geir, for instance, the working-class man who talked about his stay-at-home mother with humour and loving respect, simply cannot stand 'ladies' talk' and feels completely suffocated by it:

> *I don't think they talk about anything. No matter what they talk about, it doesn't interest me. If they talked about football, I wouldn't bother to listen to them. I can't explain it. Like up in the cafeteria here, maybe the ones I work with in particular. If there's a table of women and I sat down, I wouldn't have been able to get my food down. No, I can't explain it. But for me it's completely out there ... My cousin's husband, he's a woman, because he likes to sit in the kitchen and babble with women. So he isn't quite right in the head in my opinion. There's something wrong with him, in my opinion. The two of us have nothing to talk about.* (Geir, b. 1948)

But even among the men with more traditional views of gender, we find expressions of the necessity for men to learn to be more open and talk about their feelings or 'handle strong emotions'. Formative experiences later in their lives have made this clear. One is the experience of divorce, which made quite a few of them more aware of their own emotional vulnerability. Another is being aware that communicative skills, emotional openness and being 'a bit of a psychologist' have also become important as work qualifications (see Illouz 2007; Aarseth 2009b). Ragnar, an upper middle-class man born in 1936, and thus one of the older men in this generation, took a course in Personal Development in connection with work and has decided to send his two teenage sons to this course too, in order to help developing their self-esteem and positive attitudes.

A different way of extending masculinity is found among some of the other older men in this generation, who had children at a late age and whose focus is less on psychological self-development than on the wish to become a different kind of father and combine this with a responsible masculinity. Trygve, middle class and born in 1919, is a case in point. As a young man he lived a very adventurous life as a sailor, hunter, mountaineer and participant in the resistance movement during the war. Even though he connects his choice of being a present father to how old he was when he had children, it doesn't even occur to him that the tough 'masculine' values of his youthful activities should be incompatible with being a warm and caring father. But even in the stories of Trygve and the other men who chose to become more present fathers than was usual in their generation, gender differences frequently appear, not so much with reference to body and appearances, but in different orientations and psychological capabilities. Helge, who shared both housework and childcare in his marriage, says that there are, after all, also innate gender differences. He refers to his own children's toy preferences and says that there *are* differences '*even if the mother and the myths say otherwise*'.

In different forms, new versions of masculinity and old gender dichotomies live side by side in the men of this generation, whether they want to reform their own role radically or not. But their adherence to gender difference does to a very limited degree lead them to support their fathers' gender complimentary model. Gender difference is no longer seen as a moral order, but rather as a fact of life, most often connected to body and sexuality, but sometimes also to psychology and behaviour. This is not well adjusted to the women's ideas of gender as mainly a dimension of social convention, power and inequality, and their striving to become more like their fathers. Thus, this generation also enters their marriages with latent gender tensions on board, but it is a different sort of tension than in the previous generation.

The Battle of Gender Equality

The middle generation established their own families in the 1960s or earlier, before the Women's Movement or modern gender equality politics gave words and direction to the discontent they felt with their own parents' model of gender complementarity. But that a mental change had already taken place is seen in the fact that none of the women imagined becoming full-time housewives as young women, but wanted to combine family and work. They did so by choosing jobs where this balance was easier to accomplish (teacher or nurse), working part-time or staying at home only when their children were young. They wanted to combine a life inside and outside of the family, and they also wanted a more open and equal relationship with their children than they had experienced with their own mothers. Many of the women remember some pressure from parents and in-laws, who were alarmed by their returning to work after maternity leave and who feared the negative consequences for the children. The fact that the women ignored this critique indicates the presence of a new generational project from the women, even though it was not yet formulated in terms of gender, and even less in feminist terms. It appears not to have included much reflection on gender relations in the family either. As we saw in the previous section, the women's emotional reactions to their childhood family included negative feelings towards the housewife-mother, not towards the working father. This may have made them initially blind towards the fact that a change in the female role in the family also presupposed a parallel change of the male role. The question of what husbands thought about their wives taking up paid work—a pertinent question in the previous generation—does not make sense anymore. The men we interviewed did not seem to have reflected much upon what consequences their wives' employment would have for their own situation. Many of them said in the interviews that they knew they wanted to be closer to their children than their own fathers had been and to contribute to an emotionally better upbringing. However, this is seldom formulated either as a wish to share the work at home in general or to engage less in work outside the family.

Although the *life project* of the middle generation is less defined than that of the previous generation, it does have a clear direction, especially for the women but also to some degree for the men, in the respect that it moved towards *combining work and care* within and outside of the family. This life project met the increasing need for female labour in the expanding welfare state in the 1970s and 1980s, and, as a consequence, gradually also the need for men's presence in the home. Thus, also in this generation we can see an historical moment where the biographically formed subjectivities, including a specific way to feel about gender, and the structural and cultural conditions reinforced each other to create social change in gender relations. The political structures in the form of kindergartens and family policies adjusted to the dual-career family came as a result of this change during the 1980s and 1990s.[6] This generation started their own families in a political and personal 'void'—they knew what they did not want, but not exactly what they wanted or what this would imply in practice. Lacking clear alternative family models or new family politics, many of the young couples of this generation soon drifted into a relatively traditional gender practice—albeit with the important change that the women *did* work on a more steady basis outside the family than their mothers had done and the men *did* engage more in the daily life of their children than their fathers had done. There are very few men in this generation who do not know how to change a nappy or cook a simple dinner; a huge change from their parents' generation. Still, the insufficiency of this arrangement, especially when it came to the women's orientation towards combining work and care and the fact that women, through their paid work, became less financially dependent on the men contributed to a high number of divorces in this generation. In our sample more than a third of the 33 parents were divorced when we met them in 1991.

---

[6] Family research indicates that the change in Scandinavian fathers' participation in childcare came from the 1980s onwards (Brandth and Kvande 2003; Lorentzen 2012). Thus, our middle generation who had children in around 1970 represents a generation in between traditional and modern fatherhood. The mixed practices we find in this generation in our sample probably reflect this transition in daily life. That a transition took place during these years is also reflected in the statistics of how many people in different cohorts supported the idea of equal sharing of housework and childcare at the time of our interviews (see Hansen and Slagsvold 2012).

The majority of the women in our sample had had full-time or close to full-time paid work their entire adult lives, interrupted only by relatively short maternity leave or breaks to pursue further education. This also applies to the wives of the men we interviewed. Some stayed home for a number of years while their children were small, but returned to full-time or part-time work when the youngest child started school. None of the men stayed home, but two middle-class fathers, Trygve and the husband of Vigdis, worked reduced hours in order to take care of their children. In all the women we see a rather strong work identity and a concomitant devaluing of housework. A good deal of the women say they hate housework and that their house is a mess, whereas others say they like some aspects of it, for instance, cooking, gardening and interior decoration, and see these activities as relaxing and de-stressing. From being a female work skill, cooking and other home activities have attained the character of hobbies or creative practices.

There is no clear model of family practice in our middle generation. This is telling in itself: the missing model reflects a state of transition and new ways of doing things are learnt along the way, sometimes at high cost. In an historical period where women entered the job market on a large scale and neither clear family models nor explicit norms for how to organise family life were available, it also makes sense that practices were shaped by individual trajectories and experimentation. The majority of the men and women in this generation describe mixed practices in their marriages, with led to much discontent and eventually to divorces.[7] All interviewees with 'mixed practices' are born after 1940 and most of them disidentified with the same-sex parent. In these families the woman works on a regular basis outside the home, full-time or part-time, but is also seen as the one who has the upper hand with care and housework. The men take part in the children's upbringing and describe themselves as much more present than their own fathers were—they talk with their

[7] It is important to remember that what we know from the interviews are the subjective experiences of the general arrangement in the family and whether it is felt as satisfying or not—we do not have data on the actual division of work. It is also important to keep in mind that the men and the women are not couples (see Chap. 3). It is an established fact that men and women report differently how housework is shared, both tending to overestimate their own contribution (Kjeldstad and Lappegård 2009; Dworking and O'Sullivan 2007).

kids daily, are active in driving them back and forth to leisure activities and are also often engaged as coaches. They have different levels of 'helping-out' behaviour in the house—some have to be activated by their wives while others have predefined tasks like vacuum cleaning or washing the floors, in addition to gardening, tending to the car and repairing the house. Quite a few men think that they ought to help out or be present more than they actually are, but find it difficult to do it both because they are very engaged in their jobs and because their wives seem so much more competent. The mixed pattern crosses social class and political views. Per, who is modern and politically radical middle class, has a close relationship with his son, but with regard to housework he admits that '*traditionally my wife has been much more responsible than me. She is better at pure logistics*'. The working-class man Geir, the son of Gunnar who had the special '*knack for caring for children*', says that he has been a very involved father to his three sons—from getting up at night with the babies and later paying close attention to their sports activities. He has no objections to taking part in the housework and he finds it quite fair to share as both he and his wife are tired when they come home from work. In practice, however, it is actually his wife who mostly cooks dinner, but from the defensive way he describes this, it is still clear that the norm has changed:

> *I admit that I'm not always that good, but sometimes I get it together ... I think it's to do with habit. Usually we come home at the same time. Then she usually heads for the kitchen to start making dinner. And I don't react until I'm asked to fry the meat or set the table or something like that. Then I get up and do it. Maybe those are things I could've done without being asked ... When it comes to food, when it's things I know how to do, it's fine. But I absolutely hate things like cleaning the floors and vacuuming. I can't remember the last time I cleaned the floors. I've passed the task of vacuuming over to Glenn [his son].* (Geir, b. 1948)

The discrepancy between new norms and old practices results in a good deal of what has been described as the 'in principle men' of this generation (Jalmert 1984): men who agree that sharing is the right thing to do, but who, unfortunately, do not find sufficient time to do it. The image offered by the Norwegian psychologist Hanne Haavind (Haavind 1987), who investigated work division in families with small children in Norway in around 1980, rings true for most of the families in our sample in this generation: modern fathers have the skills to do all kind of household tasks, but it is up to their wives how much they actually do and 'everything she has not explicitly delegated to him falls on her' (Haavind 1984a, b).[8] This also applies to the men who have invested in developing 'feminine values' in themselves. Maybe the combination between closeness to their mothers and their attachment to gender difference makes them play both sides? Half of the men who talk about mixed practices are divorced and explain the divorce in terms of both practical and emotional problems. Egil, whose father Einar thought of divorce as an act of irresponsibility, says:

> *Well, you could say it became very, I felt that it became pretty tiring after a while. It was really rigid, and I guess it has to be when you have, you always have something to do, you have all kinds of commitments. You don't take time for yourself and each other.* (Egil, b. 1949)

These men have experienced conflicts with their former wives about the children after the divorce and regret that they did not fight harder to get custody. They do, however, think that they have managed to preserve reasonably good relations with their children after the divorce.

Among the women who talk about mixed practices in their marriages, we find even more divorces. Some of them give lively accounts of 'in principle men', like the middle-class woman Jorun, who recalls how her husband was lying on the sofa reading Marilyn French instead of doing the dishes. The discontent with their husbands' lack of participation was clearly boosted by their educational experiences and later the feminist movement. Most of them drifted rather incidentally into gender-conventional educations as young women, but the educational experience itself made them discover a larger world than just their own

---

[8] Holter and Aarseth offer another interpretation of women's activity and men's laziness with regard to housework in this generation where everybody agrees that work *should* be shared equally: it is less threatening to masculine identity to say that one is lazy or does not have the time than to display one's lack of skills and submission to the still-dominating female standard of how housework should be done (Holter and Aarseth 1993: 164).

family. When their children were born, they gradually realised that their lives were becoming like those of their mothers and they reacted with shock and divorce. They describe a process where they became more and more conscious of the situation, '*until I got so conscious that I got divorced*'. Nina says that she experienced how '*the centre of gravity suddenly changed, suddenly you were properly trapped*'. This became particularly clear for her after she and her husband moved to a new town because of his job:

> *In a way I noticed there that we weren't equal ... I had better results from university than he did, had more friends than he did, I was the extrovert one, I was the one making friends for us. There he was suddenly the important one in town, while I was at home and the only thing I had to look forward to was him getting home from work and eating dinner ... That was the first time in my life that I felt ... that I no longer was master of my own life. It was a truly terrible time.* (Nina, b. 1943)

Nina's account illustrates how the gendered division of work loses legitimacy when it cannot be connected to complementary skill sets. The orientation towards having a family and the romantic dreams that restricted their choice of education when they were young was not about becoming a housewife.

On each side of this 'normal chaos of love' (Beck and Beck-Gernsheim 1995) we find some families with a more traditional organisation of work and care, and some families who share more equally. Few in these two groups are divorced. The men in the traditional families identify very much with their work and career, and they hardly participate in the housework. Their workload has also limited how much time they could spend with their children. Ragnar, who is upper middle class, says that perhaps he could have had a bit more contact with his son, but '*there's nothing that grates between us ... Absolutely not ... He is doing his thing and I'm doing mine*'. He believes there should be clear agreements between the spouses before having children about who will stay at home and take care of them. He is not against women taking up paid work, but since he was the one who made the most money, it made more sense that his wife was the one to stay at home. The women from middle-class families with similar traditional arrangements are strikingly less content with the situation. They are all full-time working women who are either married to men whose work implies frequent absences from home or who have not succeeded in making their husbands take their share. They have resigned themselves to the state of affairs even though it makes them very overworked and tired at times, and they have experienced intense conflict between their own career and family obligations. In some ways this family arrangement may be seen as a repetition of the middle-class families with educated and working mothers from the previous generation, but with the important difference that housemaids are not around anymore. Turid, who is upper middle class, says: '*I think it has been working much because of me.*' Her daughter Tonje finds the unjust arrangement ridiculous and Turid tends to agree: '*I do see that it's not right that one person sort of goes clear of everything … Imagine if Tonje married a man like that—it would never work!*' Clara's daughter Cecilie, who has the same upper-middle class profession as her husband, struggles hard to combine job and family:

> *Work takes a massive toll mentally, it does. Then it can be hard to get home and sense … that the children demand just as much. And a husband who maybe doesn't understand that you're tired and have to do most of the work at home, right. Even if he probably understands, but he doesn't see the problem, because he also has enough on his plate.* (Cecilie, b. 1944)

In the few examples we have of working-class families with a traditional organisation of work, both men and women seem to be more content. In these cases it was the woman who wanted to stay at home with the children and the husband agreed to this priority even if it meant a somewhat lower standard of living. In their own experience it is not an exact repetition of their parents' model: Arne says that he has a closer relationship with his children than his father had with him, even though it is his wife who had most to do with their upbringing. Solveig emphasises that she has not been as occupied with her own home as her mother was, but has taken part in the larger environment in her community, for instance, by being a volunteer in child and youth work for many years. So, in the midst of reproduction, there is also change.

The informants who talk about a more radical gender arrangement share both paid work and care work on a relatively equal basis (and we here generously include the cases where the men's cooking may most often be for special occasions or of a lower standard than the wife's—Helge, for instance, characterises his cooking as '*dad food*'). The women in these families have strong work identities and most of them disidentified with their own mothers.

For the men, the identifications are more varied.The focus of the men who shared more equally is first and foremost their children, and this is not described in terms of duty, but as a positive investment. They experience good and close relationships with their children today:

> *It has been very stimulating and interesting to be a stay-at-home dad. And nice. Of course it was terribly tiring when they were young. There's only two years between the oldest and the twins. So there were days when I didn't have time to read the paper. But ... I have that ... I think it has often been more fun to be with the kids than with adults ... It is important not to create anxiety and guilt in the kids. I feel like I've got three children who are cheerful and happy and easy to be around, and they haven't created any problems so far.* (Trygve, b. 1919)

None of these 'new fathers' talk much about their jobs; it seems that their wives at least in periods have been busier in the world outside the family than them. A combination of experiences in their own childhood and a later life event appears to have been decisive for the choice of becoming an involved father. Trygve says that he would not have had the self-confidence to make this choice as a 30-year-old. Some of them experienced difficult childhoods that fostered in them a strong desire to give their own children a better psychological environment. This has probably made them receptive to grasp later chances in life, primarily in the form of wives who wanted an equal sharing of the care work and an economic situation and a modest lifestyle that made it possible for the couple to choose untraditionally. Trygve was also influenced by the radical discourse of psychoanalysis in the 1930s. Another case is Willy, who is lower middle class and remarried and became a father at a mature age. His second wife suggested that he became the principal care person for their youngest child since she had night shifts. He describes this with gratitude towards his wife, as a gift she gave him, and also how it boosted his skills:

> *I had taken care of the other children too. But not quite as consciously and wholeheartedly as I did with Vegard. Then I really consciously went for it. Kept her away from the care work. And I cared for Vegard and I washed diapers and I cleaned him and even mended his clothes. For 17th of May* [the national day of Norway] *I even made him a new suit. Everything like that.* (Willy, b. 1925)

The last hands-on father is Helge, the son of the upper-class boy Harald who chose to become a farmer. Helge, who is upper middle class himself, resembles the few men in the previous generation who identified positively with both parents and were closer to their children than other men of their generation. However, Helge criticises his own parents' gender complementary marriage and says that from early on he knew that he did not want to marry a '*house-keeper*', a way to describe his parents' marriage. This decision was then radicalised when he married a woman who became a feminist around the time of the birth of their children. While she was busy with feminist politics, he stayed home and took care of the kids:

> *Well, she was, she lived in so many milieus. She was so engaged in so many other things. And was out flapping in all directions and then it was me who was home to care for the children and the house too, when I came home from work. I worked all the time. And we had a nanny. When we came home we made dinner and tended to the children and put them to bed and so on. I did most of it, I'd say ... But then Women's Liberation came along and then everything turned around ... She thought she had sacrificed herself terribly to be home with ... I thought that was completely grotesque.* (Helge, b. 1938)

This marriage ended in divorce. Helge appreciated getting rid of all the nagging and he is glad his new wife has managed to become liberated without being a torment to others. When he met her, he felt the joy of '*embracing a woman who is a woman and not a Protestant*'. Helge blames the Women's Movement, but does not regret that it led him in to a different kind of father role. For him, as with the majority of men in this generation, the increased presence in childcare also led to an experience of strong attachments to the children and to a questioning of the mothers' custody priority in case of divorce. Helge achieved an agreement with his wife of shared custody.

The stories of the women with more radical patterns of sharing are less dramatic or spectacular. It is not a single biographical event that led to their practice, but rather a gradual development that came with their increased engagement in education and work, and their partner's positive attitude to sharing. They describe the sharing at home either as something principally important for them (middle class) or as a matter of practicalities (working class). These women also experience conflicts between work and family, but more in terms of feeling guilty for maybe having let the children pay the price for a dual-career family: '*Torn in all directions. Feeling inadequate. Feeling guilty*' is the way Vigdis summarises it, the only woman in this generational sample who had a husband who worked part-time in order to take his share at home.

The gender battle in this generation reflects the gradual change of what gender meant for men and women over the course of their lifetimes. For the women, it was an often paradoxical appropriation of autonomy, towards more individuality and less gender. For the men, it was an often reluctant appropriation of intimacy, but without giving up the importance of gender difference. These different trajectories created much emotional and practical turmoil for this generation, but it is worth noting that the experience of divorce radicalised both genders' support of gender equality. For all in this generation, the battle of gender equality also shaped them as a different sort of gendered parents to their children.

Equality versus Difference

None of the women in this generation are negative towards gender equality. For the majority who had negative or bland relationships with their mothers, their feelings merge with the discourse of women's rights and modern gender equality politics. For those with more positive relationships, it is rather the compassion with their subdued mothers that feeds into their feminist engagement, as we saw with Olaug, who described how her preoccupation with women's rights started when she as a seven-year-old saw her mother wear herself out for the family. Most of the women in this generation say that they did not care about gender equality questions as young girls; the engagement came during the 1970s, after they were married and had children. Their positive attitude is not surprising when taking into account how little gender difference appears to be part of their own grown-up gender construction. Why shouldn't individuals be equals? The views of the women in this generation vary from a radical stand for women's rights and against individual discrimination to a general support of gender equality politics addressed at a group level, and to a more pragmatic individual approach where justice comes second to necessity. Whether the fight for gender equality should take place mainly inside or outside the family is also a dividing line. Educational level combined with their experiences in marriage influence their stand here.

The overall pattern is that it is the women who share on an equal basis, or who divorced in frustration at not getting the husband to share, who take the radical stand. Many of them are class travellers. They all received higher education and were often radicalised as students. Few of them have been directly politically active; rather, it is the injustices in their daily lives at work and in the family they address, and they have been consciously communicating these lessons to their daughters. Olaug, for instance, has taken care not to make her daughter too good at housework in order to prevent her being stuck with this in her later relationships with men. Hanne says that she and her daughter Hilde '*fight the women's struggle all the time*' in the family. In this struggle they have constructed themselves as a new kind of women, different not only from their mothers, but also from traditional norms of femininity. This gives some problems with keeping up the solidarity with women as a group, an issue that will become much more pronounced but also much less guilt-ridden in the youngest generation. As middle-aged, they still identify with women's rights, but say that they are not as radical today as they used to be. Some of them admit that they became a bit extreme, for instance, in insisting on sharing everything according to a ruler.

Other women in this generation, with or without higher education, but with more traditional gender arrangements in their families, or those who chose to stay in marriages with mixed practices tend towards formulating their support in terms of gender quality politics:

it is important and desirable to share the work both within and outside of the family, but this should be applied neither too mechanically nor in a way that ignores taking into account that there *are* some gender differences in physical strength. Equality in work and care may coexist with gender differences in other areas. Solveig says she actually appreciates men who still open doors and pull out the chair for a woman, and that she cannot see why gender equality should be incompatible with that. Turid and Astrid, who live with a traditional gender arrangement in the family, say that they are interested in gender equality mainly professionally in their work as teachers. Those who are least engaged in gender equality—but not against it—are a group of women with little further education, who share domestic work fairly equally in practice, but without making it a gender issue. They think jobs and work in the home should be divided fairly between men and women, but since they find this is largely already the case, it is nothing to make a big deal about. Gender equality is most important in relation to work and in society at large, but they do not see the point in struggling against gender differences in other areas of life and they distance themselves from what they see as exaggerated gender policies. Like her mother Borghild, Berit is the most sceptical among the women in her generation:

> *I've never been a feminist … this gender equality business. But I can agree that there are many things in society I think that … That revolt that happened a few years back, yes, at the beginning of the seventies, I thought that it was maybe … if not exaggerated then a bit much at times, that … it went a bit too far, to put it like that, in many ways.* (Berit, b. 1949)

Among the men in the middle generation, the distaste for the Women's Movement is more pronounced. We already heard about Helge's bitterness about how his wife's engagement in the Women's Movement destroyed their marriage. Ragnar is also quite upset on behalf of '*traditional women*'. In his account we see a defence for the equity he finds inherent in the old gender-complimentary division of work, as well as an emotional reaction towards the aggressive femininity that emerges as a contrast to the mild and kind motherliness of the feminine carer:

> *I remember in the worst redstocking[9] period, we went to parties and there were quite a few women in my wife's circle of friends who were redstockings. And we started talking, and I told them exactly what I thought of them: I think you are ruthless. You're making these great Norwegian women, who have given their all for their families and society, you're making them feel really inferior. Just because they haven't worked outside the home. And that made me furious. That these know-it-all redstocking girls could brand an entire generation like that.* (Ragnar, b. 1936)

The men who shared childcare and domestic work and were not divorced also thought the feminist rhetoric of the 1970s was over the top. Their distaste for radical feminism also has to do with their preoccupation with preserving sexual and psychological gender differences. The idea of equality in sharing the work within and outside of the family in a fair way is a much more acceptable idea than feminism and women's rights. In contrast to the women, educational level does not interfere much with their standpoint on gender equality; rather, it is the practice in their own family that guides their view, in addition to a relatively close match with their parental identifications. Those who had positive relationships with their mothers are in most cases positive to the idea of gender equality, although their practice may lag behind, and those who have daughters are even more so. The men who have traditional arrangements in their marriage have the least to say about gender equality. The upper middle-class men Ragnar and Magne say that this is not an issue that engages them much or that difference is exactly what they find attractive about the female gender. This emphasis on sexual difference does not necessarily lead to a negative stand to homosexuality. Two men, both with traditional gender arrangements in their families, make references to homosexuality. One is Magne, who says that he believes more diverse sexualities will become a normal thing in the times to come:[10]

---

[9] In Scandinavia the word 'redstocking' is often used as a popular and sometimes condescending reference to feminist activists in the 1970s.

[10] The other is Arne (b. 1930), who espouses the opposite view by saying that he thinks that gay men are not 'proper men'.

> *Gender roles are more or less indistinguishable now. There aren't housewives who stay at home and the roles at work are mixed as well, so why not sexually too? So I don't disregard the possibility that they're having sexual interaction with both boys and girls. And I'll say that's almost natural, the way they grow up today. I'm not saying it's necessarily natural, natural is a relative term, but naturally in relation to your environment and the times you live in … You can't judge, I think it's got a lot to do with our environment. That's why I really like having diversity … What I'm trying to say is that things are getting more equal. But a lot of what makes a woman attractive, and now I'm talking about myself, is that she's different from me.* (Magne, b. 1938)

The men who have mixed practices in their marriages think that sharing housework is OK and they are quite positive towards gender equality in the workplace. The working-class men Geir and Jan feel that companies with no women are 'old-fashioned' and that men who cannot bear that women surpass them in position and salary are pathetic. However, they react negatively towards the idea that gender equality should make women into men, including the negative aspects of masculinity. In addition, the middle-class men who want to reform masculinity by embracing more feminine qualities are aware of the danger that too much equality could threaten the difference that makes women attractive to them and talk about women's biology as special and unique. Only the two still-married men who share work and care with their wives are unconditionally in favour of gender equality. They support women's rights (although they also share the aversion against what they see as the exaggerated feminism of the 1970s and 1980s) and want their wives to be partners in all areas of life. Trygve thinks that too many women have a double burden today because many men are shirking their responsibilities. Willy says that there should not be any '*class difference*' within the family. But even for these gender equality-embracing men, the worry is that too much similarity may come at the expense of femininity, romance and sexuality. The discomfort of being the criticised gender, the effort it takes for some of them to follow up housework in practice, and the importance they attach to sexual gender difference make almost all men in this generation somewhat awkward in the way they address the issue of gender equality, even though they support it in principle, especially at work or on behalf of their daughters. Gender does not represent an economic role or a moral order as for their fathers, but a fact of life that must also be taken into account in the struggle for gender equality. The men's road to gender equality could initially be said to have been less personal, for instance, more connected to gender equality politics at their jobs. However, their increased presence in childcare and their experience of strong attachments to their children gradually also gave them a personal engagement. This seems to be the most important emotional link to gender equality for men in this generation, but it came later than that for the women. There is a time lag, but also partly a different agenda: for the men, gender equality is a care project, while for the women, it is a project of sharing more equally both care and domestic work. For the radical women, it also entails being involved against the sexualisation and objectification of the female body. For the men, the experience of being more actively participating fathers raises the question of gender equality from the men's perspective, especially in connection with divorce and child custody. In the account of Egil, we can see how the intensity increases as he moves from talking about women's rights at work to men's rights after divorce:

> *Girls can do a lot of jobs just as well as boys, and I guess I think there should be gender equality in that regard and that there should be equal pay for equal work. I think that. But I don't think one should strive towards becoming the same. I think there should be differences between boys and girls. And if we're talking about these things, what annoys me the most about the things to do with gender equality: those girls who've worked hard to show the places they've been treated unfairly, but they've probably been aware of places where men have been treated unfairly too. But I don't think many women have fought for that, in the situation of separation and divorce. It's clear who the loser is there. I don't think many of those working with gender equality have cared about that.* (Egil, b. 1949)

7

Welfare Society, Gender and Individuality

Towards Degendering Work and Care

> *They take turns doing it, it depends who is busy, they're very good at … taking turns. He's mum's dishwasher, as she likes to call him since my dad often does the dishes. He vacuums if he's got time off, or if mum hasn't had time to do it, but … it's mostly mum who does it since she's at home during the day, she usually works evenings and nights. So during the day the flat is empty and then it's very easy for her to do it while nobody is running around … My brother and I always have to vacuum and tidy and dust our rooms ourselves, mum doesn't touch them. The only thing she says is, 'you're not allowed out of this house until you tidy your room, because now it looks bloody awful'.*
>
> *Q: Are you thinking about leaving home?*
>
> *It's sort of in the back of my mind … but … not something I've sort of gone and wanted to do, because things at home are quite nice and all right, sort of.* (Beate, 18)

Beate comes from an urban working-class family. In her family both parents have always worked full-time and they have also shared the care for their children and the housework in their small city apartment. Beate perceives it as equally shared and mainly as a practical matter, but indirectly conveys that her mother is the main person responsible. She also thinks her mother is the boss at home. Beate does not mention any unequal treatment of her and her younger brother, whereas her mother Berit admitted in the interview we had with her that she tended to ask Beate to help more at home than her brother because she is so much easier to ask. Beate tells us that the family members have a lot of fun together when they go out to eat or on holiday, but also at ordinary weekday dinners at home—which are not every day as some of them may be at work or busy with other activities—when they can all sit and tell jokes and laugh their heads off for hours.

All the 34 informants in this generation are born around 1972 and grew up in Oslo. We do not find any clear class differences in how the parents share work and care. What they describe mirrors the mixed practices that we just heard about from their parents, but with less attention to the gender divisions. Many in the youngest generation have been taken care of outside the home before they started school at seven, reflecting the high prevalence of working mothers. The different variations of private and public care they talk about reflect the lag in daycare facilities in the 1970s. Full-time kindergarten was the most prevalent solution in our middle-class families, whereas being at home with the mother before starting school is seen more often in the working-class families, albeit not in the majority of cases. In some of the more gender traditional middle-class families, the mother also stayed at home for a few years.[1]

How did the parents' historically new gender practices and their struggle with gender equality affect the young generation's experience of work and care in the family? A first observation is that the mothers' work outside the family is as visible in the interviews with this generation as the fathers' role in upbringing and care. Yet there is a tendency for fathers to be more in charge of following up the offspring's sporting activities and

[1] A radical shift in attitudes to daycare occured in the 1980s, the decade of mass movement of mothers into the labour market. Whereas in 1979 only 21 per cent of parents with pre-school children thought daycare was good care for children, 50 per cent thought so a decade later. The rise reflects a cohort replacement, but is also related to the mother's education. The fact that a majority of our youngest generation attended daycare in the 1970s reflects the high educational level of mothers and that they grew up in Oslo, where the daycare coverage was best (Ellingsæter and Gulbrandsen 2007: 663–665).

driving them back and forth to leisure activities, and for mothers to do more of the daily nitty-gritty care work, like checking homework and making sure there are clean clothes to wear to school (see also Holter and Aarseth 1993; Aarseth 2008). Behind the assumed gender neutrality, it is the mothers who in most families are described as having the main responsibility for the housework. Still, for the youngest generation there is nothing strange, comical or special about men doing housework, as was the case in the previous generation. Housework is not per se feminised, even though women do more of it than men. The organisation of work and care in the family may explain the lack of explicit gendering of money and consumption, which we saw in their parents' generation. Even though fathers in general earn more than mothers—because mothers more often work in the public sector and fathers in the private sector, or because there is more part-time work among mothers—this is not associated with and not primarily understood as a gendered pattern.

Having two working parents, or living with a single parent, also means that this generation of children assist much more in the household compared with what most of the parents did at that age. This is also confirmed in studies of time use from the period when this generation grew up.[2] At 18, both women and men in the youngest generation say that they help out at home with things like tidying up, vacuum cleaning, emptying the dishwasher and cutting the grass. Paul, who is upper middle class and the only one with a mother at home (she ran her own business from home), is the sole informant in this generation who says he never helped out at home. At 30, he regretted this as it had taken him so long to learn these necessities of life when he moved out. Daughters more often than sons mention specialised tasks like doing laundry, cooking and baking, and some of them complain about the low level of their brothers' proficiency in housework. However, only one young woman, Tonje, said that she was expected to do more work than her older brother. Sons of fathers who participate on a more equal footing with the mothers tend to give more detailed descriptions of their own chores, which may indicate a higher

[2] In the mid-1980s, Norwegian 10–12-year-olds helped out in the household nine hours a week on average. Children with working mothers or highly educated mothers did more than children with stay-at-home mothers, and girls did two hours more work a week than boys (Solberg and Vestby 1987).

level of skill: they occasionally may cook dinner, clean windows, clean the bathroom or hang out the laundry. Helge's son Henrik, who is upper middle class, even knows how to knit. But also the 'in principle men' of the middle generation appear to be quite active in making their sons do their household duties. The working-class father Geir, who admitted he did less at home than his wife, monitors his son Glenn on his duty to vacuum the house. In spite of the girls' generally higher level of skill, it seems fair to say that taking part in the housework is relatively degendered for this generation of children. The chores may be felt as more or less boring, but none of the young men describe them as feminine or something they should not do because they are boys.

All this indicates that gender norms with regard to housework have moved, even if practice is lagging behind. Housework has become less gendered partly because mothers now combine it with paid work outside the family and partly because the other family members participate, or think they ought to. This may lead to a masking of practices that are in fact still gendered, but it may also contribute to a degendering on a symbolic level when such gendered practices are interpreted as an expression of individual preferences. In fact, the youngest generation's quite paradoxical feelings of gender reflect both. They praise their mothers' skills (more than their fathers') in gendered areas like cooking, gardening, childcare and interior decoration (in addition to her career), but are very careful to assure us that this is *not* an expression of a gender order. Daughters say that even though their mothers may like housework, they do *not* have 'dust on their brains', and sons describe their mothers' greater share of housework as an expression of their individual likes and dislikes.

Some of the young men and women from middle-class families remember elements of the non-sexist education of the 1970s, for instance, in the kind of toys they were allowed to have (no Barbies for girls, no guns for boys). These rules may testify to the intentions some of the more radical mothers had of giving their own children a more gender-equal upbringing than they had had themselves. Many of the fathers also seem to have adopted this educational goal, for instance, by supporting their daughters in sports and criticising their sons for being too lazy with housework. However, the pressure towards more gender-equal norms in the family may also sometimes come from the children themselves. The gendered division of work and care has lost legitimacy in the eyes of most of the young women and men, and not to share the housework has become a sign of injustice and being embarrassingly outdated. Mothers who stayed at home with the children when they were little or fathers who do too little around the house are criticised—or explicitly excused by reference to unfortunate circumstances—by their children, or both. It is especially the middle-class girls at 18 who are very sensitive towards the mismatch between norms and practices. They criticise both lazy fathers and inconsequential mothers. Guro, whose parents share the housework relatively equally but do different tasks, remarks caustically that her father '*makes himself helpless*' in the kitchen and has to be told 15 times how to turn on the dishwasher. In the interview at 30, however, she thinks that they were '*unusually gender equal for that generation*'. Hilde, whose parents share the work meticulously, is critical of her mother's limited insight into the family economy and of her father playing more football with her brother than with her when they were younger: '*it was because I was a girl, I'm sure of that!*' Tonje, the daughter of Turid, who finally had to give up getting her husband to participate in household work, tried to make work schedules where all household tasks alternated between the family members. To her indignation, her father just signed the schedule as 'Sisyphus'. Frequently it is the mother who is made responsible for the lack of gender equality in families with a traditional division of work. Pia says this about her mother, who tried to get her husband to participate more, but eventually gave up:

> *I like to call mum a really good gender equality theoretician, but not so good as a practitioner. She has been in the gender equality committee at work and stuff, but I don't think she's been quite as good at it in practice at home.* (Pia, 18)

For most of the men in this generation, and also for those of the women who grew up working-class and later became middle class, the critique of their parents' gendered division of work is rather formulated as adults and in light of their later experiences. For instance, Morten, who comes from an upper middle-class family with a traditional work division, says at 30 that he had liked the fact that his mother stayed at home when he was little, but that he later realised that it didn't make him independent enough. Anders, who grew up working class, had a mother who stayed at home until he was 16. In the interview at 18 he said, with a little laugh, that this was quite nice because '*then you got food*'. In the second interview, at 30, he distances himself from that kind of old-fashioned gender pattern, but also partly excuses it as a possible preference of his mother's:

> *There were husband tasks and wife tasks, according to the old standard. She did everything. Can't remember having seen my dad vacuum a single time ... but my mum likes to keep things tidy, so she ... it wasn't exactly terrible. They did the dishes together, otherwise she mostly did everything.* (Anders, 30)

Stine's working-class mother, Solveig, stayed at home with the children for many years, and Solveig emphasised herself in her interview that she was not a housewife in the same restricted way her own mother had been, but was engaged in the local community. At 18, Stine was very supportive of her mother's choice and wanted to do the same. At 30, however, when she has become a preschool teacher, she is more critical of her mother and says that she is a quite controlling figure in the family, and that she is not able to see things outside of her own perspective.

In light of the parents' gender battles and the many divorces, it may be surprising that their children actually describe their families in a much more positive way than the parents described their own stable parents. In this generation the relationship between parents and children has moved towards partnership and support rather than being a relationship of authority.[3] We see this in the many negotiations between parents and children and the exposure to the adults' quarrels, as well as in the allowance for the children's critiques of the parents (for instance, as we have heard, not living up to the standards of modern gender equality). We see it in the children's empathic perspectives on their parents' problems, whether it is divorces, marital problems, difficulties in their jobs or hav-

---

[3] Bengtsson also describes this distinctive new kind of relationship between parents and children in her generational study. The young women and men born around 1970 describe an emotionally open family: 'They talk about open conflicts and antagonisms between the generations, but also about much warmth, happiness, freedom and humour between parents and children' (2001: 178, my translation).

ing chosen the wrong profession. Vilde's way of describing her middle-class father, who actively took part in the childcare, exemplifies the tone:

> *I feel, and I think dad does too, that he hasn't been able to do what he wanted to do because he hasn't listened to himself. He has done what others, when he was young, advised him to do. [So when he applied for a new job it was] a way of realising his dreams.* (Vilde, 18)

The atmosphere of this new partnership in the family is also present in the way that the daughters especially describe the family first and foremost as a relational universe. It resembles Gidden's concept of "pure relations", a modern logic of love and intimacy between spouses where one stay together not because of practical reasons or moral or material necessity, but because the relationship is experienced as emotionally satisfying in itself (Giddens 1992). The idea of pure relations may also have contributed to the deconstruction of generational borders: as emotional and vulnerable human beings, we are all equal. The marked lack of expressed sibling jealousy in this generation also points in this direction. Some of those with divorced parents feel that the parents are softer and less demanding towards younger half-siblings, but they also '*understand*' that the context has changed and appreciate being seen as grown-up.

The mutual obligations of partnership combined with busy, working parents have also, as we have already seen, brought children's work back into the family, but tasks are related to what is needed in the family rather than gender. In this way one could say that the *mentality of individualism* that we saw emerging in the middle generation has now actually acquired some *traits of collectivity*: everyone should do what they want, but since some work simply has to be done, everyone should also contribute. This does not necessarily work smoothly between children and parents: after the debate about the appropriate time to come home at night, the most frequent topic of quarrels between parents and teenagers is the issue of tidying up. The debate is not about whose responsibility it is, but about who has the right to tell others when and how it should be done. The process of degendering work tasks also leads to the necessity of considering a more general principle of justice.

New norms of gender equality influenced not only families in the 1970s and 1980s, but also, and much more explicitly, schools. Gender researchers in and outside of Scandinavia provided the first descriptions of male dominance in the classroom in the 1970s, and in the Nordic countries the 1980s became the decade with a strong official gender equality policy at school. Girls assumed a stronger and more active position in the classroom in this generation (Öhrn 2002; Nielsen and Davies 2008). In our sample, many of the men in the youngest generation report either being unruly in school or having academic problems (working class) or being too lazy, but still clever (middle class), whereas only a few of the women felt uncomfortable in school. Still, both women and men in this generation share the understanding of the necessity of an education. The young men who experience academic problems at school know that there are few alternative routes to success. For the young women, the necessity of an education is experienced almost as a duty in a context where it is expected for a girl to be autonomous and have a career. The women aim higher than their mothers: they want good educations and good careers, and in this way they display higher ambitions and a stronger achievement orientation. The favourite educational choices of their mothers—secretary, teacher, librarian and nurse—are almost non-existent in the aspirations of their daughters. So are the efforts to adapt their career plans to a future family. When asked why she entered high school, Jorunn's daughter Jenny, who is middle class, answers: '*Well, that's what you do, isn't it? … and if I was doing it, why not choose the best school?*' Their choices of education after high school are more varied than what we saw in their parents' generation. Nevertheless, the majority still chooses relatively gender-typical or gender-neutral educations and the class difference is clear: both girls and boys from middle-class backgrounds go for more extensive education than working-class girls and boys.[4]

[4] These patterns of educational choice are also found in national statistics (see, for instance, NOU 15 2012).

Respect: Identification with Parents as Individuals

The youngest generation's descriptions of their parents are more varied and differentiated, and in some way less emotional than those we heard from the previous generations—there are fewer conflicts and expressions of strong sentiments like admiration or anger. Asked if she admires her mother, Elsa's daughter Eva, who is middle class, says: '*admire and admire, I respect her*'. The parents emerge as fully fledged persons with good and bad sides, as fallible humans rather than idealised or rejected psychological objects in the narratives. Feelings of identification or disidentification with a parent are understood in terms of the parent's personality rather than of his or her gender. Often the young women and men pick and choose different parts of parents and other figures they identify with when they describe their own personalities, without always being quite aware what comes from where. Still, the most marked change compared to the previous generation is that we see less emotional disidentification with the same-sex parent (see also Bengtsson 2001). There are some similarities in the positive way in which the youngest generation relate to their parents with the identification patterns of the eldest generation: not only in the positive attitude to the skill sets of their parents, especially the same-sex parent, but also in some of the men's more muted images of and the women's warmer relationships with the opposite-sex parent. However, less prominent mothers may now also be seen as strong figures and not as victims for whom their sons should feel sorry, and warm fathers are not always the main figure representing a bigger world to their daughters. In any case, both identifications and disidentifications with parents are now filtered through the basic idea of 'being yourself'.

Sons: Fathers as Doers, Mothers as Talkers

The men in the youngest generation resemble their grandfathers in that they talk much more about their fathers than about their mothers. Almost all of the young men are fond of their fathers and describe in detail their personalities and activities, their good sides and where they have potentials for improvement. For instance, Egil's son Erik, who is lower middle class, says about his father that: '*He is quite sorted. He pretty much knows what he's doing. He has quite a good temperament, I do too, actually.*' He goes on to describe his father's abilities in sports and how he has supported Erik without putting pressure on him. He thinks their relationship is good, but also that his father works too much and that they could spend more time together.[5] The young men tend to see themselves more on a par with their fathers. Whereas the oldest generation talked about personal traits as being 'transferred' to them down the generational chain and the middle generation used the phrase 'to be like' one's father or mother in a more personalised way, several of the middle-class men in the youngest generation turn the generational hierarchy upside-down. Magne from the middle generation talked about how he inherited moral values from his father, whereas his son Morten says about himself and his father: '*We are different people, but he is quite like me in many ways.*'

Some of the older fathers are targets of much of the same critique as in the previous generation concerning their outdated masculinity and emotional closure, but the critique is more conciliatory because the sons now know them better as persons. Rune, the son of the upper middle-class Ragnar who described a rather distant relationship with his sons, confirms that they do not talk a lot, something Rune wishes they did. He says his father has a certain '*air of a general-director*', but also that he is '*of the old, kind sort*'. Anders says about his old working-class father Arne:

> *He is like the definition of a 1950s–1960s type dad, who likes detective novels, and his car, and fixing things, or building things … He is a man totally devoid of interests, in a way, I've never understood that about him, I've never quite gotten him … It is hard to describe him, very kind, very practical, conservative.* (Anders, 30)

The fathers are described as much more present than in the previous generation. This presence not only make the sons' critiques of them more

[5] According to the *Gender Equality and Quality of Life* survey carried out in 2007, men from cohorts that match our middle and youngest generations say that they would have liked their fathers to be more present in the family. For those born from the mid-1980s onwards, the number drops—probably reflecting the fathers' increased presence in childcare from this period of time (Holter et al. 2009). See also Brannen (2015) for similar findings among men in the UK.

balanced, but also allows for a more uninhibited identification with what they feel to be positive sides of their fathers' masculinity. Glenn says that he likes his father's authority and that he has more respect for him than for his mother. When his father sends him or his brothers to their rooms, then he knows who is in charge: '*you just know that he's been there*'. He identifies strongly both with his father Geir and his grandfather Gunnar: '*I belong with them.*' Another father-identified son is the middle-class boy Trond, the son of Trygve, who worked part-time to care for the children in the family. He describes his father through his love for nature and hiking, his rationality and intellectual orientation, and as one who defines happiness as '*having a family*':

> *He has many of the traits that I have, I think. He reads this intellectual Danish newspaper [laughs]. He is—I think he is a sort of man of reason. He is halfway intellectual. And ... he is quite wise, I think. He has a lot of wisdom. I have a very positive view of him, he can help me with essays and many weird things ... He has meant a lot. He has maybe—he has influenced me a lot. Many of the thoughts I have, I have probably adopted from him.* (Trond, 18)

The present father is a *doing* father, not a talking one—or if he talks, it is about sports, politics or intellectual issues. The middle-class sons see their father as knowledgeable and intellectually stimulating discussion partners, as we heard from Trond, but they rarely talk about personal or emotional things. At 30, Paul says that he and his father like each other's company and that they discuss a lot of political and moral issues, but he still find the father's emotional intelligence limited. Paul judges himself to be more in touch with his own feelings and better at 'seeing' other people. Even the three young men who grew up with the participating fathers—Trond, Henrik and Vegard—find their fathers somewhat emotionally limited. Henrik, for instance, thinks that his father '*doesn't get to show a lot of his feelings*'.

The lack of communicative skills shown by fathers seems to be relatively unchanged, in spite of the fathers' critique of their own fathers in exactly this respect. For middle-class boys, this is seen as a shortcoming, whereas working-class boys appear more comfortable with it because they see themselves in much the same way. Erik says: '*It's not like—father and son sitting down having a father-to-son talk in the evening, we have never done that. Never been big talkers, any of us really.*' None of the sons report a negative relationship with their mothers, and the middle-class boys in particular think they resemble her as well in some ways: '*I have gotten a bit from mother and a bit from father*', Trond says. This identification with both parents may also be the case in families where the mother has a more traditional role in the family or the father's masculinity is seen as outdated: Morten says that he is '*a dreamer like my father*' and that they share many fields of interest, but that he is more like his mother, who was a stay-at-home mum for many years, when it comes to logic, structure and leadership. Anders finds his mother more intelligent and interesting to talk with than his old-fashioned working-class father. Still, the mothers' qualities are seldom elaborated upon and analysed in the same intense way as those of the fathers. The description of the mother is less pronounced and sometimes laced with a somewhat condescending tone. Mothers are more often than fathers described primarily in the context of the sons' needs: she is kind, she may help with school work and she is often the one with whom they can talk about emotional issues. Most of the sons feel emotionally closer to their mothers than to their fathers. Where fathers emerge as the parent who does things, mothers emerge as the communicative ones. On the more negative side comes the mothers' obsession with tidiness or a tiresome tendency towards control and nagging. But in contrast to what we saw among the grandfathers, we do not hear about the subdued mother for whom to feel sorry. In the narratives of the sons, she is rather taken for granted as the kind and understanding person she is. This may be a result of their young age, but it probably also reflects the fact that modern mothers who have their own life outside the family rarely fit easily into the role as victim.[6]

In spite of working mothers and more present fathers in this generation, the different roles of mothers and fathers in the eyes of their sons are surprisingly unchanged. Fathers do, while mothers talk and feel. Even when a father does his half of the childcare and housework, his mascu-

[6] Margot Bengtsson (2001: 169) finds that the mother is generally seen as the dominant personality in the family in this generation.

line assets of knowledge, wisdom and tough outdoor activities take up most of the description of him. But talking and feeling are not inherently perceived as incompatible with the masculine doing; rather, it is something the young men value and would like to see more of in their fathers. Yet it is something that comes in *addition* to the doing, not something that should replace it.

Daughters: Responsible Mothers, Warm Fathers

The talking and the doing are not quite as divided by gender in the young women's descriptions of their parents, but the ways in which mothers and fathers combine doing and talking are seen as different. Mothers are described as accessible for talk and practical care, but also as important conversation partners and advisers to their daughters. The mother emerges more as a separate person in the women's narratives compared to the men's. Mothers are seen as competent at their work and in organising the family, as well as responsible and engaged in a lot of things. For instance, two of the women from the middle generation, Jorun and Grete, who reported very angry or difficult relationships with their mothers, have daughters, Jenny and Guro, who relate in a completely different way to them as mothers:

> *My mother is very nice when you meet her, and very professional in her work. And she gets very angry when people don't do what they are supposed to do. There is no suffering in silence, or bending down your head; I can be like that too. I admire the way when she is stuck in something, then she really commits herself to carrying it through, not trying to escape from things like my father often chooses to do. But I'm not sure that what is right for her is right for me.* (Jenny, 18)
>
> *Very spirited, not a typical [laughs] stay-at-home housewife, you could say, she doesn't fit being at home, she is the kind of person who needs to be out and about, and she is very young at heart.* (Guro, 18)

Most of the young women say that they take their mothers' combination of career and family as a model for their own lives, but they want better education, different jobs, less stress, fewer divorces and more equal sharing of housework. Like the eldest generation, and in contrast to the middle generation, the women in the youngest generation place themselves in their mothers' world—however, since it is a world of both talking and doing, it is a world that is no longer so clearly defined by gender. In this way, the young women's identification with their mothers appears to be less gendered than the young men's identification with their fathers. It is also likely that the mothers' own borders vis-à-vis their daughters have become clearer than in the previous generation, not only because of the mothers' lives outside the family, but also because the daughters are allowed to test these borders through quarrelling.

A huge majority of the women in this generation report a good relationship with their mothers, but we still find more women than men who have difficulties with their parents, especially mothers. In these cases the mother is seen as selfish in the sense that she does not meet the needs of the daughter because she has prioritised her own career or a relationship with a new partner at the expense of her children. The daughters experience this as a betrayal and they often express ambivalent feelings of resentment and longing. One of the middle-class daughters feels abandoned by her parents after their divorce, but her sore feelings come up especially in her relationship with her mother:

> *Maybe she doesn't care about it—like, doesn't care about my life ... I imagine that ... she has the ability to understand me and I have the ability to understand her because we are quite similar. But at the same time I feel a lot of the time like we don't understand each other too.*

Also in this generation, difficult relationships between mothers and daughters seem to be about boundary conflicts. The daughter feels that the mother is either too controlling or too detached—or both. Inger's daughter Ida said at 18 that she felt her mother overwhelmed her with her own problems. At 30 Ida described her as '*a typically emotional social worker who feels and reacts and thinks afterwards, and I don't really like that type of people, because I like people who don't explode all over other people's boundaries—but of course I love my mother too*'. The relative power balance between the parents is also important: if the mother complains about and is frustrated because of a dominant or non-participating husband, the daughter tends to see the mother as the problem and describe her as nagging and controlling. Other psychological studies of mother–daughter relationships have also found that there is no automatic link between working mothers and autonomous daughters, but that this depends partly on the mother's capacity to combine autonomy and intimacy with regard to the daughter and partly on an equal relationship with the father in the family (von der Lippe 1988).

Almost all the young women in this generation talk about good relationships with their fathers too. Like the young men, they remember having lots of fun and doing activities with fathers. Middle-class daughters also identify with their fathers' knowledge. If the father has higher education, he is often the one who emerges as the knowledgeable and intellectual person in the family, even when the mother has the same level of education. Jenny at 18, who is the granddaughter of Johanne who compared her father's knowledge with an encyclopaedia, identifies strongly with her father's intellectual skills tells us that she was given the nickname '*the encyclopaedia*' in her class in secondary school. She sees herself and her father as the intellectuals in the family, and her mother and sister as the more social and emotional ones. Ida, who had a difficult relationship with her mother, says at 18: '*I am a clone of my dad*'—they share a taste in music and are both rational and stubborn.

Quite differently from what we heard from the sons, fathers are often described as emotionally accessible by the daughters. They are more often depicted as warm, emotional, temperamental, generous, fun or a bit charmingly grumpy (see also Bengtsson 2001). This adds a tender tone to the young women's descriptions of their fathers. Hilde, who otherwise identifies with her more intellectual mother, says: '*I have a lot of tenderness for my father, like. I always have. It's a little strange…*', whereas the description of her mother is more straightforward: '*I'm pretty happy with my mother. To put it like that.*' Compared with the previous generation, the roles of mothers and fathers seem almost reversed in the eyes of the daughters, but with the important difference that a close father is less threatening to the girl than a close mother. Vilde, who has a father who worked part-time in order to share the care for the children, uses almost the same phrase about her father as Grete in the previous generation did about her housewife mother: '*I have kind of… been the biggest thing in his life, I'm kind of everything to him, and he does absolutely everything for me.*' But the meaning has changed and now exemplifies how good the relationship is between father and daughter. In some cases the young women describe themselves as '*daddy's girls*' when they were little, but say that they identified more with their mothers when they came of age. Still, the tone is seldom as tender and loving when they talk about their mothers—here we also see a repetition of the experience of the eldest generation. The ambivalence towards the same-sex parent is also present in case of the young women in this generation: while it is always seen as a positive thing to be like one's father, being like one's mother is not always so. Middle-class girls characterise their parents as relatively equal in power and status (even if they may also criticise the father's laziness with regard to housework) or dominant in different areas. Conversely, we heard the working-class girl Beate put it more directly in that '*mum is kind of the boss*' and describe with tender irony her father as '*cowed*' or somebody who '*accepts everything*'. We may here see the return of the fragile masculinity of the grandmothers' stories, this time caused by the competence of mothers and daughters in fields that earlier belonged to men. Especially in the cases where the mother also exceeds the father in terms of education, the daughter describes the father with a mixture of irony and compassion. In cases where the father has little education, the young women often support him when he is criticised by their mother. Hilde feels that her mother tends to use '*dirty tricks*' against her father even if she is often right in terms of the point she is making. Stine says that her working-class father is not so clever in discussions: '*then I end up on mum's side, but other times I kind of feel like dad is so stupid that I have to help him along a bit, right*'. Keeping up dignified masculinity seems to be a project that the daughters and the sons share.

The tenderness towards fathers may to some extent disturb the young women's equality projects, for instance, through producing excuses for fathers' blameworthy neglect of housework or for not following up as divorced fathers. However, when we meet the daughters as 30-year-olds we hear more critical voices towards these fathers, sometimes in parallel with a process of sorting out relational problems with the mother. Only those fathers who were in fact good fathers—even if they did not do their share of the housework—have kept their adult daughters' admiration and love. The reworking of parental relationships between the first and second interviews is much more salient among the women than among the men. It may of course reflect the fact that more women reported problems in the relationships with their parents at the age of 18. Yet it also applies to some of the girls who thought the relationship was fine when they were 18, but later found out that things were more complicated. As a result of this, we find a majority of women who at 30 either identify with both or with none of their parents.

Gendering Bodies and Degendering Sexuality

Both women and men in the youngest generation talk a lot and in great detail about their bodies, and this interest in the body is no longer an exclusively female affair. Just like their grandfathers and fathers before them, the men in the youngest generation report that their bodily changes were gradual and that the puberty of girls is probably a much more dramatic affair, but they do actually have narratives of wet dreams, growing hair in the groin and armpits, and change of voice pitch. 'Puberty' is now a commonly used concept and regarded as a relevant topic also among the men and 'flaws' is a term that this generation of young men makes use of without any hesitation. Being small, too fat or having a small penis are frequent complaints—in addition to red hair and freckles, acne, a big nose and a tendency to blush. Anders, who at first denies having any bodily problems, ends up talking for a long time about his acne problems. The list of flaws indicates the relative preoccupation with appearances in the youngest generation of men compared to the previous ones or, perhaps more importantly, it is a preoccupation that they do not perceive as unmasculine. One bodily theme that is recognisable across the generations of men, however, is the matter of size. This obviously includes the size of the penis, where comparisons in the school shower are still mentioned as shameful experiences. But the issue of size is more general: to be '*tall for one's age*' or '*one of the tallest in class*' is referred to as an important asset, almost negating other flaws. Just like their fathers, the young men regard bodybuilding as a form of contemptuous and effeminate self-indulgence. Men who '*feel up their own muscles*' are '*icky*', Joar, who is lower middle class, says. Vegard, who actually lifts weights and has developed his muscles, hastens to give a 'manly' reason for this activity; it is not in order to look good, but in order to be able to help out in a situation of need: '*I've always been afraid that if there's an emergency or something, this is a little sick … I wouldn't be able to do anything … I guess I exercised in order to be strong and to get some use out of it.*' The size and strength of the body is evidently an advantage in the competition between boys, but it is also seen as an asset when it comes to girls. Vegard had at times felt that he was almost objectified by girls: '*when I was 16, I was sort of the bodybuilding type. There were a lot of girls who I kind of dated, who were with me because of how I looked*'.

This fear of being objectified is significant, since it reveals the ambivalence associated with the new trend of bodily preoccupations.[7] Some of the men define—just like the male generations before them—any such interest as feminine, and remain indifferent when it comes to clothes and leave the shopping to their mothers. Others are interested in fashion, studying films and magazines for inspiration. Among the young men who are preoccupied with style, we also find those who are explicitly 'anti-fashion', which in some cases seems to become almost a mania to set oneself apart. Rune has a long coat bought at a flea market, demonstrating his boundaries both against his mother, who wants him to dress nicely, and against the socialists at school by actually putting on a suit, and finally against the conservatives (with whom he is politically aligned) by refusing to wear the expensive and exclusive brands that are their uniform. This is a case where the more general mentality of individualisation seems to be turned into a drive for uniqueness—a drive that is much more prominent among the men than the women in this generation (see also Bordo 1999). The young men in our study seem to be involved in a precarious testing out of the borders of modern masculinity, where a weak and vulnerable body remains problematic. It is therefore remarkable that they actually admit to such vulnerability to a greater extent than the generations before them and even invest in body projects in new ways within

[7] The idea that men today are metrosexual narcissists is not confirmed by our youngest generation. The concept metrosexual was first used by Mark Simpson (1994), but became a media hype in 2002 when it appropriated by the advertising industry (Pedersen 2005).

some (masculine) limits. Nevertheless, they also seem to experience their bodies as rather self-evident facts. Seen in connection with their parental identifications, it appears that a close and positive relationship with a mother who cares for her son's body (also when it comes to his appearance, giving advice on clothes) and a father who is actively involved, for instance, in his son's sports activities promote a strong embodied sense of masculinity as self-evident.

Among the men of the middle generation, we saw an increased focus on the female body. This is a much more ambivalent issue in the youngest generation: at age 18, Stian stresses that '*boobs and thighs*' were more important to him when he was younger, whereas Henrik at the same age is clearly apologetic about the fact that a nice body on a girl means a lot since '*it shouldn't*'. However, at 30 the men admit that bodily gender differences are important—and that they were important at 18 too: '*you couldn't look like the back end of a bus and have a lovely personality*', says Anders at 30, looking back at how he and his friends saw girls in high school. This emphasis on bodily difference is not seen among women to the same degree, so it may indicate that it has a specific significance in securing a sense of masculinity. At 30, Henrik does not feel that there are any differences in the skills and capacities of women and men, but at the same time he wants more intensity between women and men, and thinks that women should emphasise their femininity to a greater extent. He finds it difficult to explain what he means by femininity, but feels it has something to do with body, clothes and charisma. According to him, neither men nor women should dress in grey and try to become invisible, but he finds it especially problematic when women think that they have to behave and look like men in order to succeed in a career. Since he is clearly in favour of gender equality both at 18 and 30, this indicates that the issue of bodily and aesthetic difference in this generation of men is experienced as a separate aspect of gender, partly following its own logic, and not necessarily in tension with degendering in other areas, as it was for the men in the middle generation.

Among the young women, the generative body is no straightforward matter. The problem is not lack of knowledge as in the previous generations: they all know what menstruation is and most of them depict the transition as rather undramatic. The young working-class women are even glad to feel grown-up and 'normal'. For the middle-class girls, however, the bodily transition is more disturbing: Vilde remembers that she was proud *not* to get her period since that meant that she worked out a lot, something her father appreciated. These middle-class girls are even more negative with regard to their menstruation than the women in the eldest generation. The period is characterised as '*a real bother*', '*hellish crap*', '*a little strange*', '*embarrassing*' or directly '*icky*'. Eva, who could shout across the classroom that she needed to borrow a tampon, tells us that she is completely disgusted by the blood. Across all three generations of women, bodily appearances and looks represent an area that is much less surrounded by taboos than generative development and maturing processes. The differences between the two eldest generations were a greater differentiation of flaws and assets, as well as a drastically increased energy (and resources) invested in bodily improvements. In the youngest generation the detailed catalogue of flaws is replaced with a general preoccupation, bordering on obsession, with the body's size, shape and weight (see also Bordo 1993; Brumberg 1997). It is an issue that is strongly present in the interviews regardless of whether the women feel overweight or not. The vast majority have been dieting, and quite a few have, as one of them puts it, had '*a touch of anorexia*'. To almost stop eating makes one feel good, in control. Oda, whose mother as a young girl used to compare her weight with that of Miss Norway, first assures us that she does not have a problem with her body and then admits reluctantly that she often gets annoyed with herself if she eats without having worked out. On days like that she throws up:

> *I was completely exhausted when I was doing ballet, and I just ate and ate and ate when I was done. I was so exhausted. And that's when I became dissatisfied and threw up. Oh! Yuck [silently].* (Oda, 18)

Others make it a point that they have never been on a diet. The awareness of fat seems to pervade the body images of all the women in this generation, but the experience of the body is still quite varied.[8] There is

[8] There are specific class, family and generational histories that make some of young women more vulnerable to body norms than others. Studies have shown that they often come from the middle class, where there is the double pressure of being both pretty and clever at school (see Buhl 1990).

a stronger polarisation in the youngest generation where some women experience greater success when it comes to disciplining themselves, since there is hardly any indifference involved. The polarisation is also quite striking when it comes to social background. None of the women from working-class families report a negative relationship with their bodies, and most of the ones with a positive body image are mother-identified and have a positive relationship with an attentive father. Stine describes how she showed off her new dresses in front of her father, since he was '*the only man in the house*'. Reproductive and bodily femininity appears to be more threatening to middle-class girls. They also seem to receive more ambiguous messages from their parents, ranging from feminist celebrations of their first period to hints about watching their weight. Their relationship with their fathers is based on intellectual qualities than a positive evaluation of femininity. Perhaps it does not involve a direct devaluation of femininity, but rather neutralises its embodied aspects? The experience of gendered embodiment may therefore be a greater subjective obstacle for a father-identified girl than it is for a mother-identified boy. Feminine appearance is a demanding act of balance for a middle-class girl: not too little, not too much, and appropriate in time and place (see also Ambjörnsson 2004). The more or less suspect femininity that a young middle-class girl has to avoid in order to become a modern, autonomous girl might also no longer be represented by her own mother in the way it was in the middle generation, but rather might be experienced as a more obscure, inner threat to her perceived identity. The body that is so central to modern self-construction has become a potential enemy, which they either manage to control or that lets them down by being beyond their control (Rudberg 1995). Thus, in spite of the young men taking a much more active interest in their appearance, there are only sparse signs that men and women in the youngest generation have become more similar to each other in the way they talk about and relate to their bodies.

Among our informants, the 'risk group' with regard to anorexic tendencies seems to be father-identified athletic girls from the middle class, who hate becoming what one of them describes as '*a proper female*'. At the same time, there is a female family heritage involved, sometimes going as far back as the grandmother's generation. Oda remembers how her mother used to stand in front of the mirror and complain about how fat she was, while her daughter who stood beside her clearly saw that *she* was chubbier than her mother.

When it comes to sexuality, there seems to be more degendering going on—both in practice and in norms: at 18, more of the women than the men have had heterosexual intercourse, which coincides with figures in national statistics for their generation (Pedersen et al. 2003). Many of the young women have had one-night stands; others had their sexual debut in a very short relationship that only lasted a few weeks. To have several partners is no longer regarded as a moral problem—although both genders are aware of the fact that girls who '*sleep around*' get a worse reputation than '*players*', which is an exclusively masculine term. The possibility of being the object of negative labelling does not seem to direct the young women's behaviour to any great extent. They initiate sexual relations more often than their mothers did, or at least they feel that they *should* be able to. In practice it is still rare and is clearly felt as a risky business. The risks are evidently connected with fear of abuse, but even more with the fear of being seen as an 'exposed girl' (Nielsen and Rudberg 2007). To the young women in our sample, an 'exposed girl' is *not* a girl who has several partners, but rather a girl who has sex to please others, not because she really wants to. They insist that when and how to have sex is seen as an individual choice. The ones who 'wait' until they are in a steady relationship do not argue in terms of morality (like their grandmothers) or risk of pregnancy (like their mothers), but in terms of what they felt as right for themselves. The young women still connect love and sex, but not as strongly as the middle generation. We can actually see some signs that love is becoming more problematic than sex for the youngest women. Eva loudly proclaims that '*sex is fun!*' and positions herself as a sexual subject, even asking one of her male friends to '*deflower*' her because she thought she was being left behind at 16. Still, the cheerful facade seems to cover up many painful complications: to have sex with someone you love is definitely risky. Eva gets '*uptight*', '*deadly nervous*' and prays '*God, let him want somebody else*'. The fear that she shares with other middle-class girls is to lose herself in a heterosexual relationship (see also Kleven 1992, 1993). To fall in love implies being open and vulnerable, with the danger of being evaluated and rejected on account of something experienced as genuinely one's own and yet totally out of hand. '*In a way I want to have the upper hand, I don't want to care about them as much as they care about me, if you know what I mean*', Anja says. This may indicate that the newly gained autonomy in young women has to be safeguarded and that especially heterosexual relations are still connected with the danger of dependency and asymmetry.

These changes seem to appear somewhat paradoxically at the historical moment when at least some of the men are heading in the opposite direction, striving for an integration of sex and intimacy. The tendency to reject the idea of one-night stands is in our data actually more pronounced among the young men. Emphasised in their arguments is the importance of '*feelings*' in order to have '*good sex*'. The crucial thing is to know your partner well, Kim says, which makes it possible to open up and tell each other about one's needs and desires. One-night stands are therefore condemned as '*a cut between the head and the heart*', as Henrik puts it. Joar and Vegard also describe their own sexual debuts on one-night stands as horrible—Joar got a stomach ache but felt that he had to oblige, while Vegard felt directly attacked:

> *Suddenly she's pulling my arm, you know, and she drags me into the room, and you know, I totally panic, right, and then ... we were going to try and stuff, but it didn't work because ... she was a bit tight.* (Vegard, 18)

However, this also reveals that these men are still ambivalent towards female initiatives (see also Dworkin and O'Sullivan 2007). Some of the working-class boys mention girls who are sexually frivolous or unbearable when they get drunk. The middle-class boys think that sexual morals ought to be gender-neutral. Some of them actually prefer active girls, not least because that also reduces the risk of getting rejected. That a girl should be sexually active and initiate a relationship is not only accepted but also even demanded by most of the young men, since sex should be a reciprocal affair:

> *I remember once when ... when she just lay down and waited for me to do everything. I just put my trousers back on and went to sleep on the sofa, 'I can't be bothered with this, the doormat belongs outside' ... I don't want it just to be me, only thinking about myself.* (Vegard, 18)

Thus, it seems that sexuality for these young men should be within a relationship in order to be enjoyable. This clearly goes against the trend in the previous generation of men who defined sexuality as an uncontrollable and almost brutal urge when they were the same age. However, the integration of love and sex among the men does not mean that sex gets reduced to intimacy. Vegard, who is among those who most emphatically underline the importance of feelings in order for sex to be good, is also quite certain that it involves two different dimensions:

> *Well, I don't feel more attached during the sex act or anything like that. It's more that I feel safer and things like that, if you can hold each other and cuddle and stuff… I feel like when you sleep with someone, it becomes more … cold, like, because you don't get the same connection, because then you're busy with something else than thinking about each other … but of course it is, I don't know [laughs] maybe there's something that you have to get out of your system, kind of [laughs] … then you can fall asleep in each other's arms afterwards.* (Vegard, 18)

There is much less desire involved in the descriptions of sexual encounters among the women, and their characterisations are actually not so different from the ones given by the women in the middle generation. Many of them depict their first time as a painful affair, involving blood and horror, while others laconically state that it was no great experience. In addition to Eva, who proclaimed that '*sex is fun*', only Stine, who also had a painful first time, actually describes sexual excitement where '*the bodies live together*'. When feelings enter the picture, women still tend to talk about sexual experiences in relational terms, as the ultimate intimacy, sometimes as a testimony to their erotic power over the boyfriend, in addition to being a way to feel grown-up. The sexual experience itself is not highlighted, and we recognise some of the instrumentality from the women of the previous generation, although not as explicitly. The question is whether explicit sexual desire is still defined as a masculine affair even though both norms and practices are more degendered and individualised. Does this imply a gendered inertia when it comes to questions of the body and sexuality that seem to go slower or even resist other degendering processes?

However, neither such inertia nor the emphasis on sexual difference among the men influences the attitudes to non-normative sexualities in this generation. As with Magne in the previous generation, sexual difference and heterosexual choice are seen as a question of one's own individual taste rather than as general norms. It may actually be the other way round— that increased diversity also reduces the heterosexual choice to being one among other possible choices and thus legitimates the talk about experiences of sexual difference. When asked about homosexuality at 30 and whether this was an issue that occupied them in high school, the answers illustrate that the 1990s was the decade when gay and lesbian rights were on the agenda and the first steps were taken towards cultural and political inclusion.[9] At first many of them said that they had neither thought nor talked much about it around 1990. At the ten-year reunion for their high school class, it had turned out that two girls from one of the classes were in a same-sex civil union, which had come as a complete surprise to everyone. Some had, however, known gay people from sports, political organisations or colleagues of their parents', and had whispered with others about it. It was also clear from what some of them said that homosexuality was indeed present in school and among their peers in the late 1980s, sometimes as a bit of a worrying issue. A gym teacher in high school had been openly lesbian and at that time the students thought it was odd, one woman even remembering it as '*icky*'. A few had experienced that a close friend had come out as gay or lesbian and remember the awkwardness they at first felt about it. They had needed time to reinterpret their friendship, but it never led to a break. Those who were late in getting a boyfriend/girlfriend remember wondering silently if they might be gay or lesbian. At 30, this timidity towards the issue had disappeared. Most of them now had gay/lesbian friends and colleagues, or had experienced that a parent or a spouse came out as homosexual or bisexual. They do not condemn non-normative sexualities, but struggle with defining new rules of relationships. One man in our sample had a wife who had come out as bisexual and who had argued that this also made him free to have sexual

[9] The law on registered partnerships of same-sex couples was adopted in 1993; same-sex marriage was legalised in 2009.

relations with other men. As he did not desire other men, he could not see the great justice in that. They later divorced and he says that: '*I think I'd choke if my next girlfriend reveals that she's bi, that's like ... if she thought I'd think it was really cool, I don't think she'd get the desired reaction.*' One of the women in our sample had had a short affair with another woman in London in her late twenties, but realised that she was not really sexually attracted to women. She finds women more beautiful than men, but she does not desire them. One of the men told us at 30 that he had felt insecure of his sexual identity when he was in high school (something he did not tell anybody at the time) and that he had gone a few times to gay bars in his early twenties to find out if he was sexually attracted to men. He chose to engage in heterosexual relations after that. He says that he now feels secure in his heterosexual identity, but that he knows that it is possible for him to fall in love with a man. Henrik, who emphasises his attraction to sexual difference, also says that he loves to flirt with both women and men, but that Norwegian men are not good at it. Thus, also in their attitudes towards non-normative sexualities, we recognise this generation's combination of attachments to gender difference, gender variability and individual choice.

Individuality and Gender

The combination of partly degendered, partly still gendered structures and practices, and the belief in individual preferences creates many paradoxes in the reflections on gender in the youngest generation: gender exists, but is irrelevant, or should be irrelevant, or maybe not? Gender is experienced as less of a straitjacket in this generation and a returning claim is that it is really up to each person how he or she wants to be, regardless of gender. This seems to match well with their interpretation of the work division in their families, and also with the feeling of gender we heard about in relationships with their parents: seeing themselves as a combination of their parents' personalities and interpreting identification with same-sex parents as non-gendered. The working-class boy Anders says about his general experience of degendering:

> *The roles have become blurrier now. You're not expected to fill a particular role. Earlier it was like that, you were supposed to be and do like your father, it was divided back then, it was boy and girl. Now the roles are much more blurred. You can become what you want and be what you like.*
>
> *Q: Do you find that easy or do you think it's difficult?*
>
> *No, I think it's easy. You can, well, do exactly what you want to do, there's no … yeah.* (Anders, 18)

The problem of the middle generation—knowing what kind of man/woman they did *not* want to be, but not knowing what they wanted instead—has more or less disappeared. Both women and men in the youngest generation can talk at length about what kind of person they are or want to be, and this is mainly expressed in gender-neutral terms like being open and honest, social, active, easygoing, independent, flexible, stubborn, talkative, depressive or good-natured. The emphasis lies on '*being oneself*'. For the working-class informants, being oneself is most often equivalent to being relaxed and ordinary and not intolerant of others. For middle-class informants, it is elaborated on as being a special person, unique and not easily fitted into predefined identity boxes to do with gender, political opinions, clothing or lifestyles (see also Simonsen and Ulriksen 1998; Jensen 2001). There are gender differences, however, in how this desire for uniqueness is expressed. Among the women, it is about being authentic and coherent, the person you *really* are; among the men, it refers to being different and unpredictable, to be free, courageous and surprising or even provocative. The point of not fitting into a box is stressed by combining identities that others may see as incompatible: to be an intellectual *and* a surfer, to be serious *and* a hedonist, to like music or films that are normally seen as contrasts, or alternately to defend right-wing and left-wing political views to confuse others about one's political stand—'*I don't like being a stereotype*', Anders says. We saw the same in Rune's ruminations about what to wear. They admire other boys who are '*interesting personalities*' in this way. In only two of the women—both middle class and both strongly identified with their fathers—we find some of the same desire to be special and provocative to others.

Gender also exists on more explicit and quite stereotypical levels. Even though both men and women are at pains to explain that these stereotypes do not apply to everybody, that people are individually different, the ways in which they describe the positive and negative traits of girls and boys are rather uniform. The good thing with girls is that they are often smart, more social, and can talk about emotions and personal issues (thus, boys should try to be more like this). The bad thing with girls is their tendency to talk behind people's backs and making drama (which girls should try to do less). The bad thing with boys is that they often try to appear tougher than they really are and that they are not good at talking about emotional issues (at which boys ought to be better). The good thing with boys is that they are more active, direct and straightforward, and that they can have more fun (thus, girls should try to be more like this). The only thing women and men seem to disagree on is that the women tend to emphasise girls' greater maturity and responsibility, whereas men find this a myth and an expression of girls being too serious all the time. Compared with the previous generation there is more emphasis on both positive and negative traits in both genders, which makes it easier to pick and choose one's own self-construction or ideals.

Among the women, femininity is extended and redefined in many different ways. Eva, for instance, defines femininity as something that may be combined with independence and dignity. Her ideal woman is '*a liberated woman who does what she wants in life and who doesn't let herself be dominated by other people nagging and stuff, but who is simultaneously feminine and, in a way, keeps her feminine side*'. In their gender-neutral self-descriptions, the middle-class girls tend to stress ambitious and independent aspects, while the working-class girls emphasise the social and outgoing aspects of their personalities. The irrelevance of gender is also seen with regard to sibling rivalry: the girls may feel overlooked in comparison with new siblings, especially half-siblings from their parents' new marriages, but they almost never interpret this in terms of gender, like we saw among the middle generation. Thus, the general picture is that the young women generally perceive themselves and others in terms of individuality, but that gender still occupies secure ground when it comes to looks and appearances. For the working-class girls, dressing in a feminine way is a positive thing—'*to radiate that I am a woman*', as Stine expresses it—and most of them also prefer men who look and behave in masculine ways. Most of the middle-class girls, on the other hand, distance themselves from an overly feminine style, which they associate with being '*dumb and blonde*': '*trousers pulled up, and, like, wearing a lot of make-up, and … doing the secretary-track, no clue about politics*' (Ida) or '*shopping centre girls, very common, with a lot of make-up, who quit after high school and things like that*' (Nora). The middle-class girls do not look for dominant men, but rather their 'equal', and prefer men who are gentle and emotional—something they tend to think is the case with many men if you just get behind their facade.

When we meet the young women at 30, their experiences were that gender held more significance in the world than they had thought at 18. Some of the middle-class girls—not least those who chose 'masculine' educations and jobs—had experienced a contradiction between their educational or occupational choices and their alleged potential as girlfriend material. Ida had found out that '*a great way to escape men who harass you is saying that you study physics!*' Or, conversely, when Tonje goes to a bar and wants to meet someone, she never says that she is a doctor, but just that she '*works at the hospital*'. Then the men in the bar automatically assume she is a nurse. But quite a few of them have also experienced that they were more influenced by traditional gender patterns than they had expected, especially when it comes to men. Some had experienced being swept off their feet by infatuations (and ignoring their work in such periods) or they had become submissive to dominant men in ways they hardly understand in retrospect. The majority of them say at 30 that they have experienced life to be more complicated than expected, not least with regard to gender and their trust in their own strength. Guro, who chose to study natural sciences, says:

> *I guess I was extremely confident! [laughs]—before I messed up those exams [laughs] … I had an extremely strong faith in myself, I don't think I was scared of anything, really. I didn't hold back at all, I wasn't very used to being considerate towards others.* (Guro, 30)

These experiences have not made them more gender-conformist—quite the opposite. They understand more about gender as a power structure and how this even permeates their own selves in ways that have been surprising and quite shocking to acknowledge. They have become more aware of subtle gender oppression both in themselves and in their relationships with others. Only with regard to pregnancy and childbirth do we find some who have become more respectful towards biological gender differences. Ida, who firmly believes that individual variation is more significant than gender group differences, says that it was an ambivalent experience becoming a mother since she has a '*masculine*' personality, but that the experience also taught her a lesson about biology:

> *I would've loved to be born a man!—my husband would've been a better woman than me ... But at the same time you can't have your cake and eat it too. It would have been much easier for me to choose an academic career had I been born a man, because then I wouldn't have experienced that biological process and all those hormones. Because I'm* <u>*very*</u> *academically keen and actually very ambitious and very perfectionist. But that* <u>*can't*</u> *be combined with toddlers. I'm born a woman, I've had children, I'm married, so ... yes.* (Ida, 30)

The young men distance themselves from bragging and macho masculinities. To be emotional and open, to do housework and take care of one's children are not seen as unmasculine, but rather as desired qualities in men. Stian says that he is '*not afraid to cry*'. Most of them have female friends whom they give credit for having taught them to become better at '*opening up*' and talking about feelings. For most of the working-class men at 18, relational talk still tends to be more of a girls' thing, whereas the middle-class men demonstrate a much higher interest in interpersonal relationships and psychological aspects than the majority of their fathers did, their grandfathers notwithstanding. But in contrast to the women, who reflect more on their relationships with others and who have a more ironic view of themselves, the psychological perspective of the men is, as in the middle generation, often centred on their own personal development and taken very seriously. Trond, for instance, tells us at 18 that '*finding yourself ... I feel like I'm constantly developing. I think it's very healthy, I think it's very healthy always to develop, even if it can be very tiring and very hard always to consider yourself*'. Still, gender is more present in the men's self-reflections and the absence of masculinity appears to be more of a threat to them than the absence of femininity in women is to them—or to the women themselves. These limits of degendering are also reflected in the leisure activities in this generation, where girls have become active in football and hockey, but boys have fewer choices. Henrik, who originally wanted to dance ballet, ended up with flamenco instead because it felt less stigmatising. The mixing of gender traits may still raise the question whether they are seen by others as 'man enough':

> *I'm not a tough guy like [mentions two boys in his class], that kind of … a cliché, like—a macho type guy … I got a comment from [a girl he is interested in] the other day, that she thought that … that I'm not much of a man, sort of.*
>
> *Q: What did she mean by that?*
>
> *Well, she means that … that I'm not … that I'm not very tough. I'm not particularly bothered by masculine … signalling masculine characteristics, I guess. But I think I'm tough when I'm supposed to be tough, sort of. I can make it through a snow storm … But then I thought—I figured out—that's what I want to be. I don't have a need to demonstrate that I'm a man, hey ho, and I choose that lifestyle. My mother has always been a member of women's organisations. So I sort of always think of girls as my equals. I mean, she can do the same as me. I can't stand girls who're supposed to be weak … they annoy me. She should be part of it, everything I want to do, like, all those activities.* (Henrik, 18)

The men who have had fathers who participated in caring for them are those who are most explicitly occupied with the issue of masculinity, and their reflections on gender resemble those of their fathers, but also transgress them. Their own chosen identity combination is understood as 'masculinity' plus 'something else'. The 'something else' is not primarily seen as feminine, but as an extension and improvement of masculinity. Vegard describes himself as both '*down to earth and serious*' and as '*an emotional person*' who cares for others and likes to help if anyone has a problem, but still he does not like '*to be prevented from doing something I'd like to do*'. Henrik says that the ideal man is one who can '*show feelings and still keep some of what makes a man a man*'. This desired manliness is not about male authority, making money or having a career, but about being a physically strong, courageous and playful man. So far they resemble their fathers. However, they also embrace a kind of masculinity that re-emerges on the other side of the addition of soft values to masculinity. Trond says that he thinks gender roles are disappearing, but that this in itself may lead to men becoming more engaged in doing tough masculine things like parachute jumping. Asked how he thinks a man should be, he says:

> *A man ought to know how to bake bread. I don't know how to do that yet, but I'll learn [laughs]. And he ought to be helpful, do the dishes ... So—I don't know. I like to—I think—I find men who are a bit—who support the male ideal in a way—I think that might be healthy too. That you should be a bit—I think a man can be athletic and—I think a man should impress a woman a bit. Not be a completely soft man. I think that role is lost because—I think women might want men like that, but I think women want men who are men too. And men want women who are women too ... Yes, that he embodies some male ideals. He can be ironic about them too. But to show that he is—that a man can be fresh and sporty and that men are decent creatures.* (Trond, 18)

These young men are also those who most strongly expect a parallel gender mixing in girls: they like feminine girls, but in combination with being able to carry a backpack or rise early in the morning to join them skiing at dawn. They detest girls who are weak, passive and dependent: '*I want a grown-up woman, like*', Henrik says, and by this he also means a girl who is not dependent on him, but has her own life. The value they put on their personal freedom here seems to work as a support for gender equality. However, it may also be a version where support of gender equality is based on contempt for traditional femininity. Many of them say that they cannot stand '*stupid girls*', meaning girls who are too occupied with their looks and with dating. Intelligence and sportiness are more important than looks, but if it can be combined with good looks, even better. Some of the men with gender-traditional fathers instead prefer feminine girls. The girls should have '*a certain capacity*' in order not to be boring, but they should not be '*hyper-intelligent*', Rune says.

At 30 the men have become clearer in their opinions on bodily and psychological gender differences and see them not only as facts of life, but also as things that make life worth living. They do not see big differences in the skills and capacities of men and women, but there *are* differences related to appearances and preferences, they say, and this should be allowed. Even the middle-class women at 30 are more open to this idea.

Nora, who at 18 spoke with contempt of dumb and blonde working-class girls, asks at 30 why on earth women should have to dress boringly or as men to be taken seriously. It must be possible to look good, even sexy, *and* have brains, she says, and adds that she finds it important to challenge the norms regarding this. Anders has also become aware of femininity through his own daughter. It surprised him—his ex-wife is tough and wears black. He understands this perceived femininity in his little daughter as her inborn individuality, but not as inborn heterosexuality:

> *She's this sort of girly-girly girl. She's born that way, we didn't stand a chance, we tried … to do everything, but she's all in for pink, no boys' stuff, no cars, nothing, it has to be nice and pretty, and … she's the most girly person I've ever encountered—without having her parents to thank for it … We actually think she's a lesbian, she's terribly fond of girls and wondered if it was okay to have a girlfriend. Now she claims she's in love with a boy, though, but it doesn't matter to any of us.* (Anders, 30)

Compared with the previous generations where the tensions in the marriages were described as tensions between the life projects of women and men, the youngest generation appears to a larger degree to live out those tensions within themselves, regardless of gender. There are gender differences in terms of how these tensions are expressed, but at the same time it is also the case that the life projects of men and women in this generation have become more similar. The project is to combine work and care and what was earlier seen as feminine and masculine virtues in behaviour and personality—to be social and caring, active and daring—but also to keep up the gender difference when it comes to appearances and sexual attraction. As children in school they have competed on the same level, with the girls often more academically successful than the boys, and in their families both girls and boys have been expected to take part in the household work, with the girls doing somewhat more than the boys. As young adults they enter an educational system and a job market where the degendering has become an unquestionable norm, but where practice sometimes runs counter to theory. In this way the ambiguous practice they experience reflects their own confusing feelings of gender.

Striving for Work–Family Balance

In the youngest generation we know more about the wishes and expectations of future practice than about actual practices. The main bulk of the data stems from an age where none or only a minority had children of their own, and the analyses and conclusions about the practice of the youngest generation as adults will therefore be more preliminary than for the previous generations.[10] Eight informants, however, were interviewed a third time in 2011, when they were approaching 40. These interviews indicate the changes in life from being 30 to being 40 and may also illuminate what life phases mean for attitudes to gender equality as a practical and political issue. These eight interviews at age 40 will be analysed separately in Chap. 8.

Among the young men there was a clear connection between the work division in the families they grew up in and what they anticipated for their own life when they were 18.[11] The majority of them grew up with fathers who took part (to varying extents) in housework and childcare, and mothers who worked outside the family (part-time or full-time) from early on. At 18, these young men with participating fathers saw children and family as central and sometimes even the most important aspects of their imaginations about the future. They said they would like to stay at home themselves for a period of time with their future babies, and that the children later should attend full-time kindergarten.[12] They wanted to have enough time

---

[10] At 30, all informants had completed their secondary education, except for two of the working-class informants, Anders and Beate, who had made their way into the job market without formal qualifications. One man and eight women had children; two of the men were going to be fathers in the near future. Since we re-interviewed 19 of the 22 women and only six of the 12 men, the difference in who had become parents may, in fact, be smaller. However, it may also reflect the age difference between women and men in when they become parents for the first time. In 2000 in Oslo it was at age 30–31 for women and age 33–34 for men (Statistics Norway, Statbank, Table 05530). At 40 we interviewed three men and five women and at this point in time all of them had children.

[11] In a study of Nordic youth, Øia (2011) found that boys with working mothers have a more positive attitude towards gender equality than other groups. Bjørnholt (2015) found that caring fathers do not automatically become models for their adult sons; it depends on the mother's role in the family. In our sample, caring fathers seem to produce sons for whom caring relationships are important, but these men also have a positive relationship with their mothers, who they see as competent and with a life of her own outside the family.

[12] The father's quota was not yet introduced when we interviewed them in 1991 (see Chap. 4).

with their families. Vegard, who was cared for by his father when he was little, said:

> *I want a relaxed life where I can enjoy myself with my loved ones and understand, know them, the people around you. Both emotionally and things like that. I don't want a family where everyone sort of runs in separate directions all the time ... I'm not a male chauvinist or anything. I think it's fine that the man cooks dinner at home and vacuums and so on. I don't mind that.* (Vegard, 18)

Trond, who had his father at home part-time, took into consideration that he needed some more skills in household work before he could move out from the parental home, and he saw these skills as essential for taking responsibility for himself:

> *I live at home now, so—I feel that I might get better at things like that once I move out and feel that I have to really do those things myself. Then you have to take responsibility for your own life, like, then you have to—then there's nobody to bake bread for you, like, and you don't get your meatballs automatically.* (Trond, 18)

These young men also imagined their future spouses to be working and thought it would be unproblematic if she were more educated or made more money than them. When we met these men ten years later, they held the same views. Anders, the only father among them at that time, had taken the father's quota of the parental leave; he had wanted to take more than the four weeks, but for economic reasons had to go back to work. The couple later divorced and now had shared custody. If he has another child, he wants a 50/50 share of the parental leave and the care—and not to get divorced. Henrik is at 30 a bit worried about the prospect of children because his wife comes from a country where it is unusual for fathers to stay at home and take care of housework and childcare. He says it will be him who will have to insist on sharing.

In contrast to the family-oriented men, the majority of the young men who had grown up in families with more traditional gender roles, where the father did not take much part in the housework and the mother stayed at home before the children attended school, did not include family and children as central in their plans for the future at 18 (Anders was an exception here—the fact that both of his parents were very old seems to have facilitated his recognition of their outdated gender arrangement, something that was less evident to men with younger gender traditional parents). In their visions of the future, the emphasis was on travelling, education, self-development and careers. They were either sceptical towards or had not yet seriously considered whether they wanted children or not. Rune said he would leave it to his future wife to decide. When asked directly, they had some reservations against the gender-equal vision of future family life. Paul admitted that even though both men and women lose out in traditional gender roles, it has also been a '*very, very, very long tradition that women have stayed home and men have been out hunting*' and, thus, difficult to change overnight. They were not negative to the idea of sharing the work at home as long as their future wife was not a nag:

> *I mean, if I lived with someone, then it's, one thing is that* <u>*I*</u> *did the dishes every other day, and changed diapers and stuff, but if she was to go around and, like, all the time say things like 'Yes, now you're doing the dishes because you're a man, you're supposed to do it too', then I'd be annoyed, because then, then* <u>*they*</u> *make us feel guilty all the time.* (Rune, 18)

Working wives and kindergarten for children were OK, but they had more reservations: it might be better for children to be taken care of at home during the first years—maybe they could do it themselves, but they had not really thought about it. They would not insist on taking a part of the parental leave if their wives wanted to have it all. They were prepared to share the housework—but if the wife were at home, it would be quite natural that she would take care of it, Morten said at 18 as well as at 30. It was also OK to a certain degree that the wife would earn more than them—as long as it did not make her aloof and they themselves were not expected to stay at home. Rune admitted, however, that '*at the bottom of his soul*' he probably would feel like that would be a '*small defeat*'. At 30 these men still retain much of the same attitude. Morten, who is expecting his first child at this point, plans to take the father's quota, but otherwise he thinks his wife will take the role as the main caretaker. His wife has her own business and earns almost as much as he does. He himself now works as much as his father did, even though he was critical of this at 18. He does not want any conflicts regarding housework. Should any problems arise, he will take a practical approach, hiring someone to do the cleaning, for instance. In this case the division of work resembles the previous generation, but with some adaptation to the fact that the partner works and to the dominant discourse of work-life balance. In other cases there is more reverence of the discourse of gender equality in the family, but without the subjective conviction and desire of the men who themselves had fathers who had participated more in childcare and housework. At 30 Rune thinks that he had actually been doing most of the housework in his previous relationship, but he also adds '*but I wasn't pussy whipped!*' Paul also had a relationship that included cohabitation behind him when he was interviewed at 30. He had appreciated that his girlfriend had clear ideas about what constituted men's work and what constituted women's work because this meant that both could do what they liked the best. But in the long run he felt suffocated by her nesting. He anticipates problems with combining work and children: if he has a child in a new relationship, he imagines that he cannot continue in such a creative job as he has now. He says he feels split between not wanting to have a family and not wanting to be socially isolated.

The connection between attitudes to gender equality and the division of work in the families in which they grew up is less clear-cut for the women. A traditional division of work may rather boost the young women's critique of their parents, and spur them on to wanting something different for themselves.[13] Anja made it clear that she did not want to marry someone like her own father, who is always busy at work: '*if I ever get a husband and have children, I certainly hope that he too will take care of those children*'. Tonje also expected her future husband to be participating more because '*times change*'. Thus, it seems that the general discourse about gender equality has had a more independent impact on the girls, while the boys to a greater degree need a model in their own family of upbringing to get the point. All the young women wanted to combine

[13] Øia (2011) found that wheras a positive attitude to gender equality was part of a more general radical political attitude for boys, girls were to a higher degree positive to gender equality independently on their political stand. It may be some of the same phenomena we see surface in our sample.

family and job or career—only a few were unsure about whether they wanted children, and no one wanted to become a stay-at-home mum for an extended period of time. Whereas the middle generation chose education and jobs from the perspective of their future family lives, the youngest generation instead juggled how to fit a future family into the career they wanted. At 18 they struggled with getting these things to fit together in a much more specific way than the young men. Hilde described children as a kind of reward that comes after education, as something she '*just has to treat herself to*'. She said about the future: '*I think my most concrete imaginings are on the family side, but it's kind of on the career side I want the most.*' The working-class girl Line made detailed calculations:

> *Let's say that I start my studies when I'm 21 … well, that'll take three years, so then I'll be 24 … so then I'll work for a year, then I'll be 25, and then I can, then I can get a leave of absence … and then … and then I can have a kid. If we say one kid … well, I'll be at home for a year, then I'll be 26, then work for another year, or two years, say 28, then I can have another … so I'll be at home with them for about a year, then send them to kindergarten, then work.* (Line, 18)

Some of them simply concluded that the father would have to step in, but few wanted him to go so far as being a stay-at-home dad for an extended period of time. Also in this generation, social class appeared to influence the women's wishes for their family life more than those of the men. At 18 some of the working-class girls felt attracted to the idea of staying at home for some years while their children are small, but said that it would depend on economy. They reacted positively to the idea of the father staying at home for a period of time, but had not really thought about it, and wondered whether he would be willing to do so. They thought housework '*ought to*' be shared equally, but were not sure if it would happen. The working-class girl Kine said that the most important is that someone is at home when the child is young and that she '*probably would demand that everything is to be shared equally*'. However, she might like herself to be the one to stay at home, at least for some years. The value of sharing housework and childcare was much more prominent among the middle-class girls; for them it was a requirement, not an 'ought' or a wish.

Their career orientation was also stronger. They did not want to have children until they had finished their travels and their education, and were established in a good job. Oda said that she '*wouldn't be happy without a job*' and Jenny plainly stated that she '*would go crazy by staying at home*'. However, this was not without ambivalence, since they did want to have a family and believed one should spend time with one's children, both because this was good for the children and because they would like to for their own sake (here we see some critique of the too-busy mothers of their own). Charlotte and Tonje, who grew up in families with a more traditional work division, were explicit about sharing the housework, but were still attracted to the idea of staying at home for some years when they have children. Tonje became a bit defensive about this when the interviewer followed this up with specific questions about how long she would be at home for if she had the three children she said she wanted: '*it's not like I'll be a stay-at-home housewife, we're talking the two first years, right, but after that I'll be working full-time from eight till four, and then spend time with my children and family afterwards*'. For most of the middle-class women at 18, the idea of staying at home for a period boiled down to wanting to take their share of the parental leave. They were more positive than the men towards the idea of being the main provider while the husband is taking care of the child. In contrast with their mothers, their career plans were not subordinated to their family plans—quite the opposite, in fact. But they were, to varying degrees, aware that problems might lie ahead.

At 30 all the women, apart from those who are on maternity leave or sick leave, are in full-time jobs. They are now all in favour of kindergartens and a very few of those who have children stayed at home beyond the maternity leave. Half of those who are married or cohabiting have a partner who has a lower level of education than their own, and only one has a partner with more education than herself (whereas the men's partners are generally on the same educational level as themselves). Some of the women have experienced problems in being or earning more than their partner. Guro has a fiancé who says that it does not matter to him that she makes more money than him—but he still has to bring it up all the time, which irritates her. Tonje also talks about a previous boyfriend who always needed to assert himself because she was a medical doctor. She found this difficult—'*it would've been easier had I been a nurse*'. When we meet them at 30, three of them are on sick leave because of stress or being burnt out, a thing we do not find among the men interviewed at 30.[14] Those who do not have children mention that it is difficult to fit a potential parental leave into their career schedules. However, the most frequent reason for postponing having children is the fear of what they, consistent with modern feminist lingua, name '*the gender trap*', referring to experiences as well as research that indicate that gender equality in the family only lasts until the arrival of children (Kjeldstad and Lappegård 2009; Kitterød and Rønsen 2012). They discuss it with their partners, many of whom think it is time for children; they set terms and conditions, but still feel troubled by the prospect of losing freedom and control of their lives. Pia, who at 18 was one of the few who said that she would like to marry a stay-at-home dad, is now very aware of how income inequality plays its part in reproducing a traditional gender division in the family:

> *I'm very happy that he and I earn the same amount, oh god! I'm happy about that! And I don't want him to race ahead of me in salary. And had I known ten years ago what I know today, I might have thought more about money than I did when I chose my education.* (Pia, 30)

Hilde, who like Henrik has a partner from another country, is also aware that she is the one who has to be careful not to jeopardise gender equality. They are discussing children now, and she will be very aware not to stay at home too long with the children in order not to '*form an eternal gender pattern*'. Tonje, who at 18 thought about staying at home for a couple of years with each child, does not think this will happen anymore because she has career ambitions. She is single now, but thinks that household tasks should be shared when people move in together. Considering '*that's what men are like today*', she does not expect this to become a big issue.

Judged both by research (Holter and Aarseth 1993; Kjeldstad and Lappegård 2009; Hansen and Slagsvold 2012; Skrede and Wiik 2012) and by the eight young women[15] who already had children at 30, there

---

[14] Sick leave has been stable or decreasing for men since the 1970s, whereas it has been rising for women. In 2009 employed women's sick leave was 60 per cent higher than men's (NOU 15/2012).

[15] Four middle-class girls had their children before they had finished their studies, whereas three of the four working-class/lower middle-class girls who had children had waited until they had finished their education and were working.

are reasons to be troubled. Whereas most of the couples without children at 30 seem to share the housework rather equally, the general experience of those who had children is that gender equality at home was not so easy to put into practice as they had assumed. The middle-class girls Eva and Mari describe it as a major problem of male irresponsibility that has already led to divorces for both of them. They say that becoming mothers made them grow up and become responsible, but the same thing unfortunately did not happen to their partners. Those who are not divorced talk about their partners' passivity or laziness as a bit annoying. It is especially the housework that falls too much on them. Stine, who did not care about gender equality much at 18, changed her mind after she got higher education and says that: '*I can't wait for the day when he'll be competent enough to actually get the vacuum cleaner when he sees those breadcrumbs and I don't have to say anything.*' However, some also admit that they find some aspects of the gendered work division nice, for instance, women who say that they appreciate having the partner take care of repairs and technical tasks.[16] Maybe the point is not so much doing exactly the same, but doing what one is best at, some of them wonder at 30.

The women with children are more content with their partners' role as fathers than as housekeepers. Most of the men who were entitled to it took out their earmarked weeks of parental leave. Nobody has taken more than that, which the women wish they had done in order to bond earlier with the baby, but they still give their partners credit for being close and involved fathers. This also goes for those who were later divorced. The fathers have adhered to the agreed-upon system of visits and one has moved from another Nordic country in order to be closer to his child. Ida, who switched to working part-time after having two children, says that her husband is actually '*a gentle man*' who leaves his job early and very punctually every day in order to be together with the children. However, there are also other reasons for her reduced hours. One is that she experienced that her '*psychic landscape*' was totally changed when she became a mother; another was a new pregnancy that came quickly after

[16] Kjeldstad and Lappegård (2009) find that women are keener on sharing the 'feminine' or 'neutral' parts of the housework than doing or sharing the 'masculine' housework. Men seem to be equally happy regardless of whether they share or do not share!

the first child was born. Finally, she could not cope with the male culture in the profession she had chosen and became ill from stress:

> *I'm not tough enough to work in that business, I'm not masculine enough, I'm not aggressive enough. You have to like your job more than you like your personal life. If I hadn't had children I'd have happily jumped aboard. Very stupid—because where is the gender equality?* (Ida, 30)

The general picture at 30 is that also in this generation it is the women who are in charge of both planning and performing a larger bulk of work and care in the home (see also Holter and Aarseth 1993; Holter et al. 2009). This presents a different picture from the one we saw for the family-oriented men in this generation, who see themselves as participating equally in housework and care. There may be different reasons for this discrepancy (apart from the obvious one that the stories we have from both parties are one-sided, as we do not have their partners' views). One is that the men may be less aware of the housework done by their partners or that they disagree on its importance. The other is that the general level of expectation of equal sharing has probably increased compared with the previous generation. In this case it is possible that men actually do more, while women are still disappointed by their contribution.

Freedom versus Equality

Nobody in the youngest generation is against gender equality, but it varies in terms of how important they find it as an issue to discuss and how many reservations they have: maybe there is still some way to go until full equality is reached, but the issue is uncontroversial as things are moving or ought to be moving in the right direction. As the equality-minded Anders says at 30, when asked about his opinion on gender quotas: '*Is that still a debate, I thought that was over.*' At 18 most of the girls could rattle off the standard phrases of official gender-equality politics, but did not always see themselves in a gender perspective. Their political engagement was instead directed towards issues like anti-racist work or environmental protection. For many of the boys who had lived together with smart girls all their lives, the topic did not feel very urgent either. At 18 the boys agreed with the general idea, but did not like all the fuss about it—'*forced gender equality*', as Morten describes it—that imbues the entire male gender with a collective feeling of guilt. Rune said that one has to accept that '*it'll take a while until all the old male general-directors die out*', maybe with a hint to his own old general-director father. Policies like gender quotas and the cash-for-care reform bring forth many pros and cons in the interviews, as there is a shared reluctance in this generations towards normative claims of behalf of others: cash-for-care is problematic because it makes the mothers, not the fathers, stay at home; however, if women want to stay at home, then maybe it should be their choice? Gender quotas seem a bit of an exaggerated measure, since women are smart enough on their own—but they might still be necessary. Tonje says at 30 that for her own part she does not want to '*come in through the back door*', but is more open to the idea that men are needed in women-dominated work environments. Nora, who both at 18 and 30 holds radical views, says that moderate quotas are alright, but not more radical measures '*because I think I'm good enough to fight on an equal footing, and if I don't make it that way, I'd feel that it'd be a disservice to me*'. This is a generation of young women who have been brought up with a strong belief in that they are as good—and often better—than their male peers, and this does not resonate with the idea that they are in need of help and support. Charlotte thinks at 30 that gender quotas may have been important in earlier times, but now it is more urgent employing quotas for different ethnic groups.

Evidently, the issue of gender equality sits uneasily in connection with their belief in individuality and the feeling that gender is not a coherent package. Thinking along the lines of group identities or coherent identities is repellent to many in this generation. They definitely feel more in line with understanding gender in terms of justice and freedom than in terms of the ambiguous concept of equality. Gender differences are seen as acceptable as long as they can be seen as individual choices. The prevalent view is that people should share work according to their likes and skills, and not in accordance with formal equality in every dimension. 'Sisterhood' is not a buzzword in this generation. Kine, who at 30 struggles actively against the gender discrimination at her workplace, admits that she feels suffocated by the idea of a '*women's community*'.

Charlotte finds the whole issue of gender equality boring because she thinks it is not external commonalities but the '*internal commonalities*' between people that are important. The tension between the individual approach and the moral engagement against discrimination makes even the radical girls reluctant when it comes to the feminist struggle. Pia and Hilde were among those who at 18 engaged positively with the issue. Pia said that '*the thought of depending on a man sends shivers down my spine*'. And on the survey filled in before the interview in 1991, Hilde wrote the following voluntary comment answering a question about gender equality: '*usually men do not have the same double workload as women to. Men often get paid more to do the same job as women. We have to do something about that!*' However, as they tended to see gender equality as an individual rather than a structural issue, they did not follow up these radical views with action. Hilde says at 18:

> *I wouldn't want to be one of those standing screaming on the barricades and so on, because I know my uncle's partner, she's very 'red' and has always been involved in the Women's Movement and things like that, and I must say I admire her for a lot of the things she has done. But at the same time I don't agree with a lot of her opinions, because she's radical in things that I'm not that radical in.*
>
> *Q: What kind of things?*
>
> *Well, the entire social structure, really. I think that ... I mean, when ... I guess I'm of the opinion that you've made your bed, now you must lie in it.* (Hilde, 18)

She instead identified with her mother's way of struggling for gender equality:

> *Not outwardly, but within the family, I think, and I know she's said that a few times .... For example, sharing the housework equally and things like that. If you call yourself a feminist or a redstocking, it doesn't matter. It's more about knowing it, if you're doing what you want to and if you ... dare, yes, to be who you are, kind of.*

When women are seen as responsible for their own lives, solidarity between women also becomes less of a moral obligation and the feminist engagement tends to become weak. The women distance themselves from '*typical women's occupations*'—but not from working in the public sector, where most of them are at 30. Also class differences, which were more prominent than gender differences in their grandparents' reflections on inequalities and to some degree also in those of their parents, since many of them were class travellers, become blurred in this focus on individual responsibility for one's own success in attaining equality. The reluctance towards identifying with one's own gender group is more salient among the women than among the men, in spite of the men's stronger occupation with their own uniqueness. An evident reason for this is that masculinity and individuality have never been either culturally or psychologically at odds with each other in the way that femininity and individuality have. For this reason, ethnicity seems to be a more manageable candidate for these young women's reflections on equality. Here they belong to the majority group and do not risk victimising themselves through their political engagement for justice and equality.

Another prominent point in this generation is that gender equality should go 'both ways'. Beate is among those most sceptical of feminism in this generation, just as her mother and grandmother were in their respective generations. She argues for men's rights, but also shares the view that individual differences may override group differences. At 30, she says this:

> *Gender equality is completely fine, but then there has to be equality in all spheres … because the women who're screaming about equality have a tendency to want more than men have ever had, and that, then [loudly] I think it's going in the wrong direction again, because then it's like that, they want all kinds of rights, but women shouldn't have to do military service, right, they do <u>not</u> want that, but I think that women benefit just as much as boys from being in the military … I think it ought to be the same for everybody … even if … if women have different stuff, like, for example, if they get pregnant, which means that they have to … and they might not be as physically strong as the men, but all women <u>should</u> have a <u>chance</u> to try, even if … it's often considered a man's job because it demands physical strength, because there <u>could</u> be women who could do it, not all [loudly], but some, right, so you really have to make a judgment along the way.* (Beate, 30)

Many of the young men mention this too. Women should have access to the same jobs, salaries, rights and careers as men, but then women should also have the same duties or take their share of the unattractive and hard traditional male jobs. Vegard says at 18: '*if we're to have gender equality, then there should be equality all the way*'. The young men point to the danger of reversed discrimination, because then nothing has been attained. Egil was the only man in the middle generation who explicitly mentioned fathers' rights at divorce. This argument has become ubiquitous among the men in the youngest generation and may tell us that the power balance between men and women is no longer experienced as unambiguous.

At 30 many of those interviewed, especially the women, but also some of the men, have experienced gender discrimination against women in education and work, something they were surprised about and find unacceptable. Morten says that he at any time would prefer a female boss compared to all those messy men he has met during his career until now. He thinks, however, that women have the same possibilities so he is not particularly engaged in gender-equality politics. Anders had experienced mean male bonding against women in one of his work places, '*a very conservative place, a shipping firm, incredibly unsympathetic*'. Still, like almost all of the other men, he is against quotas, because he thinks they ought to be totally unnecessary and he fears that they will not be an effective remedy against discriminatory attitudes. Conversely, Kim experienced that gender-equality politics gave him career advantages as a preschool teacher, which he found legitimate because he thinks it is a good thing to have more men in this profession. At 30 many of the women acknowledge that gender quotas are unfortunately necessary. Like many others, Kine has seen how much more easily men get promotions and salary rises. It is so '*bloody unjust!*' she exclaims and echoes her grandmother Karen's anger at the injustice of her brother's privileges. Tonje has experienced female doctors getting much less attendance from the nurses on the hospital wards than male doctors do. But she still wants to believe that '*if a women wants gender equality, she'll make it happen*'. Hilde and Pia have not given up their radical views, including those on gender quotas: '*you have to govern a bit in order to change the culture*', Hilde says. Most of the 30-year-olds, both women and men, side with feminists in anti-discrimination measures at work and against the cash-for-care benefit, whereas opinions on other issues, like pornography, have become less straightforward than they were in the heyday of the Women's Movement. The general attitude of both women and men is that if people fancy pornography, it is their choice and sexual desires should not be the targets of the moralistic interventions of others.

8

Generational Patterns Across Time and Space

The longitudinal dimension in the study of the youngest generation helps to clarify some of the methodological effects of the design where three generations were interviewed at different points in their lives. The interviews with the youngest generation at 30 made it possible to check whether one talks differently about one's family and upbringing as a young adult compared to as a teenager of 18, and also to see whether one remembers the views held at an earlier age. The general finding in regard to the time span was that the overall content of what was said ten years earlier was well remembered, but that details may have been forgotten or reconstructed (for instance, what kind of education one thought about but did not pursue or what attitudes one had in relation to gender equality). In a few cases, emotionally difficult issues had been forgotten, while in other cases, the stories were told with almost exactly the same words. In most cases, however, it was the same content, with slightly modified details. With regard to what life phases mean for the perception of one's family of origin and relationship with parents, we heard more or less the same stories as the interviewees told at 18, but often more nuanced in light of what had happened later or as a result of having gained more life experience and maturity. This could sometimes contribute to a more conciliatory and sometimes more critical account of a parent and the family life they had lived back then. The most considerable difference compared to the narratives at 18 was a somewhat more negative experience of parental divorces at 30. Thus, the accepting approach to their parents' divorces at 18 may be due to the child's new position in this generation as a 'responsible partner' in the family. However, completely new information was only seen in a few cases connected to very difficult experiences of divorces and of parental violence.

The interviews with eight of the informants at 40 also made it possible to see what kind of family models the youngest generation actually chose and how their attitudes towards gender equality turned out in practice. When the oldest generation was asked about gender equality, it mainly triggered their reflection about how it *was*, seen in the light of the new times. For the middle generation, we get accounts of how it *is* in their present life. And for the youngest generation at 18 and 30 years of age, the perspective is how they imagine it *will be*. At the age of 40, however, the youngest generation were approaching the life phase their parents were in at the time of their interviews in 1991. They found themselves in the midst of a hectic life where the main challenge was managing the work–family balance, and the interviews therefore tended to focus on this. Thus, these interviews may contribute to understanding more about the interaction between age/life phases (the point in their lives when they were interviewed), cohort effects (the life course of a specific generation) and period effects (the way in which a given sociohistorical situation affects the experiences). It is not possible to isolate the effects of each of these sources of meaning, but from what the informants tell us about their life at 40, we can see the impact of all of them. Decisions about family arrangements and what kind of gender equality that is desired or possible to attain also depend on how the three temporal dimensions interact in each case.

Another dimension considered in this chapter is the significance of *place*. To what degree are the patterns we found in our sample products of a specifically Scandinavian history and context? To what degree do they also display similarities with, for instance, other European countries? This question is of course too large for a sensible short answer, not only because three- or even two-generational studies are generally in short supply, but also because the design, methodology and theoretical framing of the few studies that exist are often quite incompatible. That means that it is difficult to see what is actually compared. In addition, cross-national comparisons are particularly difficult because the context, whether nationally, historically, culturally or politically, for what is compared is part of the meaning of the comparison (on this point, see Bertaux and Thompson 1997; Chant and McIlwayne 1998). Instead of trying to cover everything, I have chosen to contrast my findings with some generational studies from Britain that cover the same generations, mainly the work of Julia Brannen and her colleagues, in order to catch sight of what may be specifically Scandinavian in the three generations analysed in this book.

Life at 40

The consistency from 18 to 30 in the views on how to organise one's own family holds true from 30 to 40 as well. But at 40, the informants have also experienced that things were more complex than they had thought, including the issue of gender equality. As we saw in Chap. 7, the women who had their children early found it difficult to make their partners take their share of the housework. For those who had their children later (which includes seven of the eight informants interviewed at 40), the problem is rather that their own feelings make things more complicated—in addition to the different conditions in relation to the work–family balance in working life, especially in the private sector. The family practices described by the eight informants at 40 reflect different responses to this. The norm of sharing is stronger than in most of the families in the middle generation, and the awareness of not succeeding is more acute. In order to achieve gender equality, many of the families have seen it as necessary to hire domestic help. The assumption that modern Scandinavian families substitute women's work in the family by bringing in the men instead of outsourcing the work (Hochschild 1997) may not be true to the same degree any longer (Aarseth 2009b).[1] Different family solutions

[1] A total of 11 per cent of Norwegian households employed cleaners in 2015. In the high-income families to which most of our eight informants belong, it was 32 percent (Lavik and Borgeraas 2015).

and stands on gender equality within and outside of the family will be illustrated in the following mini-portraits of the eight informants interviewed at 40—Anders, Morten, Henrik, Pia, Tonje, Hilde, Charlotte and Kine—including some connections to their generational stories. Henrik and Charlotte are third- or fourth generation middle class with academic degrees. Morten, Pia, Tonje and Hilde are second-generation middle class with academic degrees. Anders and Kine grew up working class, and of these two only Kine received some years of higher education, although not an entire degree.[2]

Henrik and Anders have adhered to the relatively gender-egalitarian practices they advocated at 18 and 30. At 40 they each have three children and both they and their wives are working full-time. *Anders*, a working-class boy who did not receive any higher education and now works in administration in a private company, has remarried. Neither he nor his wife has particular demanding careers. He says at 40 that he was never very ideologically preoccupied by gender equality, but that it became a practical matter for him when he had to do his share of the work at home, and that he wanted to be a different kind of father to his children than his father had been to him. He formulates a strong inclination to have another kind of family than his parents' gender traditional arrangement, and he finds sociobiological babble about '*alpha males*' completely stupid. He come from a working-class family chain where all the men—his grandfather Anton, his father Arne and he himself—had the most positive parental relationship with their mothers. Anton and Arne were as adults also strongly identified with their jobs, something Anders is not. He is the only man in the youngest generation who talked about a strong desire to have a child when he was only 20 years old and who had one a few years later. He says he and his wife share the childcare 50/50 and he describes '*a quantum leap*' in terms of how much time parents devote to their children now compared to when he was little. He gives vivid accounts of his three daughters and how he has had to give in to their cravings for pink and glittery clothing: '*they become little girls*

[2] In terms of recruitment, Anders, Morten, Pia, Tonje and Kine came from the new suburban high school, while Henrik, Hilde and Charlotte from the old academic high school (see Chap. 3).

without you having anything to do with it'. He supports the father's quota for parental leave, but thinks it is long enough as it is now (at the time of the interview there was a suggestion to extend it from 12 to 14 weeks). He has well-qualified views on interior decoration, but since his wife likes another style, he leaves it to her to decide. He believes he does a fair share of the housework, but his wife does not agree, so they quarrel a lot about cleaning. He finds this quite tiresome and wonders if the marriage will last. Compared to his parents, he is very modern man when it comes to gender equality. His positive relationship with his mother and dis-identification with his father in combination with low career ambitions may explain his active turn towards the family. In his case, however, his partner puts some limits on what he is allowed to participate in at home, for instance, that she wants to decide about the interior decoration. His pragmatic attitude to gender equality is a pattern that bears similarities to what we have encountered in some of the working-class families in the sample, but in Anders' case clearly in a modernised and reflexive version.

Henrik and his wife both have demanding jobs. He had a spectacular international career, but chose to change from the private to the public sector after his first child was born, as he never saw the child while she was awake. He loved his elite job with 60–80 working hours a week, but men in such jobs have wives at home, he says, and this is too high a price to pay: he wants an interesting wife and that implies that she has an interesting job. It is also important for him to have a good family life, close relationships with his children—and no divorce! His wife was home for a few years while they were abroad, which they all enjoyed, but back in Norway she is working again. With two full-time careers, three children and no hired cleaner, everyday life is rather hectic, and they try to use their flexible working hours and work from home in the evenings. It is quite tough because '*this isn't a sprint, it's a marathon*'. He thinks that they share things equally—apart from the periods when he has to travel. He describes ruthless priorities in the family: he has a leadership position at work and when '*the going gets tough*', he is the one who goes to work and she stays home—but '*then I also have to give back much more afterwards*'. He is a warm supporter of the father's quota, even if he was not able to take it himself when the first child was born because of his job. An incentive is absolutely necessary to get men to do it, he says, and it is important because '*a baby is a fantastic way to ground a man … to be contaminated with small children's love affects your choices later*'. The first time he was on parental leave, he had plans to renovate the house, but soon had to realise that he hardly had time left for his daily shower. He is the son of Helge, the hands-on father in the middle generation who did not want to '*marry a housekeeper*', but who later felt deceived by the Women's Movement. Henrik, however, saw his mother as a positive and competent person, who, he says, also had good looks. He believes that he has always been more in favour of gender equality than most girls and refers to the influence of his feminist mother. He gets irritated by women who do not fulfil their potential or do not dare to '*go for it*'—or who think they have to become unfeminine to do so. He likes beautiful women with the capacity to make their own choices. At 40 he has experienced that life is more complicated than in his mother's feminist agenda. He appreciates sexual difference, but also thinks that individual differences are often more salient than gender differences. Today he feels somewhat estranged from the whole concept of gender equality, but emphasises that he certainly needs '*no moral lecture on gender equality*'. He believes in diversity, has organised courses at work about it and thinks that diversity also is key to economic growth. Henrik, who is among the most gender-radical men in the youngest generation, combines a positive relationship with his mother with having had a hands-on father. In his case, however, the demands of a high-powered job—and how important this job is to him—work counter to the full gender equality he feels committed to. Old melodies interfere when 'the going gets tough', and it was his career that brought the family abroad, not his wife's. From what he says in the interview, his wife accepts being in a good second place.

Morten, who at 30 was among the more traditional interviewees in terms of his views and who said he did not want to quarrel about housework, has at 40 just hired cleaners for his wife '*to help her*'. They also have three children, and even though he somewhat routinely admits that '*well yes, it's the usual, you have to try to balance your job and the lives of your children*', he talks with much greater engagement and at more length about his career. When asked about the father's quota, his first response is: '*what's that?*' He has to ask his wife during the interview what exact age and grade his young sons are in, and his part in the childcare is to take them skiing or engage in their leisure interests. He sees himself as career oriented and is building up his second business now, which he hopes will turn out to be a very good economic investment, and he has taken economic risks in order to succeed. He does not feel like '*coddling the children 24/7*'. He wants to create things and do things that interest him, whereas he sees his wife as a more '*all-round*' type. His nine-year-old son defends him by saying that '*dad doesn't do a lot at home, because there isn't space in his brain*'. It has caused tension in the marriage, but his wife switching to a part-time job solved these problems. She has a small business of her own and at the interview at 30 she made the same amount of money he did. But now that she is working part-time, it is also fair that she does most of the household work, he says, just as he said at 18. This is also a generational chain with positive relationships with both parents, although the mothers had more traditional roles in the family than in Henrik's case and the fathers higher professional status than in Anders' case. Morten's grandfather Martin was one of the warmest supporters of gender complementarity, idealising the kindness and moral superiority of women. His father Magne also thought that the old gender system, with clear roles for man and wife, was preferable because it led to fewer conflicts than what he had experienced in his own marriage. He was a creative man and an independent thinker, but also one who appreciated being alone and concentrating on his own things. At 30 Morten described his father as a dreamer and his mother as the strong and logical person in the family. He says that he prefers a female boss at work, but admits that he considers himself more similar to his father. He cannot imagine being happy without being deeply engaged in his job. The most important in a family is to find individual and flexible solutions, he says, yet the solutions he comes up with all sound very gender traditional. Morten resembles the 'in principle' men from the middle generation. He pays some lip service to discourses of gender equality, but is happiest if he is allowed to concentrate on his job while his wife takes care of the children and the home. Setting up his own business is risky and gender equality cannot be given priority in this situation. It does not seem to be an important issue for Morten either as long as he can avoid quarrels with his wife and see their arrangements as fair and flexible.

The five women are fairly consistent in their views at 30 and their practices at 40 as well, but the bodily processes of pregnancy and breastfeeding influenced them more than they had believed they would. They have one or two children each and are all in full-time jobs. At 40 Tonje and Pia, both with academic degrees and married to men with the same educational level and also working in the public sector, describe very equal relationships in regard to childcare, housework, careers and salaries. *Tonje*'s husband gives high priority to family life and she sees him as a man with many androgynous sides. He takes more interest than she does in interior decorating and he lays the table beautifully when they invite people for dinner. He claimed the full father's quota and she does not need to tell him what needs to be done in the house. She does, however, keep the overview and most of the organisation—she thinks it is like that in most families, and she does not mind. They have hired au pairs in order not to have too stressful a life, which would be bad for the children. Both Tonje and her mother Turid[3] had admiring but also somewhat distant relationships with their fathers and ambivalent relationships with their mothers. This complicated Tonje's youthful protest against her parent's traditional division of work when she tried to write lists that included her father and her brother in household tasks. However, she was also among those who at 18 were positive in relation to the idea of staying home for some years when she had children. At 30 this had changed because she had become very dedicated to her professional career (the same profession as her father), but she still believed that a woman could attain gender equality if she really wished to—something she at 40 thinks has, in fact, been the case for her. At 40 she says she is engaged in gender-equality politics, but she also wants to be allowed to think that there are inborn differences and that this does not automatically mean that women are oppressed. She does not experience any of the gender discrimination at work she mentioned at 30, but she admits that having children sets women back. She sees this as a fact of life rather than discrimination: '*Well, that's the way nature works, we're lucky to be able to be at home together with the children!*' She thinks it would have been boring when it came to erotic

[3] The grandmothers of Tonje and Pia were not interviewed. Pia's grandmother was dead and Tonje's grandmother declined to be interviewed.

attraction if there were no differences between women and men. This does not concern capacities or personalities—she finds a good mixture of feminine and masculine traits in both herself and her husband—but about appearances and different approaches and opinions on things. In this way she advocates a model of gender complementarity when it comes to attraction and desire, in the midst of a very equal division of work and care in everyday life. Her emphasis on individual rights and on bodily difference may be seen in connection with her positive identification with her father and an improvement of her earlier ambivalent relationship with her mother. However, engaging in a demanding career and having a partner who appears to be quite gender radical have also given her more space for the principal support of gender equality than she to some extent had at 18.

Pia was also very upset with the work division between her parents, but she sided with her mother against her father, even if she also thought that her mother could have stood up to her father more. Pia's mother Paula was the oldest woman in the middle generation and had worked her way up to a high position in the private sector, but at the same time gave full attention and service to her family. This eventually led to her experiencing a burn-out early and retiring when Pia was in her twenties. This is a chain of mother-identified daughters. Paula had a mother who urged her to get an education and to put her own life before her obligations to her parents. However, Paula also had a very tender relationship with her father and married a man who had had a sad childhood and to whom she wanted to be kind. Whereas Paula was mild and compliant, her daughter Pia appeared a more self-assertive woman—albeit one who in her early twenties suddenly found herself in an oppressive relationship with an older man. She pulled herself together and left him and found her present husband, with whom she shares 90 per cent of the household work equally (only a few activities like changing tyres on the car, chopping wood and using the sewing machine are traditionally gender separated): '*We work until we are done.*' Having a cleaner come in every second week is also helpful. But to have children is a big change in your life and you have to prioritise, she says. For this reason she did not apply for a leadership job that she probably would have gotten. It has been easier for her husband to make such choices because he is less career-oriented and ambitious than she is. He has taken more of the parental leave than the father's quota (and because of that caused a few raised eyebrows at his work place), and had wanted even more. But Pia insisted on taking eight months so that she could nurse the children at least for the six months recommended by the health authorities. This has been the only disagreement between them. She thinks that the feminist agenda sometimes is too inflexible: '*I don't know if I think it's a great step forwards for the Women's Movement that mothers carry breast pumps in their lunch breaks … there's a lot of closeted nursing at night.*' But it was great to have a stay-at-home husband when she went back to work, because she felt it was so safe. Pia, who had quite a negative relationship with her father, seems to have identified consciously with her mother's skills and career, but also unconsciously with her submissiveness to dominant men. The positive part of the identification made her quite consciously go for another type of man and she is aware that this choice is what has made it possible for her to pursue the gender-equality values she has been a firm supporter of since she was 18. '*I have won the biggest prize in my husband*', she says with a happy smile. But had he been '*a climber*', she is sure that she would have lost the battle—that is a lesson she takes from friends whose husbands are in high-powered jobs in the private sector.

Hilde's experiences confirm this. Her husband has a career in the private sector, whereas she holds a PhD and works in the public sector. She was also one of the radical girls at 18 with regard to gender equality. Like Tonje and Pia, she criticised her parents' work division, in spite of it being actually quite equal. At 30 she postponed having children, as she was aware of the '*gender trap*', not least since her husband comes from a culture that is quite distant from Nordic ideas of gender equality. At 40 they have two children and she describes a sort of backlash in her own generation, not so much because of her husband's cultural roots, but because of his job. She now acknowledges that her parents shared much more equally than she and her husband are able to. He is exhausted when he comes home after long workdays, and even though she understands this, she insisted that he hired a cleaner to do his share. They share a good deal of the childcare, her husband does the shopping and she does most of the cooking and all of the laundry. Taking the cultural differences between them into account, she acknowledges that he has already changed enormously compared to the gender culture in which he grew up. She does not want to waste time on conflicts to get everything exactly equal—they have reached a level of sharing that she can live with. It also helps that her parents are now retired and live close by. Without their help, it had been difficult to manage the busy everyday life. She has had to compromise her equality standards to accommodate her husband's situation, but still claims at 40 that equality is the '*core value*' that she will never give up. She gets irritated by the double standards of older feminists: first they told young women to work as much as men, and now they also encourage them to stay at home as long as possible to enjoy their babies! In Hilde's generational chain we see positive relationships with both parents, but the mothers tend to be the more competent and rational figures, and the fathers the more social and warm figures (in addition to making more money). Both Hilde's grandmother and mother married thrifty men with lower class status than themselves. Hilde's grandmother Helga wanted more education, but had to settle for doing the accounts in her husband's growing enterprise. Her mother Hanne became a teacher and was an inspiration to her daughter when it came to being engaged in women's rights. In Hilde's case the positive engagement in gender equality is connected with her positive identification with her mother. Maybe the warm relationships she has with her father and her husband also support her willingness to make compromises. Her life situation has made it difficult to pursue her values completely, but this has not made her abandon them. She keeps her values and her compromises as two separate realities in her life and seems to be reasonably OK with the balance.

Charlotte and Kine are both newly divorced at 40. Division of work played some part in both cases, but in different ways. *Charlotte*, who holds an academic degree, says that her ex-husband '*was a modern man, but…* '—and the idea was that they should share the work equally. However, he always changed the rules to his own advantage. For some years she accepted following his career needs as well, something she will never do again. She is now a single mother with her own sole enterprise and thinks life is good. Echoing her grandmother Clara, who divorced before her daughter Cecilie was born, she does not miss a man in her everyday life, but thinks it is fun to date. She identifies with her role as a mother and her own independence. It had been great not to work—'*I'd rather be just a mum and take care of myself*—but this is not an option. With her own company she can regulate much of her time, which is the important thing for her. She was interested in gender issues neither at 18 nor at 30, and she detested all kind of stingy ideas of meticulous sharing. In her family chain there are marked shifts in parental relationships, from her grandmother Clara's very close relationship with her strong and kind mother to Cecilie, who had a positive relationship with Clara, but also felt very different from her and attached herself to her father, whom she only met as a young girl. Cecilie experienced considerable difficulties in her marriage, especially with making time for her own career. Charlotte had a negative relationship with both her parents at 18, especially her mother, whom she blamed for all the tiresome quarrelling about housework and for neglecting her children. At 40 Charlotte combines a critique of traditional gender norms as completely outdated with a new 'maternalism', where she thinks that the bodily processes of pregnancy and nursing make women and men react very differently to having children. For this reason she is also against the father's quota, which she thinks is mainly used by men to paint the house or only doing activities with the children that they enjoy themselves. In Charlotte's case we see more emphasis on individualism than on gender equality, something that, as in Tonje's case, might be related to identifying more with the father than with the mother. She did not think gender made any difference at 18 and 30, and when she later encountered gender discrimination, her solution was not to become a feminist, but to do without men in her daily life. Her negative relationship with her mother has given her an incitement to become a better mother than Cecilie was,[4] including not giving in to a domineering man as her mother did. This mix has turned into a kind of maternalism where men are not needed—other than as sexual partners if one happens to be so inclined.

Kine was not very radical when it came to gender issues at 18 either, but at 30 things had changed. She had made an impressive career in a big

[4] In their study of motherhood in a generational perspective, Thomson et al. (2011: 118) note that that young mothers who did not have a positive relationship with their own mothers often tended to invest more heavily in peer maternal cultures. This may also be the case with Charlotte. Ida (see Chap. 7)—who felt her whole psychic landscape changed when she became a mother—also fits into this pattern.

public enterprise and took some university courses along the way. This radicalised her view on gender equality and she has been fighting actively for it in the workplace. At 30 she was cohabiting and was very content with the equal division of work at home. She is the first in her family to receive an education. Her grandmother Karen, however, is one of the few in this generation who kept a full-time job after she got married because she liked it. Kine was the product of the unplanned pregnancy and arranged marriage of the working-class girl Kirsten, who had a bad relationship with her parents. This start gave Kine a difficult childhood, with young, irresponsible and eventually divorced parents and later also violence in the family. She had to be responsible for her parents from a young age: '*Kine is born an adult*', her family says about her. This resilience is probably also one of the reasons why she has managed her career so well. At 40 she is unwavering when it comes to fighting discriminatory structures at work and tells us about the difficulties that face young female leaders like herself. Privately, however, she has become more doubtful. She and her partner were both career oriented and had good salaries. They had an almost reversed division of work where he did the majority of the household work and made decisions about the interior decoration of their home, whereas she painted the house and took care of the car. She says that he has strong feminine sides and she has masculine sides, and observes that their daughter is much more feminine than she is. But she also felt that she became superfluous in the house and this made her feel even less feminine. The erotic attraction also faltered since she perceived him as not masculine enough. She had a period of being burnt out, but a leadership training course got her back on track again. This also made her realise that she wanted to end her marriage. She is all in favour of gender equality in society and in the workplace, but at home she would have liked to keep the gender roles more distinct and to feel that her contributions to the home *as* a woman made a difference. Sometimes she also wants to be allowed to be weak and taken care of, she says. She thus started out with the working-class pattern of a non-ideological, pragmatic attitude to gender equality and became middle class and ideologically radicalised. She found her own way since none of her parents was suitable as objects of identification. Her attraction to a more traditional gender pattern at home while demanding gender equality at work may be seen as an emotional bond with the gender culture in the social class she left. In her case, however, the longing she has for not always having to be responsible and in charge may also have interfered here.

In all eight cases, feelings of gender from their own families of origin, both class-wise and individually, and the projects they had for their own lives at 30 were partly maintained and partly changed. What changed them in the intermediate decade were material and structural circumstances, the education and the work they undertook, and the partners they chose, in addition to the surprise at the experience of the biological dimensions of motherhood, and in some cases also their own psychological and erotic attraction to gender difference. This also informs the emotional basis for the political stand they take towards gender-equality politics. As a generation they share an emphasis on individuality that does not work well with the idea of a gender battle between two groups. They tend to go for compromises rather than to fight, including the compromise that a divorce may be. They think that people should be allowed to stick to their preferences and that gendered choices in some areas can live well with gender equality in other areas. The issue of the new market-driven gender separation of childhood—pink for girls, blue for boys—is not something they find important to engage in. '*They've expired, those issues*', says Henrik, and it is difficult to find anyone among the eight interviewees at 40 who disagrees with him on this. The equality-minded Pia says that there is a '*high dress factor*' among her little daughters and that she cannot see this as a problem as long as they can play freely. Tonje says that '*such things are completely insignificant, it's not worth fighting the kids on it*'. As a default she buys pink and purple for her two daughters because then she knows everyone is happy.

Judged from the eight interviews at 40 and with a glance at the bigger sample interviewed at 30, it seems like that the variations in family models and practices of gender equality can be related to the interviewees' parental identifications in combination with their choice of job and partner. The most important precondition for a gender-equal practice among the men seems to be a positive relationship with the mother and a perception of her as having been equal in status with the father. This may indicate that the father's role for positive identification with gender equality is more indirect (see also Bjørnholt 2014). The men's engagement in gender equality is seldom based on the value of fairness in itself, and it is not a wish to deconstruct sexual difference. The leitmotif of gender equality for them is to get a close relationship with their children and/or to get a better relationship with their wives, and the extent to which they succeed has to do with how they balance this wish with their careers. For the women we also see the tendency that a positive relationship with the mother promotes a positive engagement with gender equality, but here the main point is justice and sharing work fairly. If the identification with the father is stronger than with the mother, the project is formulated in terms of individuality and difference rather than in terms of equality and fairness. A striking difference between men and women is that the choice of partner is much more decisive for attaining gender equality for the women than is the case for the men, and is also more important than the women's personal career involvement. A gender-equal-minded man makes gender equality in the family possible, while a man with a demanding career may work against it. This partner effect is much less visible among the men.

Made in Scandinavia?

In order to get a sense of what may be specifically Norwegian/Scandinavian in the sample analysed in this book, Julia Brannen, Peter Moss and Ann Mooney's study (2004) of working and caring in four-generation families in Britain, and Julia Brannen's later study of fathers and sons (2015) are particularly relevant to bring in as comparative contrasts. These studies work with approximately the same cohorts as we do.[5] In this way the three

[5] In the 2004 study the informants are born in the 1920s, the 1940s and around 1970; in the 2015 study of fathers and sons, the informants are born mainly around the 1940s, the 1970s and the 2000s. In order to simplify the comparison to our study, these three generations of the British studies will be referred to as the oldest, the middle and the youngest generation. The fourth generation in the Brannen et al. (2004) study—the children of parents born in the 1970s—were not interviewed. In Brannen (2015) this generation is included as boys between 5 and 17 years of age. The interviews in the 2004 study were carried out a decade later than ours (1999/2000), which means that the youngest generation in the British study was around 30 at the time of the interviews and thus similar to our second interview round with the youngest generation in 2001. The interviews in the 2015 study were made around 2010, at approximately the same time as our third round of interviews with the youngest generation. The design and interview methodology are somewhat

studies speak to each other with regard to temporality, but are separated by place. Both the British and the Norwegian samples are diverse when it comes to social class, but in the 2004 British study there are fewer cases of geographical and upward social mobility, which reflects the sampling process. It may, however, also illustrate the different timing of industrialisation and urbanisation in Norway and the UK, and also the earlier and stronger emphasis on education as a tool for attaining social equality in the Scandinavian countries. The focus of the British studies is primarily parenthood, which also distinguishes it from ours, which focuses more on childhood and youth. Where the British studies look at how different generations of parents organised work and caring for their children, our study looks closer at how children experienced their parents' work and care. Yet, the studies also touch upon many of the same issues and this makes the comparison relevant.

The social context described in Brannen et al.'s studies indicates well-known social and historical similarities and differences between the UK and the Scandinavian countries. The greatest differences are represented by England's early industrialisation and urbanisation, the impact of the two world wars, the fading of the British Empire and the large-scale immigration that followed beginning in the late 1950s, the decline of the welfare state and the strong neoliberal trends under the conservative governments from 1979 onwards. Deindustrialisation processes have also had much more sinister consequences in Britain in terms of high unemployment, massive privatisation and austerity in the public sector. Some of these trends were also seen in the Nordic countries from the 1980s (see Chap. 4); however, it did not stop the expansion of the welfare state as it did in the UK, and Nordic unemployment rates were never even close to those in Britain. This has given quite different conditions for processes of gender equality in these two national contexts in the post-war period. Brannen et al. characterise the British welfare regime as 'a mix of liberalism and maternalism' (2004: 53), which provides quite a different

different from ours, as the 2004 project includes both men and women from the same families and uses biographical narrative interviewing. It has fewer numbers of chains (12 versus our 34), but since more family members are interviewed in each chain, the number of informants are not so different (71 versus our 88). The focus of the 2015 study is fatherhood and migration and it compares 30 father–son pairs (89 informants) of white British, Irish and Polish decent.

political climate from the social democratic and equality-oriented welfare regime of the Nordic countries. It has been much more difficult for British women to take up paid work on a stable basis after the housewife era, partly because of the lack of subsidised public childcare facilities and partly because of cultural norms and policies which until the mid-1990s expected the mother to take the main responsibility for the family and the father to be the main provider. It was only from the late 1980s that women with small children startet to take up gainful work (something that happened ten years earlier in Norway), and as late as 2000, only 54 per cent of British women with a child under five were in gainful employment (the similar figure for Norway was around 80 per cent: Kitterød and Rønsen 2012). The social differences in employment according to the mother's educational level are also much larger in Britain than in Norway: British mothers with high-level education worked as much as the Norwegian average for all women in 2000 (Brannen et al. 2004: 49). Even though Norway's daycare provision was established later than in the other Nordic countries and the family ideology has been stronger (Melby et al. 2008), the situation has been very different from that in the UK, where government policy has largely neglected the needs of working parents and their children since the Second World War (Fox Harding 1996; Knudsen and Wærness 2001; Leira 2002).[6] There is a striking difference in the attitude to childcare outside the home between the British and the Norwegian informants, which may be related to this lack of a general provision of high-quality public daycare in the UK. Whereas most of the British informants in all generations in the 2004 study are sceptical of letting childminders take care of children or 'dumping' them in nurseries (Brannen et al. 2004: 73, 208), most Norwegian informants see daycare for children as a positive thing for children as well as for parents. Worries about leaving the child to 'stranger care' are simply absent in the Norwegian narratives. The concerns in Norway rather relate to what age the children should be when they start attending daycare and how long they should spend there each day (Ellingsæter and Gulbrandsen 2007).

[6] In 2002 the percentage of respondents of surveys 'agreeing' that 'a man's job is to earn money, a woman's job is to look after home and family' was only 10 per cent in Norway as opposed to 18 per cent in Britain and 34 per cent in Portugal (Crompton et al. 2007: 11).

However, the lack of daycare in the UK seems to have established a stronger bond between women in different generations: in the British study all three generations put emphasis on the importance of having grandmothers living close by, something which is mentioned only by a few of our older informants and hardly by any of the younger (an exception is Hilde in the interview at 40).

I will highlight a few interesting differences between the findings in the two British studies and our study, which may be related both to different welfare contexts, different timings and different cultural norms. The most striking difference is that the weaker gender-equality policy in the British context seems to have had consequences for the feelings of gender among the middle and youngest generations. Whereas the oldest generations in both Britain and Norway describes a childhood of poverty, lack of social security and opportunities, hard and gender-divided work, but with positive relationships to their parents' skill sets, the younger generations in the British studies emerge as somewhat different from the younger generations in Norway. In the middle generation of the British study, both women and men have more traditional gender attitudes and practices, and also less disidentification with their own parents compared to their Norwegian contemporaries. The youngest British generation, however, appears to condense traits both of the Norwegian middle generation (in terms of parental relationships) and the Norwegian younger generation (in terms of their less normative views on gender and organisation of the family).

The British studies clearly indicate that British fathers came later into childcare than Norwegian fathers. While there is a growing acceptance of mothers' employment among the British men of all generations, the gendered assumptions about what children need is less negotiable (Brannen et al. 2004: 126; see also Plantin et al. 2003). For the two oldest generations of men in the British studies, what children need is to be looked after by their mothers. Some of these men are described as 'family men' who have placed high value on being present in the family, but nevertheless seldom sharing much of the care work. It is only in the youngest generation that we find hands-on fathers, most of whom are unemployed working class (Brannen et al. 2004: 118).

The women of the middle generation in the British study share the psychological perspective of our middle generation, but to a much more limited degree the negative relationship between daughter and mothers. Most of the British women born in the 1940s rather seem to idealise their stay-at-home mothers who 'were there' and did not let their children come home to an empty house, and they do not connect this recollection with the fact that they themselves to a much higher degree took up paid work when their children started school, albeit part-time and with frequent interruptions. In comparison, the vast majority of women of this generation in the Norwegian sample worked close to full-time and only one stayed at home until her children came of age. Another difference from the Norwegian sample is that, in spite of the extension of state education in Britain in this period, girls' education was not experienced as equally important as for boys in the middle generation in the British study. The equality-oriented 'policy for the daughters' of the 1960s and 1970s in the Nordic countries in combination with a relatively anti-authoritarian upbringing and a child-centred school system may indeed have had a huge social effect on later processes of gender equality. In addition, other studies of young women outside Scandinavia from this period indicate that they typically have been met with much more gender-traditional expectations, for instance, parents encouraging them to spend time on their looks in order to find a husband, instead of getting an education (see, for instance, Esseveld 1988; Breines 1992; Ravesloot et al. 1999).

In the British studies, the critique of parents instead emerges in the youngest generation (those born in the 1970s). In contrast to their Norwegian contemporaries, they grew up with stay-at-home mothers as the norm (albeit not necessarily as practice) and with fathers who did not take much part in the childcare because they were the main breadwinners. The daughters of this generation criticise their mothers for having been too homebound and with limited horizons, and their fathers for not being present (the 2004 study). The sons criticise their fathers for their lack of emotional skills and see themselves as very different when it comes to showing their children affection (the 2015 study). The case of the couple Rachel and Graeme, belonging to the youngest generation of Brannen et al.'s study (2004: 191–197), may illustrate this dynamic of change, which is quite similar to the pattern in the Norwegian middle generation, but in a later historical context, which allowed for a more radical practice for the young couple: Rachel made a conscious decision about not becoming like her overprotecting full-time housewife mother. Graeme, for his part, wanted to become a more caring parent than his own absent and divorced parents had been. In this young couple, Rachel was at the time of the interview the sole breadwinner in the family, whereas Graeme had given up his job to take care of the children (in combination with studying for a university degree). Thus, their critique of their own families of childhood led Rachel to a strong work orientation and Graeme to a strong caring orientation. In most cases, however, this generation's critique of parents did not lead to such a radical change of gender practice. There is a much higher frequency of part-time work among the youngest generation of women in the British study compared to the Norwegian study, as well as a greater readiness to adapt work life to the needs of the family.[7] Among the young fathers, the discourse about the new fatherhood is often more of an ideal than a practice (Brannen 2015: 95). The mixture of different attitudes among the young men resembles the Norwegian middle generation, for instance, by being 'in principle men' or by presenting themselves as 'modern men' in their need to legitimise traditional gender arrangements as practical or chosen by the wife. In the Norwegian sample this pattern is seen in the youngest generation with Morten, but otherwise it belongs to the middle generation. However, those in the youngest generation in the British study resemble their Norwegian contemporaries in supporting gender equality in the individualised version, and to a large extent take gender equality for granted in their own lives. Even though family lives are not governed by one set of normative principles, as in the two elder generations, structural issues of gender frame their practices, something which is often hidden and unaddressed. Quite a few of the young middle-class fathers find that long working hours—actually longer than those their fathers worked—are a necessity in order to make a career. As Brannen (2015) points out, the job status and job flexibility in men's jobs decide to a large extent the possibilities they have in terms of becoming caring fathers. We see some of the same tendencies with the young Norwegian fathers work-

[7] Statutory maternal leave was introduced in Britain in 1976. Two weeks of paternity leave with very little pay were introduced in 2003, alongside an extension of maternal leave to 12 months.

ing in the private sector, but the provisions of the welfare state contribute to reducing the consequences of this on their partners.

If the Norwegian case demonstrates a condensed process of modernisation, the British case illustrates a condensed process of gender equality in the family and definitely under less favourable conditions. What consequences will this have for their feelings of gender? Plantin et al. (2003) demonstrate in a comparison of young British and Swedish fathers how the longer period of discourse and practice on fathering in Sweden has served to develop caring identities and skills in the Swedish fathers, whereas the English fathers appear much more ambiguous and confused. Thus, the point is that becoming a caring father in practice also has a transformative effect on men and how they see themselves (see also Aarseth 2009b). Julia Brannen (2015: 145) refers to Victor Seidler's claim that there are tensions today in what men are expected to be and who they are striving to be, as they are at odds with neoliberal notions of individualism that shape both labour market conditions and affect gendered subjectivities. It may therefore not be surprising that there are still signs of a generational delay when listening to the descriptions of their children—the young sons interviewed in Brannen (2015). These young boys, born around the millennium, describe relationships with their fathers that resemble our youngest generation: they report good and warm relationships, but also wish that their fathers had more time. They share masculine interests and activities, but are also worried about their fathers' hard conditions at work. Even if practice and discourse do not always overlap, the fathers in this generation have, after all, been more present and caring than in the previous generation, and thus they also provide their sons with a transformative model of masculinity (Brannen 2015: 166).

The division between the British and the Norwegian studies that sets out from the middle generation may also be related to the fewer numbers of upwardly mobile families in the British study compared to the Norwegian study. The cases of upwardly mobile daughters found in the middle generation of the British study do actually express more critique of housewife mothers and a stronger identification with fathers, thus resembling the pattern in the Norwegian study in the same generation. The authors indicate that there could be a connection here: 'It is possible that a weaker mother–daughter tie … may be an integral part of the process of intergenerational change and innovation' (Brannen 2004: 200). Brannen (2015) also finds that ambivalence between fathers and sons is more prominent in cases of social mobility, whether upwards or downwards. Another study from Britain, Steph Lawler's examination (2000) of mothers and daughters, lends support to this idea. Lawler's sample consists of 14 women at approximately the same age as the middle generation, and interviewed, as in our study, in the early 1990s. There are more cases of upward social mobility here compared to Brannen et al'.s study, and the sample focuses on the emotional aspects of the mother–daughter relationship rather than on the intergenerational shifts in the organisation of care. In Lawler's study, the negative and ambivalent relationships between daughters and mothers are much more prominent. The daughters' critique resembles what we heard from our informants: the mothers are accused of not seeing who the daughters 'really were' (Lawler 2000: 101). The daughters talk about invading and controlling mothers, occupied with keeping their lifeless houses clean. They are determined to become another kind of mothers themselves—with more emphasis on talking and having open communication, and on securing their own daughters' independence. This new motherhood project of theirs has not been without tensions and contradictions, but we get the impression of the same kind of friendly mother–daughter relationships as we heard about from the youngest generation in our study (albeit that in Lawler's study we only have the mothers' versions of this, not the daughters'). This emphasis on independence and being allowed to be who one 'really is' was most prominent among the class travellers. They recall feeling 'held back' by their mothers with regard to education (whereas their fathers were seen as more encouraging). Thus, Lawler analyses their negative relationships with their mothers in terms of insecurities around their class positions and a fear of returning to the mother's position: 'they experience tremendous anxieties around an identification between the self and the mother' (Lawler 2000: 102). They often describe themselves and their mothers in pairings like intelligent/stupid (in a similar fashion to some of the working-class daughters of this generation in our study). In Lawler's study, women who grew up middle class did not express any fear of becoming like their mothers and no working-class women expressed this fear either, although these women could also be critical of their mothers' limited role and might say that their mothers failed to understand them. However their mothers did not represent a threat to their feeling of being 'authentic selves' (Lawler 2000: 105). In the Nordic sample, where class journeys dominate, we find something in between: the critique of mothers for not understanding them or seeing them for who they were is similar, but the fear of becoming like their mothers is not salient. As we saw in Chap. 6, the upwardly socially mobile informants in this period found that it was their parents who were 'displaced', not themselves. It seems reasonable to explain this difference by the special features of the Nordic class journey in this period, especially the 'lock chamber' model (see Chap. 1), where neither society nor the mothers held the daughters back—quite the contrary. The compressed story of modernisation in combination with gradual class moves and the support from the welfare state contributed to a perception of the journey as a move from rural to urban culture rather than from working class to middle class, as was the case in Britain. It gave a feeling of travelling along with and not against notions of what was felt to be normal.

9

Gender: A Study of Continuities and Psychosocial Change

Looking at the three generations of women and men we have encountered in the preceding chapters, it becomes evident that huge changes in life and family patterns and in reflections on gender, as well as in the contours of a changed psychology of gender, have taken place. In this chapter I draw special attention to the changing psychological patterns, whereas in the final chapter I will integrate this into a broader frame of changing gender cultures, life forms and life choices, and will summarise how feelings of gender may have worked as emotional links in these processes of historical change.

I will first summarise, analyse and compare the relationships to parents and the perceptions of bodies and sexuality between the generations, and will see how this has contributed to changes in gender identities and gendered subjectivities. The relationship between parents and children has changed dramatically over the three generations, but there are also dimensions of the father–son, the mother–son, the father–daughter and the mother–daughter relationships that seem to be more sluggish than others. The same applies for women's and men's relation to bodies and sexuality. These relations crystallise into generational patterns in gender identities and gendered subjectivities. Over the three generations, we see a move from single-gendered to multi-gendered and sometimes degendered identities and subjectivities. There are similarities between the oldest and youngest generations in relation to a securely felt gender identity and positive parental identification, whereas the middle generation stands out in this respect. However, the deviation in the middle generation, in interaction with huge changes in the societal context across all of these three generations, contributed to a very different psychological dynamic behind the apparent similarity in the oldest and youngest generations. I will look into these changes and continuities for each gender under the headings 'The Changing Psychological World of the Men' and 'The Changing Psychological World of the Women'.

In the second part of the chapter I will return to the questions posed in Chap. 2 about the historical character of theories and will examine the observed changes in psychological gender from the perspective of different psychoanalytic theories that have evolved in the historical period of our three generations. The analytical level in this chapter will also be *the dominant patterns of feelings* within each gender and generation, which becomes the background of which individual variation emerges, are seen and interpreted. In order to remind the reader that I am describing changing patterns of generations rather than the individual variations, I will use 'gender identity' and 'gendered subjectivity' in the singular to designate a particular generational pattern. The focus on this general level also entails that my use of psychoanalytic concepts and theories on gender and development which address individual dynamics and unconscious fantasies will necessarily have to be somewhat speculative. Furthermore, as the data concerns the feelings of gender as they emerged in the interviews (cf. Chap. 3), it is also important to keep an eye on both the element of retrospective interpretation of feelings and the conditions at different points in life that may have had an impact on them.

The Changing Psychological World of the Men

Fathers and Sons

As we have seen, the main pattern of relationships between fathers and sons has changed from a filial, admiring relationship in the oldest generation, to a bland, sometimes ironic but rarely directly conflictual relationship in the middle generation, and to a more mutual admiring relationship in the youngest generation.

It is not difficult to see in this a connection to the social status and the presence of the father in the son's life. The fathers of the oldest and the youngest generations were clearly more present in their sons' lives, but in the oldest generation this was combined with a more pronounced generational hierarchy between parents and children, and also with a more direct experience of the father's authority and hard physical work to provide for the family. An interesting effect of this change is the tendency of more centrifugal identifications (Laplanche and Pontalis 1973: 206) in the youngest generation, where the father resembles you instead of you resembling your father.

The bland relationship with the father in the middle generation is correspondingly related to the more distant father in the breadwinner/carer family, but may also have been amplified in this sample of socially mobile sons: the father is not only absent, he also represents an outdated masculinity. There are few signs of phallic phantasies—superman fantasies—connected to the absent father among men in this generation, but the idea of masculinity is diffuse and this may be connected to their childhood experiences of distant fathers. The sons of this generation criticise their fathers for being unavailable and for being what Holter and Aarseth (1993: 51) have termed 'emotionally handicapped'. Those who had more present fathers are not impressed by their fathers' emotional competence either, but here the critique is mixed with a positive identification with their masculine assets.

It is only in the oldest generation that the father emerges as a powerful figure who one may not be able to match. Competition and possibility for humiliation are connected much more clearly to the same-sex relationship for men in the oldest generation than in the two younger ones. Nancy Chodorow (2012) suggests a special 'Achilles complex' between fathers and sons—where the son feels humiliated by the father's power and privileges and therefore comes to fear passivity. Seen from this perspective, some of the critique we hear from the sons about fathers letting their wives work too hard might be interpreted as a projective identification related to their own fear of being let down by their fathers.

Yet, it is not a punitive father that emerges in the oldest generation, but an admirable one with positive social qualities, like having something, being something or doing something—he is, as several of our older informants described him, 'the jack of all trades', and this makes the sons proud. What Jessica Benjamin describes as the identificatory love for the father (1995: 57) shines through for these informants, whereas it is absent among the few who had more socially withdrawn fathers. In the middle generation the bland relationship with the father makes him unfit as either a strong or a threatening figure. This implies that the threat of the Achilles complex is more or less gone. However, the sons are also left to construct for themselves what it means to be a man, and some of them appear quite obsessed with this question in the interviews.

In the youngest generation the sons seem to incorporate the fathers' strengths and qualities into their own identities. The relational basis of this incorporation seems to be more caring fathers; however, this dimension of care is not explicitly mentioned. Actually, most of the boys had wanted their fathers to be even more present, and they also see them as less emotionally competent than their mothers (see also Brannen 2015, who finds that men want their fathers to have been more present, no matter how much he actually *was* present). It appears that a caring parent, regardless of what sex, tends to become someone taken for granted, the invisible background of one's own unreflected wellbeing. The fathers of the youngest generation are described more as doers than as talkers, but the many doings of father and son seem to have established a safe emotional attachment, and against this background the sons emphasise and identify with their fathers' 'masculine' virtues, like being knowledgeable, competent and physically fit. The middle-class fathers in our sample may not be the jack of all trades as the old working-class fathers were, but they nevertheless embody some of the modern masculine qualities that the sons consider to be important. There is less emphasis on the father's work, career, status and possessions than there was in the oldest generation; rather, it is the personalised masculine virtues he embodies for his son that seem to give the sons a secure subjective sense of being male. It is the playful, creative and physically courageous masculinity they identify with. This masculine identity is seldom constructed as complementary to femininity. In fact, this is only seen in a few of the stories of the working-class boys, who, being located in the middle-class and girl-dominated sphere of academic high school, may have an unconscious wish to defend their fathers' status by denigrating feminine activities. The predominant pattern, however, is that the positive identification with their fathers' masculinity does not exclude identifications with more 'feminine' values and activities. It is a question to what extent they gender these qualities at all: what it means to be a man may include all sorts of qualities regardsless of whether they have been culturally associated with masculinity or femininity earlier. It resembles what Lynne Layton describes thus: 'The capacity to enjoy being a man without repudiating identifications with women seems to lead to something new, something that is not dominant in the culture and that the term *androgyny* does not quite capture' (1998: 189). Masculine gender identity in this generation, especially among middle-class boys, is rather connected to the feeling of being unique and unpredictable than to a specific cultural content.

Mothers and Sons

The patterns of mother–son relationships display a similar but inverted picture, changing from seeing the mother as a kind and self-sacrificing but also quite invisible person in the oldest generation, to an upgrading of her subjectivity and a much stronger attachment to her in the middle generation, and to a positive but also somewhat taken-for-granted figure in the youngest generation.

The connection to the interpersonal world of family arrangements is less straightforward than in the case of the father–son relationships, which may indicate that more intrapsychic interpretative work is going into the sons' relationships with their mothers. In the oldest generation, the relationship with the mother is strikingly understated and mainly comes up in connection with her working too hard and the good food she served. When asked directly, they admit that she was the one they sought out for comfort, but this is not an unsolicited memory. The victimisation of the mother may be a way to repudiate her power and project their own feelings of weakness and dependency. As Corbett

(2009: 47) argues, masculinity is here constructed outside of shared recognition and bears the stain of the unmarked position. However, the men also want to defend their mothers as 'other' and take care of her as strong men should. According to Benjamin (1995: 102), such attitudes of paternal protectiveness may also indicate latent maternal identifications. The weak mother in need of male protection is in particular seen in the accounts of the men who grew up in working-class and rural families. The mother is acknowledged more as a separate person in the interview with the one middle-class male informant we have in this generation.

In the middle generation the mother is more visible. She is described as someone who had deserved to get more out of life, but she is seen as a kind, capable and caring person. She is not described with the joy and pride that is seen in the older and younger generation when sons talk about their fathers, but rather as 'the mother blanket' (Holter and Aarseth 1993: 93). However, there is much less disidentification with feminine weakness in this generation of sons: the mother is not only a kind and warm person, she also does important things in the eyes of her sons in terms of her emotional competence and availability. The mother is primarily a love object, but in a limited sense is also a 'like subject' (Benjamin 1995). We may in this respect see traces of what Ken Corbett identifies as an internalised mother–son dialogue, which 'offers solace in the face of normative cruelty, and holds out the hope these boys need to imagine themselves otherwise' (2009: 114). Yet, the sons' sense of being different from her may have protected them from feeling overwhelmed by her services, as is more often the situation for the daughters. The sons of this generation identify as men, but since it is not clear what this implies or whether it is seen as something to strive for, this aspect of their gendered selves becomes less positive. The absent fathers also seem to give the masculine identities of their sons a defensive character: how do you defend yourself as a man if you do not know what it means to be one? For this reason it may be more vital for the men in the middle generation than for the men in the youngest generation to keep a watchful eye on the holding up of gender difference, something that complicates their efforts to incorporate and integrate the feminine qualities they value. The impression we get from some of the 'new' men in this generation is that they use their openness towards the emotional field to develop and secure their own individual autonomy rather than to recognise women as like subjects. Those who combined a positive relationship with both parents direct their increased affinity for the emotional sphere into becoming hands-on fathers to their own children. Compared with the oldest generation, the appreciation and capacities for the relational field have increased for almost all men in the middle generation and, in combination with new societal possibilities to become more caring fathers, this was an important resource for changing the feelings of gender in the following generation.

The mothers of both the oldest and the youngest generations worked hard, the mothers of the oldest generation most often doing physical work and the mothers of youngest generation in full-time and mostly middle-class jobs. It is not that their sons did not see their mothers' hard work, but the older men tend to explain it as an irregularity, something that should have been otherwise.[1] As for the youngest generation, their mothers' work and careers appear as equally disengaging to them as their fathers' do. In both generations it is the *services* that the mother provides that become her main function in her son's eyes. Still, the partnership between children and parents in the youngest generation gives the mother a somewhat more equal standing and visibility when compared with the oldest generation: she is seen as a strict and responsible person rather than a kind victim, and the sons do not describe her skills only in terms of feminine qualities from which they separate themselves. The mothers embody both masculine and feminine traits and their sons may identify with both. In this way, the mother, even if she is also a somewhat muted figure in the youngest generation, is still recognised more as a 'like subject'.

[1] Chodorow (2012: 48) describes the psychological position of 'weeping for the mother', which she finds in female patients from classical patriarchal families where the daughter has an active professional and personal life that contrasts with the lives of the mother, who is trapped in a classical patriarchal marriage. It seems that such weeping for the mother may also be found among men from working-class families; however, it is then more connected to the mother's hard work than to her entrapment.

Bodies and Sexuality in Adolescence

For most of the men we interviewed, body and sexuality emerge as very important components in their feeling of masculinity. Their engagement with bodily size and strength in comparison to other men is striking in all three generations (see also Corbett 2009). There is, however, also a change in the cultural and psychological meanings of this preoccupation. For the oldest generation, the strong male body is the working body and is thus a clear positive identification with their admired fathers, and maybe an attempt to fend off the Achilles complex as a grown and strong man. Other kinds of bodily preoccupations are felt as weak and feminine and not acceptable for a man. It is reasonable to think that there are some homophobic elements at play here, something we also heard from two of the older men (Knut and Arne), who unsolicited and with disgust connected men's bodily adornment with homosexuality.

For the middle generation, a strong body is related to physical fitness in sport rather than to work, but more importantly, their own bodies become more clearly connected to male sexuality: masculinity is not secured by work, but by having a penis that is the right size compared to those of other men. This emphasis on the sexual meaning of masculinity may be seen in connection with their more insecure masculine selves in the self–other relations: you do not prove your masculinity by becoming a strong and admirable man like your father, but by possessing a male body. The middle generation have to create masculinity all on their own during adolescence, and the loss of the possibility of becoming a man through the generational line amplifies gender polarity.

In the youngest generation penis size is also important, but other parts of the body may also add to the feeling of being a successful man: bodybuilding, skin, hair and clothing. To be preoccupied with looks is no longer seen as an exclusively feminine business. Still, there is a palpable risk of losing one's subject position and becoming the object through this preoccupation with one's own body. Bodybuilding is OK, but only within certain limits—and is best if it can be connected to the culturally safe male position of getting strong enough to protect or dominate others.

Sexuality in the oldest generation is felt as exclusively male, just as the preoccupation with the body is felt as female. The men in this generation tend to split sexuality and tenderness. Only men are seen as having sexual drives, and for some of them this leads to pretty rough seductive manners towards 'cheap girls'. For others, especially those with a sentimentalised relationship with their mothers, sexuality becomes associated with guilt because it may hurt and harm the kind and innocent woman. Women who initiate sexual contacts are dismissed as prostitutes or even monsters by both categories of men. Ideal femininity is a moral thing, connected to the inner qualities of a woman rather than to sexual appearances and activity.

In the middle generation the feelings of guilt and the protection of innocent and vulnerable women have disappeared. This does not necessarily mean that all the men of this generation behave as sexually unrestricted and irresponsible people, but some do, and now not only towards 'cheap girls'. Seen from the perspective of the men, all girls may be more or less sexually accessible and it is up to the men to test out the limits. Since masculinity is now almost only based on sexuality, this also forms their image of the attractive woman: she should look good and be sexy. She is not the prostitute of their fathers' generation, but neither is she a relative of their own kind and caring mothers. Yet, their identification with their mothers as 'like subjects' may still have made them more perceptive to the increased subject status of women in their own generation. In combination with the more liberal sexual norms in the 1960s and 1970s, this may also have conveyed an understanding of women as more active and responsible for their own acts, and thus have contributed to allaying the feelings of guilt for male sexuality that we saw in the older generation. But since masculinity is so strongly connected to sexuality, it is important to be in charge. Sexually forward or aggressive women are still felt as wrong, but now maybe more threatening to their fragile masculinities than morally condemned.

The gendering of sexual initiative is much less prominent in the youngest generation. The men in the youngest generation tend to like women who are active and who initiate encounters, but not to the extent that it makes them feel treated like objects. They prefer sexuality as part of an intimate relationship, but also experience it as two different dimensions of the sexual act. They do not see homosexual relationships as either condemnable or, in some cases, as necessarily unthinkable for themselves, Yet, all the young men in our sample say and they personally prefer heterosexual relationships and connect this preference to an appreciation of bodily difference: when it comes to love and sex, they want women to be attractive *as* women. However, this sexual role is only a part of their feelings about femininity: they want women who are strong, clever and independent—*and* sexually attractive.

Changing Patterns in Gender Identities and Gendered Subjectivities in the Men

We see changes both in the men's gender identities and gendered subjectivities, and different kinds of tensions between and within them. For the oldest and the youngest generations, gender identities are felt as secure in the sense that the question of what it means to be a man is not problematised. This is less clear in the middle generation. However, the *content* of the gender identities and their interchange with gendered subjectivities are very different in the oldest and the youngest generations. For the old men, almost everything is implicitly gendered—work, strength, money, food, care, behaviour, body and sexuality—so much so, in fact, that it is difficult for them to *see* gender at all. This single-gendered identity fits well with the single-gendered subjectivity that makes them thrive in the men's world and attracted to the culturally defined masculine activities in a gender-complementary order. The price for this single-gendered identity is that they have to split off culturally defined feminine qualities in themselves and project them onto the women. The main axis of conflict in men in this generation is found *within* their gendered subjectivity, not between gender identity and gendered subjectivity, and not in relation to the sociocultural context either.

In the middle generation, the content of masculine identity becomes both narrowed down to include mainly sports and sexuality, and widened by incorporating some feminine qualities through the men's stronger identification with their mothers. The insecurity of what it means to be a man leads to a troublesome double identification where they keep circling around the question of whether their valuation of care and intimacy makes them feminine. There is a tension between sameness and difference within their gender identity, but also a tension between gender identity and their less updated gendered subjectivity: they were the receivers of their mothers' service as boys and did not learn to be in the caring position themselves. Thus, as adult men they struggle with pursuing the feminine values they embrace and their emotional need for establishing a gender difference, which is no longer guaranteed by a complimentary gender order. However, the sociocultural demand for a new father-role represents a chance to integrate and maybe gradually degender some of their own 'female' identifications. This may also open up for more multi-gendered subjectivities.

Like their grandfathers, the youngest generation do not feel it as problematic to be men, and they relate positively to culturally defined masculine aspects of their fathers like playfulness, courage and knowledge. In contrast to their grandfathers, however, they do not negate their attachments to their mothers and culturally defined feminine qualities like intimacy, care and preoccupation with looks and appearances are not seen as a threat to this subjective sense of maleness. They tend to degender many of these qualities and instead emphasise their own unique way to combine them. This echoes Lynne Layton's claim (with reference to Jane Flax) that 'some kind of core identity seem to be a necessary prerequisite for the capacity to play freely with alternating identities', while simultaneously indicating the historical conditions for this claim (Layton 1998: 185). Like the middle generation, the young men also emphasise gender difference, but now primarily in relation to their personal experience of sexual attraction. In other areas, gender difference is perceived as less important. Their experience of care as not an exclusively feminine activity, but also as a quality of their fathers seems to have established more multi-gendered subjectivities that allow them to enjoy a broader range of activities across the gender divide. For this generation, the tension is to a lesser degree present within or between gender identity and gendered subjectivity. However, new tensions may arise in connection with the sociocultural context, for instance, conditions on the labour market that make it increasingly difficult to combine work and care, even they feel it is a natural thing for them to do.

The Changing Psychological World of the Women

Mothers and Daughters

The relationships between mothers and daughters are almost never characterised with the same pride or enthusiasm we have seen between fathers and sons in the oldest and the youngest generations. The mother–daughter relationship seems to be experienced as most emotional when it is conflictual, whereas it is taken more for granted when the relationship is positive. The changes across the three generations in the relationships between mothers and daughters indicate a move away from relationships being generally positive and admiring to being quite conflicted in the middle generation. In the youngest generation, we see a pattern of friendly and respectful relationships, where the daughter sees her mother as smart and proficient, and to a large extent as a model for her own life when it comes to combining work and family.

As with the changes in the father–son relationship, it is easy to see the connection to the changing family forms. In the eldest generation the mother's proficiency occupies an important place in the household economy, and this allows for the daughter's positive identification if the mother is not too strict or perfectionist. Yet, especially in the rural and working-class families, the mother also represents the ordinary everyday life; she is frugal and sensible, not a figure of admiration and wonder like the father. The ambivalence in the identification with the mother also reflects the gender hierarchy of the family: the mother may be capable and strict, but still comes in second in terms of authority to the father. This lends both positive and negative dimensions to the daughters' identification with her (see also Bengtsson 2001; von der Lippe 1988, who find that the power relation between the parents is important for girls' identification with their mothers). The ambivalence in their maternal identifications is seen in a frequent split in their relationships with other people: nice aunts are admired more than mothers, and selfish sisters allow for a more direct critique and a projection of their negative identification. The tendency towards bitterness in the old women and their characteristic wavering between uttering critical hints and quickly taking those hints back may connect to their ambivalent identifications, in addition to being demanded by a strong cultural norm that prohibits talking badly about other people.

In the middle generation the daughters find themselves restricted by a mother whose main job is to take care of them, and the ways in which the women talk about this indicate unclear borders between themselves and their mothers. They feel monitored by the mother's omnipresence and sucked into her problems and frustrations in a way that the sons of this generation do not. The weak mother becomes the suffocating mother and the daughters are more psychologically vulnerable to this because they cannot use gender as a criterion for separation. Even when their mothers encourage them to follow higher education or not to marry too early and become financially dependent on a man, the mothers are seen as intrusive. As Lynne Layton notes in connection with patients with housewife mothers, the message 'don't be like me' is rarely a successful injunction (Layton 2004: 36). The many stories about brothers in this generation who were granted privileges may of course be a projection of the daughters' anger towards their mothers; however, from the sons' description of the attendance they received from their kind mothers, it may also very well have been a fact of the intersubjective world, leaving a narcissistic wound in the daughters of this generation (Layton 1998: 56), as well as a greater sensitivity towards injustice. The ambivalence towards the mother that we saw in the oldest generation has grown stronger in the middle generation. The daughters here do not even see the mother's work as important anymore, but as something that reduces her to a servant of the family. This seems to have tipped the balance towards a more negative identification that has been very difficult for the daughters to handle and also for the mothers to hold. The women who are the angriest with their mothers suffer from feelings of guilt because they can also see that the mother's situation was difficult and because of the unclear borders between them. Yet it is only when their fathers are unusually authoritarian or violent that the daughters side with their mothers and we see the pattern that Chodorow (2012) calls 'weeping for the mother' (see note 1). If becoming a woman means giving up one's own agency, it is a repulsive process, but there are few other alternatives to becoming a woman and a subject in this generation. The 'policy for the daughters' of the emerging welfare state that encouraged girls to do well in the educational system (see Chap. 4) amplified this psychological tension. Since many of the women in our sample did pursue higher education, we see some of the same relational trouble connected to class journeys between daughters and mothers as between sons and fathers—only that it becomes much more emotional for the daughters, and also implies a stronger identification with their fathers than the sons have with their mothers. Thus, the psychological consequences of the class journey often imply a cross-gendered identification for women that is not the case for men. This may be the reason for the much stronger 'degendering' of personal qualities among women than among men in this generation. Femininity is disparaged and projected onto their mothers. But crediting men with all the good things and women with all the bad things leaves them with a negative identification with their shameful mothers, something that again will lead to problems with self-esteem (Chodorow 1999: 83).

In the youngest generation the mother's agency and subjectivity make her a more suitable object of positive identification. The mother emerges as an independent subject because she has other things to do than merely taking care of the daughter and has a position in the world that may even induce pride in the daughter, almost like between fathers and sons—but never quite. The mother represents the bigger world to her daughter in this generation, and gender does not seem to play an important role in this. Too much focus on gender, like ideas of sister-solidarity and female networks, seems to threaten a sense of subjectivity and individuality among the daughters, but their relationships with their mothers do not. Identification with the mothers' qualities is much less gendered for the daughters than identification with the fathers' qualities was for the sons of this generation. This predominantly positive and gender-neutralised identification with the mother has an everyday and sensible character and appears to be based on basically safe attachments. The borders between mothers and daughters may also have become clearer due to the more equal relationship between parents and children where aggression from part of the child has lost its taboo. However, the psychological balance between autonomy and closeness will vary in different families and this explains why there is no direct connection between a mother's work outside the family and a daughter's development of psychological autonomy (see von der Lippe 1988). If the mother becomes *too* absorbed in her own world, she is experienced as neglectful by the daughter and this may cause a narcissistic wound of not feeling seen or loved, which in turn may inhibit the feeling of autonomy. Conversely, as we also saw in the case of the sons, the mother's care may also be something that is taken for granted, a 'mother blanket', that goes unnoticed or rather noticed only when it is absent. Even though they are a minority, there are more women than men in this generation who report conflictual relations with their parents and in particular their mothers, and this may indicate that the borders between mothers and daughters are still more potentially vulnerable than the borders between mothers and sons.

Fathers and Daughters

The relationship with the father is idealised among most of the women in all three generations and combines tenderness for the father and, in cases where it is possible, also admiration for his knowledge or position. This tenderness and admiration is strongest in the oldest and the youngest generations. The most pronounced element of idealisation is seen in the oldest generation of working-class and farmer daughters, where the father represents something that the daughters themselves cannot become, but in which they may take vicariously part through him. Belonging to the sphere of the mother's jurisdiction may also help keep the father as a good object in this generation. The father represents money, generosity, relaxedness and connection to a bigger world. But, at the same time, he may also be seen as vulnerable and in need of the daughter's help and support. As Lucey et al. (2016) argue in a paper on working-class fathers and daughters, daughters may unconsciously identify with the fathers' provider role and try to take some burdens off their shoulders. For the middle-class girls in this generation the father is a more distant figure, but is still often surrounded by the excitement of being the stranger in the family.

In the middle generation the psychologically complicated relationship with the mother gives the father a stronger psychological position as liberator for the daughter, representing a calm space outside of what is perceived as the mother's control and chaos. The psychological need for the father combined with his relative distance from the family may be the reason that the relationship with him in this generation does not have the same warmth as in the older and the younger generations. He is remembered as calm, rational and often strict, sometimes as someone who also suffered from the mother's regime and moodiness, but not as exciting as in the older generation. He seems to be needed more as an object of identification than as an object of love, and he is not remembered as someone who confirmed their sense of femininity. It is rather as 'a boy in the making' that they can hope to get his attention. This may lead to a narcissistic humiliation in the daughter where she feels her femininity as absent or devalued (see also Harris 2008). The only woman in this generation who says she felt pretty as a young girl is also the only one who remembers that her father gave her compliments on her looks. The general cultural tension between the generations in the 1960s probably also contributed to less idealisation of the father. He is the best there is in the family to identify with for the girl, but this does not mean that he is an ideal.

In the youngest generation, the tenderness towards the father is back. Fathers are seen as emotional and sweet, or more fun and playful than the sensible and serious mothers. Maybe their fathers, the men of the middle generation who wanted to become more emotionally present fathers, actually succeeded better in this in the eyes of their loving daughters than in the eyes of their tired wives? The identificatory love for the father is obvious and may, in combination with secure attachments to mothers and a culture that encourages female agency and desire, have helped the daughters to become psychological 'subjects of desire' (Benjamin 1995). However, for the middle-class girls this position is not as gendered as for the working-class girls, for whom the father more often confirms their sense of femininity. With more secure borders to the mother, the father is less needed as a liberator or a sign of separation. The father's role as the one who represents the bigger world to the daughters has become less prominent since the mother can also fill that role now, and even more so in cases where the mother has more education than the father. Girls with academic fathers admire and identify proudly with their fathers' competence, and degender these qualities in themselves (much as the middle generation did), whereas girls whose fathers have less education defend them. Also here we are reminded of Lucey et al.'s (2016) analysis that daughters of working-class fathers often sense the father's vulnerability and feel guilt or even turn away from taking higher education in order both to stay close to him and not to surpass him as their mothers might have done. This compassion with fragile masculinity was also seen in the oldest generation, whereas the middle generation of women were in need of constructing their fathers as strong. Could it be that the identificatory love for the father gives a different dynamic in women's and men's craving for gender difference? Whereas men want to preserve gender difference because it is important to their own sense of masculinity, women want to protect the men's feeling of masculinity because they sense their fragility. However, the longitudinal data with the youngest generation also indicates that the protection of the father has more realistic proportions as the daughters become adult women and see him more clearly as the person he is, not as a fantasised object, whether idealised or sentimentalised.

Bodies and Sexuality in Adolescence

The feelings connected to the reproductive body are a same-sex generational thing for the women in all three generations. The way in which they deal with this reveals something about how they relate to their mothers. Because we did not interview them about their pregnancies and motherhood, it is mainly their reaction to menstruation that we have information about. In the oldest generation it is seen as a female curse, something mothers and daughters are equally subjected to. But since it is not talked about, this does not lead to any closeness between mothers and daughters—it is the silent and unwelcome sign of womanhood. In the middle generation the menstruating female body is also felt as a negative thing, but is taken more as a fact of life and even something that may contribute to some intimacy between girls. This may be surprising when seen in connection with the negative relationships to their mothers; however, it may also tell us about the basic care that these devalued mothers actually provided for their daughters, in addition to the decreasing taboo that came with more information about sexual reproduction. It is actually the youngest generation that reacts the most strongly against menstruation, which is also the case where they have feminist mothers who celebrate their menarche. In this generation, where the relationship between mothers and daughters is more about strengthening individuality rather than gender, the reproductive aspects of bodies seem to represent a hidden and uncontrollable femaleness that comes from nowhere (see also Chodorow 2012: 151). It also connects to the increased significance of the body as identity in this generation, where the main challenge is to stay in control of it. This gives the body an ambiguous meaning with regard to gender in this generation of women. The adornment of the body represents a more positive feminine identification for the young women in all generations, but this is never connected to identification with the mother—quite the opposite. For the oldest generation it is a pure joy to do with a luxury that serves as a contrast to the frugal work ethic of their mothers. For the middle generation the adornment becomes more desperate because it is often based on low self-esteem as woman, and put in the service of heterosexual relations. A good enough body is in this generation a body that is good enough in the eyes of others. For the youngest generation the pleasure of dressing up in feminine ways is back for many of the girls, but often also with a pressure for perfection that may destroy the joy. Ambivalence towards cultural femininity is seen in their relationships with their bodies, which are felt equally as a source of pleasure, an endless demand and, if overdone, a threat to their own sense of subjectivity.

The perception and norms of sexuality represent the biggest change when we compare the three generations of women. In the oldest generation sexuality is hardly mentioned—it is projected onto the men, but the women's ownership of it is indirectly revealed in their attraction to the wild boys and the good dancers who they also understand are dangerous and not boyfriend material. The fear of pregnancy before commitment to marriage is an effective barrier to the enjoyment of sex for many in this generation. In the middle generation sexuality is still seen mainly as a male drive, but as boys gain importance as liberators from parents, the girls also engage in sexualising their own bodies to attract the boys. The loss of generational identification leaves the daughters as well as the sons in a void with regard to what it means to become a man or a woman when they come of age. Whereas the sons could identify masculinity with sexuality, the daughters take a vicarious path and try to become the special choice of a man. As Simone de Beauvoir wrote in *The Second Sex* (1949), the boy can place exhibitionism and narcissism in his penis and save the rest of his body for other uses, whereas the girl must present her whole body as an object to attain the same narcissistic satisfaction. Sexuality, however, is not only a way to assure femininity, but is also a way to assure autonomy from the parents. In this way sexuality also attains a mark of instrumentality.

In the youngest generation sexual desire has lost much of its gendered meaning, but the fear of being stigmatised for being too active has not disappeared. At 18, the middle-class girls tend to experience heterosexual love as more dangerous than sex, since an emotional commitment can make them vulnerable to dependency and asymmetric gender relations. The problem the young women struggle with is to combine love and sexuality with being an autonomous subject. The fear of being a 'fallen subject' by letting oneself be pressured into sex seems to be bigger than the prospect of being a 'fallen woman'. Class dimensions are activated here, as middle-class girls tend to project their own fear of falling as subjects onto working-class girls, whereas the working-class girls try to defend themselves against this by growing out of irresponsible sexual behaviour at an early age. In addition, the dimension of physical desire is not so clear and this raises the question of whether explicit sexual desire is still seen as a male affair, in spite of increasing degendered and individualised norms and practices.

Changing Patterns in Gender Identities and Gendered Subjectivities in the Women

The gender identity of the oldest generation of women seems to be more complex than that of the men of the same generation. The women identify with both their mothers and their fathers—the mother's competence in the household and the father's knowledge, generosity and connection to a bigger world—but the sociocultural situation does not leave any space for the development of their paternal identifications. This identification is, however, not split off and disowned; it gives them a sense of inequality in their lives and a longing for something else. Their gendered subjectivity appears to be more traditionally feminine in being adaptive to other's needs and not strong on autonomy. In spite of their longing for a bigger world, many of them retreat from using the few possibilities they actually had to pursue it. In this way their gendered subjectivity fits well with the complimentary gender order, but there are tensions in their gender identity, which are connected to their experience of inequality. The main axis of tension in the women of this generation is found between their double gender identity, their single-gendered subjectivity and their restricted sociocultural possibilities.

The middle generation disowns traditional femininity and identify with culturally defined masculine values in terms of rationality, independence, education and work, but embraces these as degendered qualities. At the same time, their increasing individual exposure in the public sphere as young women combined with their disidentification with their mothers add to their low self-esteem as women. This is seen both with regard to their bodies, the desperate need to be popular with boys and the paradoxical willingness as young women to prioritise the heterosexual relationship in pursuing the independence they want. The problem for this generation is their still quite traditional single-gendered subjectivity: they seek autonomy in the heterosexual relationships and they are dependent on being validated in intimate relations. The tension in this generation of women arises between their partly degendered gender identity and their still quite traditional gender subjectivity. The sociocultural situation gave increasingly support to their degendered identity and this led gradually to more autonomy and a late arrival of a more multi-gendered subjectivity as adults and as new feminists—often with divorce as the price.

In the youngest generation we see the same kind of secure gender identity in both men and women: to be a woman is not problematised, except for when it means unequal treatment. They identify with their mothers' feminine and masculine sides, and also to some degree with their fathers'. At 18 some of them felt femininity as a threat to their sense of subjectivity, but this is less prominent at 30 and 40, where they seem to find joy in being competent at work, having a family and playing with sexual difference as a sensual and aesthetic dimension. The problem may be that this gender identity is so wide that it sometimes wears them out. Their subjectivity is increasingly multi-gendered, but autonomy must still be guarded with more attention than we see among the men, who take their own individuality and uniqueness for granted. Layton (2004) writes about a tendency among young white high-achieving middle-class women in the USA to move away from a traditional relationship-based femininity towards a defensive autonomy where committing to relationships is seen as dangerous, or where love and work are unintegrated tracks in their lives. In our sample this reaction is visible when the young women are 18, but as adults, love and work appear to have become more integrated for most of them. Layton explains the defensive autonomy she sees in her clinical practice as an adaption to a work environment that is still strongly male. So it might be the possibility to combine a career with family in the Nordic welfare states that gives another basis for integration, in combination with the degendered maternal identifications of this generation of young women. However, the frequency of burnouts they talk about in the interviews at 30 may indicate that not all tensions are gone. The main tension in this generation of women is not between gender identity and gendered subjectivity, but what it is socioculturally possible to pursue.

Evolving Psychoanalytic Theories of Gender and Heterosexuality

How do these marked generational changes in gender identities and gendered subjectivities fit into the evolving psychoanalytic theories of gender and heterosexuality? In this section I will return to the question I posed in Chap. 2 about the temporal dimension of psychological theories. Three influential psychoanalytic theories of gender and heterosexual development were formulated in the periods of childhood and youth of each of the three generations of my study: the Oedipal model of Freud, the gender identity model based on Margareth Mahler's theory of separation and individuation, and the gender ambiguity model based on more recent feminist relational and postmodern theory. I will give a short presentation of each of these and will then bring in the psychological positions of the three generations.

The Oedipal Model: Love or Identification

The Oedipal model was finalised in the 1920s. For Freud, psychological gender differences are not present until the Oedipal crisis, where the discovery of the anatomical differences between the sexes, in combination with an increased genital libido, makes the child direct a more erotic interest towards the parents. The boy's fear of castration pushes him to give up his erotic desire for his mother and identify with his father instead, whereas the girl, discovering that she has already been 'castrated', will blame her mother and redirect her love to her father and transform her wish for a penis into a wish for having a baby by the father. Thus, gender is created psychologically by splitting identification (wanting to be like) and desire (wanting to have) (Freud 1925; Lucey et al. 2016). In the heterosexual family this is a truly gendered drama where the child at first directs love and identification at both parents (the negative and positive Oedipus complex), but in most cases ends up with accepting biological and cultural gender complementarity where one can have feelings of love for those of the opposite gender, and feelings of identification those of the same gender (Freud 1925). The Oedipal complex creates both gender and generational polarities and installs a relatively fixed gendered personality structure in the child. The boy sublimates his erotic feelings into a sentimentalised image of his kind but weak mother, thereby splitting sexuality and feelings of tenderness in himself, and directs his energy towards the men's world, where questions of size, strength and success become immensely important. The girl, after she has 'become aware of the wound to her narcissism, she develops, like a scar, a sense of inferiority … she begins to share the contempt felt by men for a sex which is the lesser in so important a respect' (Freud 1925: 253–254). The girl reacts with negative or ambivalent feelings towards her mother who refused to give her a penis and turned down her erotic love, and also often reacts with jealousy towards other children of whom she feels the mother is fonder. She finds comfort in idealising her father, and this idealisation is a substitute both for her forbidden erotic feelings and for what she was herself denied to be. In order to keep the father as a good object, she must also restrict her own activity within areas that belong to men or pursue it with feelings of guilt. Thus, 'normal femininity', according to Freud, becomes characterised by passivity, narcissism and masochism. In this way women's agency is displaced and becomes part of their eroticised relation to men (Dimen 2002: 50). Dimen describes this as a split in terms of how desire is culturally constituted: whereas men's desire is constituted as an active and adult wish ('I want'), women's desire is constituted as a passive need ('I want to be wanted'), or she is seen as being without desire at all, just as clingy and needy as an infant. In this way the fact that both wish and need are part of the longing for desire for both women and men is concealed.

The Gender Identity Model: Autonomy versus Intimacy

The second model challenges the Freudian idea that psychological gender differences are non-existent before the Oedipal phase and offers another interpretation of the Oedipal drama. A central reference here is Nancy Chodorow's book *The Reproduction of Mothering*, which came out in 1978 and where she argues that differences in masculine and feminine personalities are better explained by early object-relations than by the Oedipus complex.[2] What is achieved in the Oedipus complex must be seen as building on what happened in the pre-Oedipal period, not least during the process that Margareth Mahler has named 'separation-individuation', which starts in the second year of life. This process coincides with the age when the child learns its nominal gender and thus early gendered representations of the body and the self become intertwined with psychological tensions between freedom and safety, autonomy and intimacy. The argument has two elements. The first is that if the mother is the primary object, the separation is more ambivalent for the girl because

[2] Dinnerstein (1976) and Benjamin (1988) are, in somewhat different versions, other examples of the second model. Nancy Chodorow's and Jessica Benjamin's views on gender and development have many parallel features. In the 1990s they both abandoned the idea of two separate lines of development and put more emphasis on gender as a personal construction (see Benjamin 1995; Chodorow 1994, 1999, 2012). When I use Chodorow's (1978) book as an example of the second model and Benjamin's (1995) book as an example of the third model, it is only these specific books I have in mind, not what the authors' views were earlier or later.

she and her mother are of the same gender, and is more abrupt for the boy as he is of a different gender. Femininity will be constructed in the generational dimension: the girl is little, the mother is big, but they are of the same kind. This gives the girl's gender identity a safe ground, and her subjectivity becomes more clearly relational in its character and with good capabilities for intimacy and empathy. However, the development of autonomy and establishing psychological borders between herself and others may become restrained. For the boy, on the other hand, separation takes place in the dimension of gender, which implies a more dramatic relational cut-off from his primary identificatory object. This may give him a better capacity for autonomy, but constrains his relational capacity. Chodorow summarises the gender identity development in a way that emphasises the advantages for the girl and the problems for the boy: 'growing girls come to define and experience themselves as continuous with others; their experience of self contains more flexibility or permeable ego boundaries. Boys come to define themselves as more separate and distinct, with greater sense of rigid ego boundaries and differentiation. The basic feminine sense of self is connected to the world, the basic masculine sense of self is separate' (Chodorow 1978: 169).

The other element of the gender identity model is the sociological framing of the separation-individuation process in the post-Second World War family arrangement (white, middle-class) family, where the mother is the primary carer for the child and the father is a more distant figure. For the boy, the establishing of a masculine identity becomes more precarious when he does not have a model at hand to show him what masculinity implies. He does not know exactly what a man is; he only knows that a man is *not* a woman. Thus, masculine identity becomes abstract and negatively defined, and based on a repudiation of femininity. He will fear and denigrate everything connected with the feminine—closeness, weakness, care—and deny its existence in himself. Care may be received as long as it takes the form of service and does not turn him into a baby. For the girl the problem is rather that the closeness she has with her mother also makes her vulnerable to the mother's psychological conflicts, which again stem from the mother's own restricted agency. This means that the already ambivalent relation between mothers and daughters—where the girl both wants to stay close and have freedom—

may become more strained and conflict-ridden. In this setting, for both boys and girls, the father comes to represent autonomy and freedom, a link to a bigger and exciting world. Thus, in relation to the psychological capacities for intimacy and autonomy, the two genders seem to start at opposite ends and this one-sidedness may build weak spots into their gender identities: for women intimacy may be grounded in anxiety of conflicts and low self-esteem, while for men autonomy may be a kind of omnipotence where his own dependency is disowned and projected onto unworthy "others". In both cases, other persons are not recognised as subjects in their own right.

The Gender Ambiguity Model: Sameness and Difference

The third model is Jessica Benjamin's re-interpretation of the preceding two models in her book *Like Subjects—Love Objects*, which was published in 1995. She argues that psychoanalytic theory should decentre its theory of development by conceiving of development as continuously and ongoing reconfigurations of earlier positions. Benjamin questions both the idea of more or less fixed personalities (cf. the concept of identification instead of identity), as well as the androcentrism of Freud's model and the gynocentrism of Chodorow's 1978-model, which make either men or women the more privileged subjects in development. Benjamin's main point is that the binary opposition between desire and identification—between difference and sameness—are not sustained in the developmental process. Especially in the early stage of separation–individuation she finds that the father of both girls and boys becomes an important object of identificatory love, which cannot be attributed solely to his role as a liberator from maternal power. The father (or some other significant person who is not the mother) represents the child's first experience of 'difference' compared to the 'sameness' of the mother; he becomes 'the knight in shining armour', as Margareth Mahler describes him. However, the mother remains an important figure of identification, power and attachment for both boys and girls. She may also be the agent of separation when she enters increasingly differentiated interactions and mutual recognition with the child, but the person outside this dyad has a unique role in the development of agency and desire: 'Identification with a second other as a "like subject" makes the child imaginatively able to represent the desire for the outside world … the new feature associated with this phase, its legacy to adult erotic life, is identificatory love … [and it] remains associated with certain aspects of idealisation and excitement throughout life' (Benjamin 1995: 57–58). For girls, the identificatory love with the father is an important psychological basis for becoming able to be a subject of desire and to gain a sense of autonomy over her own body and self. For boys, it may also have narcissistic and homoerotic overtones that confirm the achievement of masculinity. In this phase where love objects can be like subjects, the child does not need to choose between the mother and the father or follow conventional rules of gender differentiation. Benjamin suggests that children use crossover identifications to formulate important parts of their selves, as well as to elaborate fantasies about sexual relations; for instance, the father can be an object of homoerotic love for the girls (Benjamin 1995: 126, 129). This 'over-inclusive' phase of gender identification is refigured by the gender complementarity of the Oedipal phase, where identificatory love is split up into love and identification, and the fantasy of object love comes to compensate for the narcissistic loss of the identification with the opposite-sex parent and the love of the same-sex parent. Envy, feelings of loss and resentment may lead to both repudiation and idealisation of the other sex now (p. 66). However, this is not necessarily the final outcome of gender identity development. Benjamin adds the possibility of post-Oedipal complementarity that may integrate the Oedipal complementarity with the identificatory love from the pre-Oedipal phase. Whereas the Oedipal form of gender complementarity is a simple opposition based on splitting, the post-Oedipal form is instead constituted by sustaining the tension between sameness and difference in a way that can make the oscillation between them pleasurable instead of dangerous. Benjamin suggests that this becomes possible if the Oedipal gender split is transcended by a symbolisation that opens up for more mature reflections on gender. This symbolisation may be fascilitated in a historical period of constant reconfigurations of gender (confer the point of Adkins 2004b discussed in; see also Chap. 1). The 'familiar' in the other can then be found by returning to the earlier phases where the child experienced identificatory love with both parents and to the transitional space of play with different nominal gender positions. Here development includes the ability to return without losing the knowledge of difference (Benjamin 1995: 74–75). Post-Oedipal complementarity may in this way regain some of the multiplicity and mutuality denied by the Oedipal form, but that exist within the line of gender development. Thus, according to Benjamin, it is not necessary to search for subversions of the gender dichotomy outside of the gender system. A more flexible identificatory capacity may be part of the story and loosens up gender as a fixed form as it 'reworks its forms, disrupting its binary logic by breaking down and recombining opposites rather than by discovering something wholly different, unrepresented or unrepresentable'. Thus, the meaning of gender may be changed from within, not by radically deconstructing the whole idea of difference.

Generational Psychological Positions

According to Raymond Williams, any useful cultural analysis begins with identifying patterns and their relationships with other patterns, 'which may sometimes reveal unexpected identities and correspondences in hitherto separately considered activities' (Williams 2011: 67). When comparing the changing patterns of feeling of gender in the three generations of women and men with psychoanalytic theories of gender and heterosexual development in mind, an interesting and 'unexpected correspondence' between generations and theories emerges: the oldest generation seems to be best explained by the Freudian Oedipal model, with its emphasis on psychological gender complementarity in the patriarchal family and the importance of the split between feelings of identification and feelings of desire (Freud 1925). The middle generation has a better match with the gender identity model, where processes of individuation–separation in connection with asymmetric parenting lead to gender differences in the development of intimacy and autonomy (Chodorow 1978). The youngest generation fits best into the gender ambiguity model, which questions the idea of two traces of development and sees difference and sameness as a continuous tension in psychic life of gender as well as in the modern family (Benjamin 1995).[3] The three psychological models were formulated during or in the aftermath of the childhoods of the three generations, and even if the fits are not seamless, the relatively better match between the models and the childhoods from the same period is notable.[4] This indicates that it is not only the theories that have changed as a result of critical work, but also the gendered psychologies they set out to describe. My claim is not that the Oedipal constellation was not present for the younger generations or that issues of separation–individuation were not relevant for the oldest. Not everyone in these generations fits into the same psychological models. As we have seen, there are important differences depending on social class, and definitely also on the many particular ways in which mothers and fathers transmit gender to their children. Therefore, there are always a variety of outcomes. But as has been consistently argued in this book, individual variation does not prevent social patterning across these variations. What emerges is an *affinity* between the generational patterns of gendered psychologies and the different theories of gender psychology. This suggests that the different psychological constellations and tensions described in these theories have had different impacts in different historical contexts. It also suggests that the reason these theories developed as they did was that they caught the contours of a changed generational pattern of the times in which they were formulated: new structures of feelings related to gender. Seen through a theoretical lens, the generational feelings of gender could be described as follows.

[3] As I was finishing this book, I came across a new article by Nancy Chodorow (2015), where she also argues for the existence of generational narratives in psychoanalytic feminist thinking about masculinity. She describes them in connection with second-wave feminism as pre-second-wave, and second-wave and post-second-wave theories, and names their masculinity models according to the classical narratives of 'Oedipus', 'Glory of Hera' and 'Wrath of Achilles'. The point I am making in this chapter is that these shifts in theories not only reflect the theoretical and political thinking of academic generations, but also indicate that processes of gender socialisation empirically may have changed in these generations of women and men.

[4] A further point could be that the theories also come from different places: Freud's from Central Europe; Chodorow's and Benjamin's from the USA. The elements of misfit seen between the Norwegian generations in my sample and the theories might be related to this. However, psychoanalytic theory has always also been part of a cross-national community, which complicates the question of origin.

As boys, the men in the oldest generation came to identify with their fathers and direct their love towards their mothers. Masculinity is constructed outside shared recognition with their mothers (Corbett 2009). The phallic idealisation, as well as the fear of humiliation we see among them, carries traces of both the pre-Oedipal and the Oedipal father, but the organisation of male sexuality as a 'want' appears to be more clearly Oedipal (Freud 1925). The split between sexuality and tenderness may be seen both in the sentimentalised image of the mother, the asexualised figures of the women they marry, the denial of their own dependency and weakness, and maybe also a fear of homosexuality. The women in this generation project sexual drives onto men and idealise their fathers as the good object. This idealisation carries traces both of identificatory love and forbidden erotic desire, yet it does not give them access to the position of becoming a subject of desire. Their own sexuality is only indirectly visible and some of them directly disown it—it is only among some of the middle-class women that we may see some traces of the 'want to be wanted' (Dimen 2002). The ambivalence towards their mother may have an Oedipal imprint, the deception of having to return to her world. To be too active (like the egoistic sisters) outside the female sphere appears to be both forbidden and guilt-ridden. The problems inherent in this 'normal femininity' of the Oedipal model, the scar it leaves on self-esteem and the masochistic acceptance of not being allowed to be a subject of desire could explain the tendency towards bitterness that is never allowed to really disclose itself.

For the middle generation, gender complementarity has become less stable and psychological gender issues seem to circle questions of sameness and difference in relations and identities. The main problem for the men of the middle generation seems to be safeguarding an insecure masculinity, which makes them obsessed with gender difference. What fits less well compared with the gender identity model is that there are few traces of a father as a symbol of freedom and autonomy. Nor do the men in our sample separate themselves abruptly from their mothers at the intersubjective level, and there are also much less disidentification with femininity than the gender identity model suggests. However, in the intrapsychic world, femininity seems to be more threatening. This leaves this generation of men with a tension between an intersubjective embrace of feminine values and an inner fear of them as being able to destroy an insecure masculinity. When it comes to sexuality, it has a more defensive character than of an Oedipal 'want'. Whereas the Oedipal organisation of male sexuality in its mature forms also includes a moral dimension of protecting women, the sexual organisation in the middle generation sometimes appears to be less mature because it lacks Oedipal integration. Instead of the protecting man and the innocent child-woman, we get a culture of boys hunting women as prey. If we turn to the women of this generation, the unclear borders and relational conflicts between mothers and daughters are conspicuous, but we do not see much of the mutual intimacy and closeness that is also an important point in the gender identity model. However, the traditional gendered subjectivity, more capable of intimacy than autonomy, the close relationships with female friends, the acceptance of the reproductive female body and the intensity in the conflicts with the mother may all reveal that the women still have deep emotional same-sex attachments. The father emerges clearly as the liberator of the daughter from the mother's control, but the emotionally more muted relationship between fathers and daughters, compared to the stronger idealisation in the older and the more warm relationship in the younger generation, reflects the model's claim that the relationship with the father never becomes as intense as the relation to the mother. Also, the mark of instrumentality in the heterosexual relation and in sexuality may indicate that the father (as well as male lovers) is a supplementary choice emotionally. The women in this generation seem to have far fewer problems in degendering the qualities they identify with in their fathers than the men have with the qualities they identify with in their mothers. An obvious explanation for this may be the cultural gender hierarchy; however, it might also be connected to a more secure basic gender identity that stems from the mother–daughter bond. The women interpret these new psychological qualities as a more modern way to be a woman, as different from their mother's way, but not as something masculine. They may feel more or less attractive as women when they are young girls, but they do not question whether they are women or not.

In the youngest generation the identificatory love, especially for the father, is evidently present in both women and men, without jeopardising their attachment to their mothers. The father is not important as a liberator—this is a role that the mother now manages well—but he represents the exciting 'difference' compared to the more taken-for-granted 'sameness' of the mother, as Benjamin (1995) suggests in the model of gender ambiguity. For the men the identification is with the father's positive masculine qualities, whereas the warm relationship described by the women may indicate that the father for them rather is important by giving a possible, but not always gained, access to the position of being 'a subject of desire' (Benjamin 1995). The mother tends to be more taken for granted, yet both sons and daughters also see her as an independent subject and identify with both her 'masculine' and 'feminine' qualities. Thus, we see contours of the more over-inclusive patterns where both mothers and fathers can be 'love objects' and 'like subjects'. The cross-gender identifications are used to formulate important parts of the self-presentation as well as to elaborate on sexual relations (Benjamin 1995: 126; Corbett 2009: 213), which suggests the possibility of a male generational bond beyond defensiveness as a source of enjoyment of play, competition, excitement, desire and mutual recognition between men. This matches our youngest generation and may constitute the psychological background to opening up to homoerotic impulses: love and identification with parents of either sex are no longer so clearly separated. We do not see the same playfulness in the female generational bond, however. In the model of gender ambiguity, the post-Oedipal gender complementarity also preserves a certain emphasis on Oedipal difference, both in women and men of this generation, especially in connection with bodies and sexuality. In the youngest generation gender has become more multiple—'different moments of the self', as Dimen describes it (2002: 57). As we have already seen, this does not necessarily or magically remove traditional gender practices, yet these practices seem to be based less on a feeling of gender in the youngest generation compared to the two older generations. Maybe it is convenient that the woman do more of the housework and care for the children, but it is neither because housework is particular feminine nor because it is unmasculine.[5]

[5] The different class composition of the generations in our sample may also be part of the picture. The two first models—which have been criticised for being reserved for middle-class/bourgeois families—seem in our case also to cover working-class and rural families, as long as they share the same family pattern of male provider and female carer. However, the more fluent and over-inclusive

There may be more tensions in the psychological position of gender ambiguity than are identified through this rather optimistic theoretical lens, and the intertwinement of multi-gendered subjectivities and other societal structures has no definite outcome. It might lead in the direction of making inequalities appear as equalities, as Hanne Haavind (1984a, b) has argued (see Chap. 1), and might generate new frustrations in a generation that thought gender had lost significance in most areas of life. The point here is not to judge the different constellations of gender as more or less successful or recommendable, but to draw attention to how different generational feelings of gender express processes of social transformation. In contrast to either narratives of liberalism or theories that make a story of decay out of the move from a strong Oedipal character to the narcissist character of modern society (see Kohut 1977; Lasch 1979), my intention has rather been to stress the historical specificity of psychological tensions and potentialities in each generation as a dynamic formation that is shaped by the past and the present of one generation, and changed further in future generations. In this sense, the story has no beginning or end and will always be open to new ways of organising life and new feelings of gender.

The Bedrocks of Gender?

In spite of the changing contours of gendered psychologies, there are also more sluggish elements that emerge when we compare the three generations. One is that *mothers are always taken more for granted than fathers*. Mothers seldom stand out as the idealised and exciting individuals like fathers often do. The relationship with mothers may often induce positive feelings of attachment and security, and mothers can embody both 'feminine' and 'masculine' qualities that their sons and daughters identify with—but this rarely produces the same enthusiasm, whether in the form of pride and admiration or in the form of warmth and tenderness, as it does with the fathers. Across the generations we have been looking at here, the father remains the knight in shining armour (Mahler

model of gender identities may have a strong connection to the middle class, where both the degendering of work and care, and the valuation of uniqueness and individualisation are indeed most prominent.

et al. 1975; Chodorow and Contratto 1992; Benjamin 1995), whereas relationships with the mother are characterised by more ambivalent feelings, especially for women. Another sluggish element is that *disidentifying with your same-sex parent seems to produce more psychological tension* in the form of insecure gender identity than disidentifying with the opposite-sex parent. It is not important whether the same-sex parent embodies the culturally prescribed gender norms or not. A good relationship can include both 'masculine' and 'feminine' qualities in the same-sex parent. A positive identification with the same-sex parent (which, of course, does not exclude a positive identification with the other parent too) means that gender identity is felt as basically secure or unproblematic regardless of what it consists of. This indicates that emotional identification with other people is not exactly the same as identification with cultural meaning. A third sluggish element across these three generations is that *the gender polarity appears to be more psychologically important to uphold for the men than for the women.* Women seem to get their feeling of gender more in the generational relation, even if the identification is negative. For the women, gender polarities are instead connected to problems of inequality (see Chodorow 1999: 28) or eroticised and used as an indirect way to gain agency and subjectivity.

I will have to leave this as observations. It may have to do with the structure of the heterosexual nuclear family, even in times where fathers have become more present and mothers more individualised. Adrienne Harris indicates that Benjamin's idea of the identificatory love of the father could be seen as a compromise between a feminist theory of gender-neutral parenting and a psychoanalytical model—and I would extend that to a cultural model—'that counterpoises active and passive, reason and madness, regression and activity' (2008: 47). We may also here have reached one of the bedrocks of Western culture—the one Simone de Beauvoir (1949) analysed in the figure of 'woman as the second sex'. In spite of many and important changes in gender relations, the position of being a subject still sits better with deep-seated cultural images of masculinity than of femininity.

10

The Processes of Degendering, Gendering and Regendering Across Three Generations

Throughout the twentieth century and during the lives of the three generations explored in this book, a change in gender contracts has taken place. The dominant family model has changed from the agrarian family at the start of the century, where women and men contributed to the survival of the family within separate working spheres, to the male provider/female carer family of the middle of the century, where providing through gainful work was the responsibility of men and taking care of the home and the children was the responsibility of women. Later models were the dual-earner family of the first gender battle in the 1970s and 1980s, where the norms about domestic work had changed without practice quite keeping up, and finally, the dual-earner/dual-carer family of the new millennium, where women and men try to share domestic work and childcare in a way they find personally fair, or, in some cases, acknowledge that it is not possible, given their preferences or conditions of the work market.

What has happened to gender in these processes? Where have they brought the project of gender equality? What place did the feelings of gender have in these processes of social transformation? In this final chapter I will attempt to summarise some of the answers that arise from the approach to gender and social transformation used in the book. I have followed Raymond Williams' recommendation to start with 'the whole way of life' when trying to understand changing cultural forms (see Chaps. 1 and 2). As a methodological consequence of this, I have not isolated feelings of gender from the context in which they emerged, but have gradually differentiated them out analytically as a particular social form. I will now put them back into the frame of the whole way of life where they belong and have their impact.

The dominant patterns of life choices of each generation make sense in the light of structural and political conditions: the agrarian family at the beginning of the century was a family of scarcity and no security net—it was about surviving, not justice. The male provider/female carer family of the mid-twentieth century could rely on increasing living standards and a policy that encouraged women to stay home. The dual-breadwinner family encountered the increasing demand of women in the workforce and an extended social security system. And finally the dual-earner/dual-carer family became possible with state-provided family–work schemes and the fact that women now were often more educated than men. The increasing pressure in the labour market also put limits on how far the sharing could go in this generation, especially in families where one or both parents worked in career jobs in the private sector. The different family form were interpreted, inspired and rationalised through dominating discourses of the time, especially the norm of obligation to one's family early in the century, the importance attached to the home, motherly care and safe childhoods in the post-war period, the discourses about women's rights and gender equality from the 1970s, and the increased emphasis on individualism towards the end of the century.

The main perspective in the book has been to explore to what degree the patterns of dominant life choices and the recognition of the discourses that went along with them also had an emotional sounding board, and to what extent one may say that the different family models were emotionally driven by feelings of gender or sometimes in tension with them. How did the changes in social gender contracts become something that women and men not only dutifully took part in, but also, to varying degrees, even wanted to contribute to? What are the emotional links between structure and agency at a given historical moment? The analysis has indicated that the emotional energy invested in life choices tends to be unequally distributed between women and men belonging to the same generations. This lack of simultaneity has produced tensions that may be seen as pressure towards change. In this way feelings of gender can be seen as active sources in processes of historical transformation.

Emotional Links

From their childhood, the oldest generation carried a deep mentality of work and feeling of obligations to their families. Work and family were fundamentally positive entities, which is not to say that they were without problems, hardships or sorrows. These feelings come in gendered versions connected to the hierarchy between men and women, the different valuation of their work, and their social positions, duties and entitlements. These asymmetries sometimes tinge the women's positive feelings about work and family with a hint of bitterness, especially towards other women who managed to get a larger share within this given hierarchical order. As we have seen, these experiences were processed in their relationships with their parents, where the women's idealisation of their fathers and ambivalence towards their mothers were stronger than the men's idealisation of their mothers and ambivalence towards their fathers. The outcome was gender identities and gendered subjectivities that existed in concurrence, but also in some tension with the changing sociocultural context. Especially at a historical moment where many signs conveyed that a new world was emerging, the father's connection to the outer world may have increased the young women's attachment to him and their ambivalence towards their mothers, whose authority was bound to the house and waning in the new times. This may also explain the more positive images of mothers in the middle classes where the mothers both had more time for the children and encouraged education and less obligation towards the family for both sons and daughters.

It is especially the asymmetry in feelings connected to femininity that represents an important emotional tension between women and men in this generation. As they came of age, the men's experiences of their own bodies constructed and confirmed the figure of the strong, working and heterosexual man, and of the exposed female body that could so easily become a victim not only of hard work, but also of the men's own sexuality. The women connected the reproductive aspects of their own bodies to the general curse of womankind, and silenced their fascination and desires for the wild and fun men. The men's feelings of guilt and moral compassion with the kind and too hardworking women are the most forceful *emotional link* identified in this generation's life choices. The men wanted their wives to stay at home so that they would not have as hard a life as their mothers, and the economic and political situation in this period made this possible. The men themselves were prepared to work hard to make it happen and at the same time to prove themselves as good and successful men. In this way they also indirectly kept up the invisible care they had received from their mothers during their childhood, including demarcating their own identities even more sharply from the female world. The price they paid was distance to their own children and a wife who complied with the arrangement with emotional reservation, indolence or silent discontent. Together they cooperated in their married life to refine the complementary gender order of nice women and responsible men. However, the emotional upgrading of femininity by the men from invisible mothers to caring wives ran opposite to the women's emotional downgrading of masculinity from fun fathers to boring providers.

The refined gender complementarity created by their parents contributed to a destabilising of the very same gender order in the next generation. The absent father and the available but often discontent mother frame the childhood of the middle generation in the middle of the century. The move from a rural to an urban setting took out the immediate meaningfulness of the mother's work in the home seen from the child's perspective, while (real) work and money became connected to men. This family arrangement created a rift in the social bond between sons and fathers and daughters and mothers. The fathers' work became more abstract as it was done outside the reach of the children, and the mothers did not need much help in their small, modern city departments. Children were sent out to play with each other instead, and both girls and boys were urged to prioritise their homework in the new co-ed school from this period. 'The policy for daughters' of the 1950s and 1960s accentuated the rift between mothers and daughters in spite of being backed up by the mothers themselves. The relatively gender-neutral upbringing in post-war Scandinavia seems to have played a crucial role in the processes of change because it could connect to many other societal trends pointing in the same direction. The positive feelings connected to family and family obligations, duty and hard work lost their material and structural basis. The disidentifications and cross-identifications with parents in this generation of children lead to the psychological challenge of redefining the meaning of one's own gender through an identification with the other. Heterosexuality became a way for the men to confirm the masculine side of their identification once they came of age, which meant that the now-blurrier gender border became important to safeguard. The women put the heterosexual relationship in the service of liberation from their parents. This put them in a paradoxical situation where they exaggerated traditional femininity in order to become free. As young adults they recognised the futility of this strategy and instead headed for becoming individuals themselves.

The tension between women and men in this generation concerns how to interpret the gender border. The women tended to see it as a source of power and inequality and wanted to degender work and care, whereas the men could identify with care work only if the gender border was upheld with regard to money and sexuality. In the narratives of this generation the most forceful *emotional link* identified in their life choices is represented by the women who wanted to be different from their mothers and more like their fathers, and who had the expansion of the educational system and the increasing demand of female labour on their side. The men complied passively as they had a drive towards becoming better fathers than their own fathers had been, but they did not identify to the same degree with housework and joint responsibility for the home. They felt attacked by the connection the women made between gender and inequality, and feared that the women would disappear as attractive sexual objects. The women's project of becoming individuals could eventually draw on the arguments from the Women's Movement and the emerging gender-equality politics. The way forward was less clear for the men in this generation. What is a man if the sexual gender border disappears or he embodies more and more feminine psychological capacities? And what happened to the attendance he was accustomed to from his mother? The result was the dual-earner family, where the norm was to share work and care, but where the men's engagement was often more in principle than in practice, which ignited the many private and public gender battles in this generation. What complicated the situation for the women was also that their emotional ambivalence, sometimes even contempt, for traditional femininity as represented by their mothers and their attraction to male liberators sometimes interfered with their relationships with other women and also could make them unclear in their relationships with men.

In spite of the gender battles and divorces experienced in their childhood, the idea of family regained a positive emotional content in the youngest generation. They saw their family as a relational universe, a place for care and communication and sometimes even fun. The busy parents and the basically good terms that existed between children and parents moved the relationship towards partnership and mutual dependency rather than a relationship of authority. The children helped out more than in the previous generation as both parents worked outside the home, and they saw their parents as fallible and vulnerable human beings, sometimes with unfulfilled life dreams, burnouts and divorces. The gradual degendering of work and care made their emotional images of the parents and their own gender identities and gendered subjectivities more open. The mixture of individualism and gender was seen when this generation came of age: girls felt less obliged to fit into norms of passivity and femininity when it came to sexual encounters. However, in practice an active approach to sexuality risked being interpreted within a conventional gender framework and positioned them as either dependent or monstrous women.

The dominant *emotional link* identified in this generation's life choices, found both in the women and the men, is the trust in the parents and the basic feeling of being first and foremost an individual with all rights and possibilities at hand. They wanted to continue the family form of their parents, but with more fairness, fewer quarrels, less stress and fewer divorces. For the young women the choice of education was not made with regard to future family obligation as in the previous generation, and from an early age they were aware of the importance of sharing work in the family. For the men the division of work in their childhood families had more emotional impact on their expectations of family life. None of them questioned the norm of sharing, but handled it differently depending on their family experiences. The partnership this generation had experienced in their childhood families moved the gender battles towards a more principal norm of fairness where doing what one is best at or likes the best seems more important than sharing everything completely evenly. The tension between women and men in this generation is the concealed re-emergence of gendered structures within the framework of a partnership. The arrival of children was also a challenge in this generation, in addition to tougher conditions in the labour market in the new millennium. The problems were mostly interpreted in terms of their own ambivalences—wanting a career, to be a good parent, to keep fit and spend time with friends—rather than formulated as a critique of their partner. The general picture among the informants we meet at 40 is that men and women negotiate the outer demands as well as their inner splits in a more peaceful atmosphere with each other than was the case in the previous generation. They either divorce or try to find a way together where gender is not relevant as an argument for different contributions, but sometimes seen as a fact of their current life or even as an attractive difference when it comes to personal relations.

The emotional links had a different gender profile in different generations and they also led to new dilemmas of gender. The choice of the male provider/female carer family made most emotional sense for the men, and the gender dilemma that emerged in its wake raised the following question: what is a woman when she is not participating in the economy anymore? The choice of the dual-earner family made most emotional sense for the women and the dilemmas that now arose were: what is a man when he is doing domestic work and care work? What is a woman if she is not caring and kind? These new dilemmas established emotional tensions not only between women and men in these generations, but, as we saw, also within the individuals. In the youngest generation the choice of the dual-earner/dual-carer family seems to make emotional sense for both women and men, but not in exactly the same way, since their psychological point of departure and the cultural interpretation of their behaviours are different. The dilemmas that arose now are: what does individuality mean for personal gender and for gender structures? Can you be equal, yet different? Also here, life choices introduced new problems: old gender structures seemed to re-emerge behind the strong belief in individualised gender. The generational view shows that when old problems are solved, new and different sets of problems enter the stage. This represents the dynamic of change where gender is continuously reconfigured in the intersections of structural, political and emotional processes.

Looking for the emotional links is a way to grasp the prereflexive dimensions of agency (Adkins 2004b; McNay 2004; Silva 2005—see Chap. 1). The emotional link has both dynamic and adaptive sides. What it highlights is that the emotional drives have a historical/socialised form and are not lagging behind structural and political change. The emotional link is not only connected with the past, it also represents the sense of things in the present, and it anticipates the future to the extent that it resonates with new discourses and new structural life conditions (Aarseth 2009a). This reflects Raymond Williams' claim that no societal structures 'come first' in generating social change: 'New forms can flow from [a] particular form and extend in the whole organisation, which is in any case being constantly renewed and changed as unique individuals inherit and continue it' (Williams 2011: 125).

Political Links

The feelings of gender that gave direction to life choices and the experiences that followed from them also informed the attitudes to gender equality we found in women and men of the three generations. Norwegian surveys on attitudes to gender equality show an increasing support along age groups (Hansen and Slagsvold 2012; NOU 15 2012), but are the different generations and genders answering the same question in such surveys? Gender equality is an equivocal concept. It can mean *justice*—the right not to be discriminated against because of gender. It can mean *equality*—that gender should be irrelevant to distributing tasks, duties, resources or privileges. It can be about individual *freedom*—the right to choose how to live one's life independently of gender. In Chaps. 5, 6 and 7, the attitudes to gender equality were described in terms of different dilemmas: for the oldest generation the gender complementarity model could be interpreted both as an expression of equity between men and women, and a hierarchical social order that cripples justice for women. For the middle generation the model of sharing raised questions about whether equality implies sameness or has room for difference. In the youngest generation it is rather the dilemma between gender equality as an approved norm and the belief in individual choice and freedom that is at stake. There are also differences between and within the generations in terms of in what areas gender equality is seen as relevant. It may concern skill sets and divisions of work, reproduction and parenthood, differences in personality and preferences, sexual norms and behaviour, style and appearances. Differences may be seen as natural or cultural, and as worth keeping or changing. Models of gender difference may survive within a general embrace of gender equality: ideas about fundamental biological or psychological differences between women and men, or that complementarity in some areas of life is practical or desirable. Thus, equality and difference, justice and freedom exist in different dimensions—and they move, disappear and re-appear in different places and different disguises. The positions on gender equality we find in the different generation are based on practices, cultural norms and feelings of gender, and these do not always pull in the same direction.

For the oldest men, modern gender equality is at odds with their own life project since it makes their own form of masculinity—and the sacrifices that came with it—worthless, and moreover makes their idealised wives a target for critique. They are occupied with the crumbling moral order in society and their critique of modern times is condensed in their worry about the increasing number of divorces. They defend the mild and kind motherliness of the feminine carer against new ideas of women becoming like men. For the oldest women, the belief in gender complementarity in work, care, skills and personalities is not so emotionally hard-wired as for the men. Women with agrarian roots rather associate the question with the asymmetries and injustice in the gender order of their childhood. The middle-class women's focus is on equal capabilities in women and men, which they think ought to be more acknowledged. Whereas the men in this generation are loyal to their trust in gender complementarity, the women are stuck in the tension between, on the one hand, beliefs in justice of gender equality and, on the other, the strong social norm of gender complementarity and gender hierarchy that they have lived with. What women and men in this generation agree on is natural differences in sexual behaviour and that the body is a women's issue. As we saw, both women and men in this generation adjust their attitudes somewhat to the new practices of their children and grandchildren, but it is not difficult to see the connection between their principal view and their generational feelings of gender.

The idea of gender equality has more emotional appeal in the middle generation, where many of the men want to develop their relational capacities and become more present fathers than their own had been, and many of the women want to get away from their mothers and have a more independent life. The views of the women in this generation vary from a radical stand for women's right to self-determination and against individual discrimination, to a general support of gender-equality policies addressing social rights on the group level, and to a more pragmatic individual approach, where issues of equality come second to what is convenient or necessary for the family. Whether the fight for gender equality should take place mainly inside or outside the family is also a dividing line. For the men the discourse of gender equality in work and care is a much more palatable idea than the discourse of feminism and women's rights which puts the blame on them. Yet, the problem of following up the housework in practice and the importance they attach to the sexual gender difference make almost all men in this generation somewhat awkward when they address the issue of gender equality, even though they support it in principle. There is a time lag, but also partly a different agenda between women and men here: for the men gender equality is about getting close to their children and preventing quarrels with their wives; for the women it is about the fairness of sharing and getting the same opportunities as men in the labour market. For the radical women it is also an engagement against the sexualisation and objectification of the female body.

In the youngest generation the emotional appeal of gender equality has diminished for both women and men, not because they are against the idea, but because to a large extent they find that it has already been achieved with regard to work, care, skills and sexual norms. They feel more like individuals than as gender, and therefore only reluctantly identify with the gender categories that are the foundation of any gender-equality policy. But since they believe gender equality is already a fact, they also become quite upset when they realise that this is not always the case. In the context of the workplace this applies to both women and men; in the context of the family the reaction comes only from women. Yet, the women's critique is often moderated by their own distaste for rigid regimes and their belief that people should do what they are best at and enjoy. This leads to a less ideological but perhaps also more disguised gender battle where, for instance, hiring au pairs and cleaners may help to keep up the belief in modern gender equality in the families that can afford them. The structural levels of gender discrimination are not always addressed or seen as something that is difficult to combat, like the work conditions in the private sector, where more of the men than the women work. Subtle discriminatory mechanisms escape the attention of even the most alert: Hilde and Pia were well aware at 30 that gender gaps in salaries are often a threat to attaining gender equality at home, but they did not connect it to the opposite problem, which they had not experienced at that time, but which Guro and Tonje told us about: that women who make *more* money than their male partners risk threatening their partners' feeling of masculinity. This complex cultural web makes gender equality much more of a demanding balancing act for women than for men. This dilemma is further accentuated as both men and women seem to appreciate gender differences in some areas. They tend to see feminists as over-the-top aggressive and ignorant of bodily issues and the pleasurable aspects of personal gender differences. They also tend to find gender-equality policies boring and preoccupied with insignificant details.

The changing feelings and norms of gender are intertwined with processes of social mobility. The least engagement with, or even resistance towards, modern gender-equality discourses is found in the few working-class chains where there is no social mobility across the three generations: the female chain of Borghild, Berit and Beate and the male chain Gunnar, Geir and Glenn. In these working-class families sharing the work is more of a practical matter—which was seen both in the relatively fair sharing of work between Berit and her husband with regard to their work hours, and in Gunnar and Geir's 'knack with children', combined with Geir's shunning of housework and women's tedious talk. In the middle-class families it is a more ideological matter and traces of traditional gender arrangements are felt to be old-fashioned and embarrassing, and must either be openly opposed, explained away or disguised (cf. Haavind 1984a, b). It may also be the case that gender differences have a different emotional foundation with regard to class. In the middle-class families in the youngest generation, gender identities are mainly expressed through leisure activities, consumption and aesthetics, whereas work, care and household are losing ground as bases for gender identity projects.[1] In the working-class families, gender identities seem to be more dependent of the work division in the family and this pattern may also continue into the next generation in cases of upward social mobility. This was the case with Kine, who had a high-powered job and fought for gender equality at work, but suddenly, as she approached 40, felt that she had become unfeminine and her partner unattractive as a man, which she connected to their untraditional gender arrangements at home. The Swedish historian Ronny Ambjörnsson says that gender often gets in a squeeze in class journeys (Ambjörnsson 1996/2005: 27). This may explain the overlaps of feelings of gender between the class of the childhood family and the adult family of a new class. In our sample this overlap seems to be more prominent if both spouses grew up in the same class and made similar class journeys. We also observed this in the oldest generation when a young rural couple settled in the city. In those cases the agrarian culture was more resistant to modern urban culture than in cases where one person grew up in the city and the other in the countryside (Nielsen and Rudberg 2006). Thus, the attitudes to gender-equality policies are connected in complex ways to gender, generation, generational relations, class and social mobility.

Degendering and regendering processes are not univocal; there may be contradictions between practices, norms and emotions. Gender norms may lose credibility, but practice may still be gendered. Housework was an example of this. The housework became less gendered in the middle generation, partly because mothers now combined it with paid work out-

[1] A pertinent question is whether gendered work and care are actually gaining ground again in the new reincarnation of stay-at-home mothers, which has become a media hype in recent years. So far, however, it seems in practice to be only an upper-class phenomenon in Norway (see Aarseth 2015) and is not visible, for instance, in terms of changes in figures of women's employment. At any rate, this idea did not seem to have any appeal among the informants we talked to in 2011.

side the family and partly because the other family members participated or thought they ought to. This could lead to a masking of still-gendered practices, but it could also contribute to a degendering on a symbolic level when such gendered practices were interpreted as an expression of individual preferences. Yet when work and care are distributed according to individual preferences, they are also often regendered again because of habits, distribution of skills or feelings of gender. Individualistic explanations of gendered choices may be seen both as an unaware reproduction of structures and as producing new understandings that gradually also affect practice. Degendering and regendering may also take place in different areas, such as a regendering of aesthetic imaginaries running in parallel to a degendering of most other areas in life.

Across the generations it emerges that positive attitudes to gender equality understood as equal treatment and equal possibilities are for the women in all three generations closely linked to higher education and often also to encouragement from their mothers to get an education, in addition to experiences of injustice in their lives. For the men in our study the link to education is not as clear. Here a positive identification with the mother, the division of work in their own marriages and whether they have daughters seem to be more crucial. Gender equality is not as pressing an issue for men as it is for women; they go along with it if needed or if they see their interests in it. However, as we have seen, practice has in itself a transformative potential: the more men participate in childcare and household tasks, the more skills they gain and the more they tend to enjoy it. Helene Aarseth's longitudinal study of families sharing a gender-equality project indicates a dynamic process: it may start as a morally driven project about equality and justice, but eventually develops into a project of joint engagement and individual desire—and in this process the different tasks that are undertaken in the family are also increasingly degendered (Aarseth 2009b; see also Plantin et al. 2003). Aarseth's point is that real change happens only when the project has moved from being an external demand to being an internally driven project that feels emotionally meaningful to the participants. This point echoes Raymond Williams' words that 'the absolute test by which revolution can be distinguished, is the change in the form of activity of a society, in its deepest structure of relationships and feelings' (Williams 1977: 420). However, it also implies that feelings of gender may sometimes delay the revolution or that new feelings may be produced at a different pace and through different types of situations than political identities.

What is striking when we look back at the interviews with the youngest generation at 30 is that many of the gender issues raised here received increasing public and political attention in the following years. In the first decade of the new millennium more attention was given to the unsolved problems or unintended negative consequences of the official gender-equality policies (NOU 15 2012): that life in the dual-earner/dual-carer family had become too stressful, that women's own priorities also contributed to the lack of equality, that there was too little focus on men's situation, that more attention in society should be given to care values and not only to what is profitable, and that gender equality in work and care could be combined with an appreciation of gender differences in other aspects of life. In different ways, our youngest informants voiced the demands of their generation for more personal choice and differentiation in gender politics already in 2001 (Melby et al. 2008; Nielsen 2004). Among the men, the wish to be at home and take care of their children or the insistence that gender equality should 'go both ways' was already present in many of the interviews at 18. Thus, these issues seem to emerge from everyday experience and this may be seen as one of the conditions for their political articulation. Political identities are also based on feelings of gender. It is not possible from our sample to decide whether there was a similar psychological readiness for new policies in the two older generations. However, from what we know of their life experiences, it seems more than likely that the educational policies in the 1960s and 1970s had a clear emotional appeal in the older generation, particularly for the women. Correspondingly, the gender-equality policies introduced in the 1970s and 1980s had a similarly strong emotional appeal in the normal chaos of love that we described for the middle generations as adults, including the men's emotional readiness to become more present fathers.

As we saw in Chap. 9, the three generations reflect the theories of gender psychology of their respective times. The same could be said about the women and the different historical approaches of feminism. With their emphasis on justice, equality and freedom, there is an affinity to the three 'waves' of feminism: from liberal and social feminism in the first-wave Women's Movement, to radical feminism in the second wave, and the post- or individual feminism in the third wave (Holst 2009). What the study of the three generations shows is that the influence may go both ways. Political mobilisation is not necessarily prior to processes of mental change in a population, but the political articulation can catch and help articulate vague feelings. The difference between the women in the oldest and middle generations illustrates this: there was no political movement to catch the discontent of the older women, positioned as they were between the first and second waves of feminist articulations (and, from what we know, none of the interviewees read *The Second Sex*, which came out in 1949). In contrast, the family policy of the time helped the men articulate their feelings of gender in a way that silenced the women and made them express their discontent in bitter remarks or in their unenthusiastic complicity as housewives. In the middle generation the Women's Movement helped articulate the frustration of the women and gave it direction. And this point of intersection between feelings and politics was again framed by economic structures of increased wealth and expanding higher education. The sensation of new normalities was based in politics, structures, feelings and everyday practices.

Gender Links

In the youngest generation women and men seem to have more similar projects, more of the same thinking about freedom and individuality, more shared beliefs that gender no longer matters and also more of the same appreciation of sexual difference in limited areas of life. However, there are also asymmetries in how this is achieved and the dilemmas that come with it. It is common to think that, due to the gender hierarchy, it is easier for women to appropriate 'masculine' values and activities than for men to appropriate 'feminine' values and activities. To some extent we have also seen this in the analyses: it was more culturally acceptable for women to do men's work in the oldest generation than for men to do women's work. It was easier for the women in the middle generation to take over and degender their fathers' skills and knowledge than for the men to take over and degender their mothers' skills and knowledge. In the youngest generation girls were more encouraged to play football than boys were to dance ballet. However, in the youngest generation the opposite is also the case: it appears to be easier for the young men to extend their masculinities with 'feminine' qualities like care and attendance to bodily appearance than for young women to become fully acknowledged as subjects of desire and power. The cultural and psychological sluggishness connected to bodies and sexuality for women more than for men keeps interfering in the degendered areas of work and care in ways that are not part of their wish to keep sexual difference alive in other areas. The young women often must walk a fine line in order not to be gendered too much or too little. They are facing dilemmas here that are more or less unknown to the men: take care not to dress up neither too femininely so you are not taken seriously at work or in a way that makes people see you as a boring neither-nor. Take care not to speak up so much that you are seen as dominant and aggressive, but not so little that you are seen as a dull woman. Take care that you do not earn less than your partner so that you will be left with the care work in the family, but do not earn more than him so that he will feel pussy-whipped either. The tribute to equality, individuality and free choice often comes with an unacknowledged contempt for traditional femininity that we also find, directly or indirectly, in both women and men in the youngest generation. The empathy with fragile masculinity that we saw in both the oldest and the youngest generations of women stands in striking contrast to the contempt for women who are gendered either too little or too much. The young women shun group identifications on the basis of gender more than is the case for the young men. The increased individualism in modern societies is in this way a double-edged sword for women in the sense that it simultaneously liberates them from old limits and inequalities *and* invites them to take part in something that is culturally and psychologically deeply coded as masculine.

Feminist sociologists have debated whether individualisation is a phenomenon that privileges men and the middle classes more than women and the working classes or whether individualisation take on different forms (Jamieson 1998; Skeggs 2003; Roseneil 2007). Beck and Beck-Gersheim's claim that modernisation gave the female biography an 'individualisation boost' (2002: 55) is on the one hand undeniably right: gender differences have become less defined and legitimised by religion, tradition and family, and women's lives have changed more than men's in the last century, especially in the areas they mention (education, work, sexuality and relationships). On the other hand, it is also the case that the combination of gender and individuality is not so straightforward for women as it is for men. For women, being an individual and being gendered tend to be two separate identities that are difficult to inhabit at the same time. For men, an extended masculinity becomes part of their individuality more easily. This appears to be one of the cultural bedrocks of gender. Already in their narrative styles we saw more emphasis on self-development among the men than was the case with the women. The middle generation struggled with integrating the 'feminine' values they identified with in their mothers, but many of them actually used the newly appropriated qualities of emotionality to extend their masculine selves, for instance, by channelling them into projects of self-development and work qualifications, as much as they used them to take responsibility for relationships with others. To be 'yourself' was an important value among all in the youngest generation when we interviewed them at 18, but while among the middle-class boys this meant standing out as unique and unpredictable individuals, it meant being one's 'authentic self' for the middle-class girls, and for the working-class girls and boys meant being relaxed and tolerant. There is not necessarily any contradiction between using emotional skills for personal development, at work or in relationships with others, but there seem to be some gendered patterns in terms of how the emotionality within these areas connects and is displayed. In spite of the prevalence of 'new men', political scientists have also observed an increasing gender gap in the political attitudes of young people, where more young women than young men adhere to the basic values of the welfare state like social reform and economic solidarity (Christensen 1994; Øia 2011). The young women represent a 'relational individualism'[2] to a higher degree, where their relational capacities are used to increase their feelings of responsibility in society at large rather than to engage in strategic self-development.

[2] The concept of 'relational individualism' is inspired by Nancy Chodorow, who first used it in an article from 1986 with the same name (Chodorow 1989). Chodorow used the concept in order to distinguish an object-relational psychoanalytic understanding of the self from a more orthodox Freudian version of autonomy. My use of the concept here is broader, as I also include the moral and political dilemmas of cultural individualisation.

The characteristic switching in the youngest generation between gender as dichotomy and gender as irrelevant may illustrate a tension between, on the one hand, gender as a dichotomous structure in our language and thinking where it is almost unavoidable to automatically 'gender' opposing qualities, and, on the other hand, an experience of increasing irrelevance of gender in practice. However, it may also testify to gender having become a more flexible dimension psychologically and through this also less substantial and threatening. It is difficult to see the appreciation of sexual difference within certain limits as only products of normative commands, backlashes or defensive reactions in the youngest generation. Gender as 'soft assembly' may be a historical product: 'Gender may in some contexts be thick and reified, as plausible real as anything in our character. At other moments gender may seem porous and insubstantial' (Harris 2002: 104). Muriel Dimen argues that the solution to the problem of splitting is not merely remembering the other pole, but 'being able to inhabit the space between, to tolerate and even enjoy the paradox of simultaneity' (Dimen 2002: 56). What I would add to this is that there are not only new spaces between the two poles, but also non-gendered spaces where the poles disappear because they are simply no longer experienced as relevant.

This addresses the question I posed in Chap. 1 about the relationship between *destabilising* a category and *weakening* its significance in different areas of life. Increased equality leads to a weakening of gender norms or makes the category of gender less important, constraining and exclusionary in some areas. This does not imply that sexual difference disappears, but different sexual preferences based on sexual difference may be experienced as more personal and less normatively constrained choices. The wish for sexual difference in heterosexual attraction expressed by many in the youngest generation is not claimed as general, unitary, recommendable or normative, but as a personal preference (until further notice). Within the youngest generation's individualist frame of thinking, it is rather a claim that everyone should do as they like, and what one likes may vary. Thus, the connection between gender norms and desire is loosened. Heterosexual choice becomes one of a number of choices. This does of course not remove the still-prevalent discriminatory attitudes and structural disadvantages of non-normative groups in society with a magical touch, but it indicates that heterosexuality may also be understood and practised within a post-heteronormative frame. The focus in this book has been the patterns of feelings of people living different kinds of 'normalised' lives at different points in time, but changes in norms do not happen in isolation from what goes on within other groups in society. Norway has become a multi-ethnic society since we did our original interviews in 1991. Sexual minority groups have become more visible, and the majority groups have become more aware and in most cases more acknowledging of diversity. The intimate lives of people from different groups also intersect more. Just looking at the eight informants we interviewed in 2011, two have non-Norwegian partners, four have worked outside Norway for longer periods of time, one has experienced that someone in the close family came out as bisexual, one has had a brief homosexual experience, one had a best friend who was a lesbian, and one said he liked to flirt with both women and men. This is a huge change compared with the two older generations in my sample. The increased openness to homosexual and bisexual impulses in themselves may be connected to the multi-gendered selves produced through their generational biographies, as well as to increased contact with people living non-normative lives, and to the new discourses on queer rights in popular culture and politics. This also shows that there are no strict borders between the different groups, and that both straight and queer people contribute to changes in gender norms and intimate life (Roseneil 2007). To return to Raymond Williams once again: new forms can flow from any particular place and extend into the whole organisation.

***

In 1991, the same year we did our interviews with the three generations analysed in this book, the Anglo-American relational psychoanalyst Virginia Goldner wrote the following, inspired by Judith Butler's *Gender Trouble* that had come out the previous year:

> *The cultural matrix that sustains the illusion of two coherent gender identities prohibits and pathologizes any gender-incongruent act, state, impulse, or mood, as well as any identity structure in which gender or sexuality is not congruent with biological sex. Thus, those genders and sexualities that fail to conform to norms of cultural intelligibility appear only as developmental failures or logical impossibilities.* (Goldner 1991: 254)

In spite of the undeniable presence of sluggish psychological and cultural structures, the multiple gender identifications in the youngest generation cannot easily be fitted into this image of looming gender binaries. Judging from the changes that emerge from the analysis of the feelings of gender in the three generations, the cultural matrix mentioned above hardly describes young people's lives in Norway in 1991. Not only did we see more multi-gendered identities and subjectivities in the youngest generation, but also that this extension had emerged gradually through complex social processes during the twentieth century. Activities and norms connected to education, work, care and ways of being and doing, have beyond doubt become less gendered. Degendering has also taken place with regard to bodily preoccupation and sexual norms and practices, but here the sluggish aspects are more pronounced. The cultural codes cannot explain why change happens, only what hampers and delays it. They do not say anything about historical conditions or the subjective motivations for taking the small steps that gradually accumulate into historical change. The many ways in which cultural codes are lived and handled are much more ambiguous than the codes themselves.

Against this claim it could be argued that the sample I have analysed lives comfortably within what Goldner calls the 'norms of cultural intelligibility'. However, the point is that in this process *the norms themselves* have become extended and more flexible, psychologically as well as culturally. The situation fits better with what Lynne Layton, with reference to Homi Bhabha, wrote in 1998: 'the "new soul" ... emerges from a process of inhabiting a sexed body and identifying with men and women in such a way as to displace timeworn histories of hegemonic masculinity and femininity' (1998: 190). Maybe we are not quite there yet, but a considerable step has been taken in this direction during the three generations we have followed.

Appendix: The Women and the Men in the Study

In addition to giving information about the chains, Tables A.1, A.2 and A.3 are meant to give a rough idea of the class positions and class travels between generations. As a rule of thumb it is the highest attained class status during the life course that is used (meaning that unemployed or retired are not relevant categories even if this was the case at the time of the interview).

Class positions are defined to match our sample by aggregating four dimensions:

- Education beyond high school (none, short, short higher (equivalent to BA level) or long higher (MA level)).
- Type of work (manual, service, housework).
- Position at work (low/high).
- Economic capital (low/high)—only used in connection with farmers or the self-employed.

Table A.1 The men in the study

Eldest generation Born 1899–1926	**Middle generation** Born 1919–1949	**Youngest generation** All born 1971–1972 Numbers of interviews
Anton, b. 1900 Farmer/fish. (l) to urban WC	***Arne***, b. 1930 Stays WC	***Anders*** WC to LMC 3
Einar, b. 1923 Farmer (l) to urban self. (l)	***Egil***, b. 1949 Self. (l) to LMC	***Erik*** LMC to ? 1
Gunnar, b. 1926 Rural WC to urban WC	***Geir***, b. 1948 Stays WC	***Glenn*** WC to ? 1
Harald, b. 1899 UMC to farmer (h)	***Helge***, b. 1938 Farmer to UMC	***Henrik*** Stays UMC 3
John, b. 1919 Urban self. (l) to WC	***Jan***, b. 1947 WC to LMC	***Joar*** Stays LMC 1
Knut, b. 1925 Farmer (l) to urban WC	***Kjell***, b. 1946 WC to LMC	***Kim*** LMC to MC 2
Martin, b. 1905 Farmer (l) to urban MC	***Magne***, b. 1938 MC to UMC	***Morten*** UMC to self. (h) 3
(not intervjued)	***Per***, b. 1947 Stays UMC	***Paul*** Stays UMC 2
(not intervjued)	***Ragnar***, b. 1936 Urban self. (l) to UMC	***Rune*** Stays UMC 2
(not intervjued)	***Svein***, b. 1949 Urban WC to LMC	***Stian*** LMC to UMC 1
(not intervjued)	***Trygve***, b. 1919 Stays MC	***Trond*** MC to ? 1
(not intervjued)	***Willy***, b. 1925 Urban WC to LMK	***Vegard*** LMK to ? 1

Table A.2 The women in the study

Eldest generation Born 1910–1927	**Middle generation** Born 1934–1953	**Youngest generation** All born 1971–1972
Agnes, b. 1912 Urban self. (h) to UMC	***Astrid***, b. 1942 Stays UMC	***Anja,*** Stays UMC 1
Borghild, b. 1911 Stays rural hw/WC	***Berit***, b. 1949 Rural WC to urban WC	***Beate*** Stays WC 2
Clara, b. 1912 Urban LMC to MC	***Cecilie***, b. 1944 MC to UMC	***Charlotte*** Stays UMC 3
Dagny, b. 1911 Stays hw/UMC	***Drude***, b. 1940 UMC to MC	***Dina*** MC to UMC 1

(Continued)

Table A.2 (continued)

Eldest generation Born 1910–1927	**Middle generation** Born 1934–1953	**Youngest generation** All born 1971–1972
Ellen, b. 1923 Stays hw/MC	***Elsa***, b. 1948 Stays MC	***Eva*** MC to urban WC 2
Fay, b. 1922 UMC to hw/urban self. (l)	***Fanny***, b. 1945 Self. (l) to MC	***Frida*** Stays MC 2
Gerd, b. 1927 Farmer (l) to hw/rural WC	***Grete***, b. 1946 Rural WC to urban MC	***Guro*** MC to UMC 2
Helga, b. 1918 Farmer (h) to urban hw/ self. (h)	***Hanne***, b. 1947 Self. (h) to MC/self. (h)	***Hilde*** MC to UMC 3
Ingrid, b. 1910 Rural WC to urban hw/WC	***Inger***, b. 1950 WC to MC/UMC	***Ida*** Stays UMC 3
Johanna, b. 1910 Farmer (l) to farmer (h)	***Jorun***, b. 1943 Farmer (h) to urban MC	***Jenny*** MC to UMC 2
Karen, b. 1924 Farmer (l) to urban WC	***Kirsten***, b. 1953 Stays urban WC	***Kine*** WC to MC/UMC 3
Lilly, b. 1922 Urban self. (l) to urban WC	***Liv***, b. 1950 Stays urban WC	***Line***, WC to MC/self. (l) 2
Martha, b. 1913 Urban WC to urban hw/MC	(not interviewed) MC to MC/UMC	***Mari*** Stays UMC 2
Nelly, b. 1913 Stays rural WC	***Nina***, b. 1943 Rural WC to UMC	***Nora*** Stays UMC 2
(not interviewed)	***Olaug***, b. 1946 Stays UMC	***Oda*** Stays UMC 2
(not interviewed)	***Paula***, b. 1934 Rural self. (h) to MC/UMC	***Pia*** Stays UMC 3
(not interviewed)	***Randi*** , b. 1949 Urban WC to LMC	***Rikke*** LMC to MC/WC 2
(not interviewed)	***Solveig***, b. 1945 Farmer/fish. (l) to urban hw/WC	***Stine*** WC to MC/LMC 2
(not interviewed)	***Turid***, b. 1947 Urban WC to MC/UMC	***Tonje*** Stays UMC 3
(not interviewed)	***Unni***, b. 1941 Farmer (h) to urban MC	***Ulla*** Stays MC/WC 2
(not interviewed)	***Vigdis***, b. 1951 Urban WC to MC/UMC	***Vilde***, Stays UMC 1
(not interviewed)	***Yvonne***, b. 1947 Urban MC to LMC	***Ylva***, LMC to MC/LMC 2

Table A.3 Overview class composition of the sample

	Oldest generation	Middle generation	Youngest generation
Number of informants	21 informants: 7 men, 14 women	33 informants: 12 men, 21 women	34 informants: 12 men, 22 women
Social class distribution (total)	WC: 5 LMC: 1 MC: 1 UMC: 3 Self.: 3 Farmers: 8	WC: 16 LMC: 0 MC: 4 UMC: 5 Self.: 4 Farmers: 4	WC: 6 LMC: 7 MC: 8 UMC: 13 Self.: 0 Farmers: 0
Generational profile	Dominant group: Rural/farmers. Only one urban WC	Dominant group: Urban WC. No LMC	Dominant group: Urban MC/UMC. No rural or self-employed
Social class distribution and gender			
WC	Men: 1 Women: 4	Men: 7 Women: 9	Men: 2 Women: 4
LMC	Men: 0 Women: 1	Men: 0 Women: 2	Men: 5 Women: 2
MC	Men: 0 Women: 1	Men: 2 Women: 2	Men: 1 Women: 7
UMC	Men: 1 Women: 2	Men: 2 Women: 2	Men: 4 Women: 9
Self-employed	Men: 1 Women: 2	Men: 1 Women: 3	Men: 0 Women: 0
Farmers/fishermen	Men: 4 Women: 4	Men: 1 Women: 3	Men: 0 Women: 0
Differences between men and women within generations in the sample	• Higher social profile among the women: – only 1 man from middle class (4 women) – no men from farms (only smallholdings)	• Only 1 rural among the men (6 women) • Otherwise the most equally gender-balanced generation with regard to class	• Higher social profile among the women: – women are over-represented in MC/UMC (16 women, 5 men) – men over-represented in LMC (5 men, 2 women) • Equal number of WC

The class categories employed are as follows:

- *Housewives (HW), urban or rural*: women who were mainly housewives while their children lived at home (no men in this category).
- *Working class (WC), urban or rural*: manual work (with or without vocational training), service work with no formal education after school and no high work position.
- *Lower middle class (LMC), urban or rural*: service work with short education or equivalent work position.
- *Middle class (MC), only urban*: shorter higher education or shorter education in combination with leading work position.
- *Upper middle class (UMC), only urban*: longer higher education.
- *Self-employed (Self.), urban or rural*: specified with regard to economic capital—low/high *(l/h)* (self-employed with low capital, for instance, shopkeepers or craftsmen with their own shop).
- *Farmer/fish., only rural*: farmers, smallholders and fishermen, specified with regard to economic capital—low/high (*l/h*) (low capital: smallholders or combinations of fishing/farming).

Class position of the childhood family is determined only from the parents' paid work. If both are in paid work and they have different class positions, it is the highest class position with regard to education that is used. If this is the mother's position, it is underlined in the table. In cases where the mother is widowed early, divorced or a single parent, it is only her class position that is used and this is also underlined. New partners of the parents/step-parents are not included.

Class position of the adult informant is determined by their own occupation.

The partner's class position is not included in the figure of the men since the data is too fragmented here. But there are no indications of wives having higher class status than the men interviewed in our sample. For the women, the partner's class position is included if it is different from their own. This is marked after a slash (for instance, MC/LMC means that the woman herself is MC and the partner LMC).

When a chain has 'gone urban', the rest of the chain is also urban (the only exception here is Harald, who grew up urban UMC and became a farmer).

Everyone in the youngest generation was interviewed at 18, most of them again at 30 and eight at 40. The number of interviews with each informant is marked in the bottom-right of the cells of the youngest generation. In four out of the eight cases who were only interviewed at 18 we do not know the class position of the adult informant.

References

Aarseth, H. (2007). Between labour and love: The re-erotization of homemaking in egalitarian couples. *NORA, Nordic Journal of Women's Studies, 15*(2–3): 133–143.

Aarseth, H. (2008). Samstemt selvskaping: Nye fedre i ny økonomi. *Tidsskrift for kjønnsforskning, 2*, 4–21.

Aarseth, H. (2009a). Situert refleksivitet: Det narrative selv mellom tilhørighet og distanse. *Sosiologi i dag, 39*(4), 7–28.

Aarseth, H. (2009b). From modernized masculinity to degendered lifestyle projects. *Men and Masculinities, 11*(4), 424–440.

Aarseth, H. (2015). 'A sound foundation?' Financial elite families and Egalitarian schooling in Norway. In C. Maxwell & P. Aggleton (Eds.), *Elite education: International perspectives*. London: Routledge.

Aarseth, H. (2016). Eros in the field? Bourdieu's double account of socialized desire. *Sociological Review, 64*(1), 93–109.

Aarseth, H., Layton, L., & Nielsen, H. B. (2016). Conflicts in habitus: The emotional work of becoming modern. *Sociological Review, 64*(1), 148–165.

Acker, J. (1989). The problem with patriarchy. *Sociology, 23*(2), 235–240.

Adkins, L. (2004a). Introduction, context and background. In L. Adkins & B. Skeggs (Eds.), *Feminism after Bourdieu*. Oxford: Blackwell.

Adkins, L. (2004b). Reflexivity. In L. Adkins & B. Skeggs (Eds.), *Feminism after Bourdieu*. Oxford: Blackwell.

Alwin, D. F., & McCammon, R. J. (2004). Generations, cohorts, and social change. In J. T. Mortimer & M. J. Shanahan (Eds.), *Handbook of the life course*. New York: Springer.

Ambjörnsson, F. (2004). *I en klass för sig: Genus, klass och sexualitet bland gymnastjeier*. Stockholm: Ordfront.

Ambjörnsson, R. (1996/2005). *Fornavnet mitt er Ronny*. Oslo: Pax.

Andersen, L. C., & H. Aarseth. (2012). Den likestilte familien i et klasseperspektiv. In A. L. Ellingsæter & K. Widerberg (Eds.), *Velferdsstatens familier* [Families of the welfare state]. Oslo: Gyldendal Akademisk.

Åström, L. (1986). *I kvinnoled: Om kvinnors liv gjenom tre generationer*. Malmö: Liber Förlag.

Beauvoir, S. d. (1949/1979). *The second sex*. Middlesex: Penguin.

Beck, U., & Beck-Gernsheim, E. (1995). *The normal chaos of love*. Cambridge: Polity Press.

Beck, U., & Beck-Gernsheim, E. (2002). *Individualization*. London: Sage.

Bengtsson, M. (2001). *Tid, rum, kön och identitet*. Lund: Studentlitteratur.

Benjamin, J. (1988). *The bonds of love*. New York: Pantheon Books.

Benjamin, J. (1995). *Like subjects, love objects: Essays on recognition and sexual difference*. London: Yale University Press.

Bertaux, D., & Bertaux-Wiame, I. (1997). Heritage and its liniage: A case history of transmission and social mobility over five generations. In D. Bertaux & P. Thompson (Eds.), *Pathways to social class. A qualitative approach to social mobility*. Oxford: Clarendon Press.

Bertaux, D., & Thompson, P. (Eds.). (1993). *Between generations. Family models, myths, and memories, International yearbook of oral history and life stories*. Oxford: Oxford University Press.

Bertaux, D., & Thompson, P. (Eds.). (1997). *Pathways to social class. A qualitative approach to social mobility*. Oxford: Clarendon Press.

Bjørnholt, M. (2014). *Modern men. A Norwegian 30-year longitudinal study of intergenerational transmission and social change*. Örebro: Örebro Universitet.

Bjurström, E. (1980). *Generationsupproret: Ungdomskulturer, ungdomsrörelser och tonårsmarknad från 50-tal till 80-tal*. Stockholm: Wahlström & Widstrand.

Bjurström, E. (1997). *Högt & lågt. Smak och stil i ungdomskulturen*. Umeå: Borea.

Blom, I., & Sogner, S. (Eds.). (1999). *Med kjønnsperspektiver på norsk historie*. Oslo: Cappelens akademiske forlag.

Bollas, C. (1987). *The shadow of the object: Psychoanalysis and the unthought known*. New York: Columbia University Press.

Borchorst, A. (2008). Woman-friendly policy paradoxes? Childcare policies and gender equality visions in Scandinavia. In K. Melby, A.-B. R. Ravn, & C. Carlsson Wetterberg (Eds.), *Gender equality and welfare politics in Scandinavia: The limits of political ambition?* Bristol: Policy Press.

Bordo, S. (1993). *Unbearble weight. Feminism, western culture, and the body.* Berkeley, CA: University of California Press.

Bordo, S. (1999). *The male body: A new look at men in public and private.* New York: Farrar, Straus and Giroux.

Bornat, J. (2004). Oral history. In C. Seale, G. Gobo, J. F. Gubrium, & D. Silverman (Eds.), *Qualitative research practice.* London: Sage.

Bourdieu, P. (1990). *Outline of a theory of practice.* Cambridge: Cambridge University Press.

Brandth, B., & Kvande, E. (2003). *Fleksible fedre.* Oslo: Universitetsforlaget.

Brannen, J. (2015). *Fathers and sons.* Basingstoke: Palgrave Macmillan.

Brannen, J., Moss, P., & Mooney, A. (2004). *Working and caring over the twentieth century.* Basingstoke: Palgrave Macmillan.

Breines, W. (1992). *Young, white, and miserable: Growing up female in the fifties.* Boston, MA: Beacon Press.

Brumberg, J. J. (1997). *The body project: An intimate history of American girls.* New York: Random House.

Bruner, J. (2003). Self-making narratives. In R. Fivush & C. A. Haden (Eds.), *Autobiographical memory and the construction of a narrative self.* Mahwad, NJ: Erlbaum.

Buhl, C. (1990). *Følelser og kropp: Behandlingav alvorlige spiseforstyrrelser.* Oslo: Universitetsforlaget.

Bühlmann, F., Elcheroth, G., & Tettamanti, M. (2010). The division of labour among European couples. *European Sociological Review, 26*(1), 49–66.

Butler, J. (1990). *Gender trouble.* New York and London: Routledge.

Butler, J. (1993). *Bodies that matter.* New York: Routledge.

Butler, J. (1995). Melancholy gender—Refused identification. *Psychoanalytic Dialogues, 5*(2), 165–180.

Butler, J. (2004). *Undoing gender.* New York: Routledge.

Chamberlayne, P., Bornat, J., & Wengraf, T. (Eds.). (2000). *The turn to biographical methods in socialscience.* London: Routledge.

Chant, S., & McIlwayne, C. (1998). *Three generations, two genders, one world. Women and men in a changing century.* London: Zed Books.

Chodorow, N. (1978). *The reproduction of mothering.* Berkeley, CA: Berkeley University Press.

Chodorow, N. (1989). *Feminism and psychoanalytic theory.* New Haven & London: Yale University Press.

Chodorow, N., & Contratto, S. (1992). The fantasy of the perfect mother. In B. Thorne & M. Yalom (Eds.), *Rethinking the family: Some feminst questions.* Boston, MA: Northeastern Press.

Chodorow, N. J. (1994). *Femininities, masculinities, sexualities: Freud and beyond.* Lexington, KY: University Press of Kentucky.

Chodorow, N. J. (1999). *The power of feelings.* New Haven, CT: Yale University Press.

Chodorow, N. J. (2000). Individuals in history and history through individuals. In M. Tymoczko & N. C. Blackmun (Eds.), *Born into a world of war.* Manchester: St.Jerome Publishing.

Chodorow, N. J. (2003). The psychoanalytic vision of Hans Loewald. *International Journal of Psychoanalysis, 4*, 897–913.

Chodorow, N. J. (2004). The American independent tradition. Loewald, Erikson, and the (possible) rise of intersubjective ego psychology. *Psychoanalytic Dialogues, 14*(2), 207–232.

Chodorow, N. J. (2012). *Individualizing gender an sexuality.* New York: Routledge.

Chodorow, N. J. (2015). From the glory of Hera to the wrath of Achilles: Narratives of second-wave masculinity and beyond. *Studies in Gender and Sexualities, 16*(4), 261–270.

Christensen, A.-D. (1994). Køn, ungdom og værdiopbrud. In J. Andersen & L. Torpe (Eds.), *Demokrati og politisk kultur. Rids af et demokratisk medborgerskab.* Herning: Forlaget Systime.

Connell, R. (2009). *Gender. In a world perspective.* Cambridge: Polity Press.

Connell, R. W. (2000). *The men and the boys.* Sydney: Allen & Unwin.

Cook, D. T., & Kaiser, S. B. (2004). Betwixt and be tween. Age ambiguity and the sexualization of the female consuming subject. *Journal of Consumer Culture, 4*(2), 203–227.

Corbett, K. (2009). *Boyhoods. Rethinking masculinities.* New Haven, CT: Yale University Press.

Crompton, R., Lewis, S., & Lyonette, C. (Eds.). (2007). *Women, men, work and family in Europe.* Basingstoke: Palgrave Macmillan.

Danielsen, K. (1990). *De gammeldagse piker: Eldre kvinner forteller om sitt liv.* Oslo: Pax.

de Coninck-Smith, N. (2003). *Reflections on the constructions of the Nordic parenthood in the 20th century.* Copenhagen: The Danish University of Education, Department of Sociology.

Den Dulk, L., & Doorne-Huiskes, V. (2007). Social policy in Europe: Its impact on families and work. In R. Crompton, S. Lewis, & C. Lyonette (Eds.), *Women, men, work and family in Europe* (pp. 35–57). Basingstoke: Palgrave Macmillan.

Dimen, M. (2002). Deconstructing difference: Gender, splitting, and transitional space. In M. Dimen & V. Goldner (Eds.), *Gender in psychoanalytic space*. New York: Other Press.

Dinnerstein, D. (1976). *In the Mermaid and the Minotaur. Sexual arrangemets and the human malaise*. New York: Harper & Row.

Drotner, K. (1991). *At skabe sig selv—Ungdom, æstetik, pædagogik*. København: Gyldendal.

Drotner, K. (1999). *Unge, medier, modernitet—pejlinger i et foranderligt landskab*. København: Borgen.

Duncan, S. (1995). Theorizing European gender systems. *Journal of European Social Policy, 5*(4), 263–284.

Dworkin, S. L., & O'Sullivan, L. F. (2007). "It's less work for us and it shows us she has good taste": Masculinity, sexual initiation, and contemporary sexual scripts. In M. Kimmel (Ed.), *The sexual self*. Nashville, TN: Vanderbilt University Press.

Ekerwald, H. (2002). *Varje mor är en dotter: Om kvinnors ungdomstid under 1900-tallet*. Stockholm: Symposion.

Elder Jr., G. H., Johnson, M. K., & Crosnoe, R. (2003). The emergence and development of life course theory. In J. T. Mortimer & M. J. Shanahan (Eds.), *Handbook of the life course*. New York: Springer.

Ellingsæter, A. L. (2012). Familiepolitikk i klassesamfunnet. In A. L. Ellingsæter & K. Widerberg (Eds.), *Velferdsstatens familier* (pp. 99–121). Oslo: Gyldendal.

Ellingsæter, A. L., & Gulbrandsen, L. (2007). Closing the childcare gap: The interaction of childcare provision and mother's agency in Norway. *Journal of Social Policy, 36*(4), 649–669.

Ellingsæter, A. L., & Leira, A. (Eds.). (2006). *Politicising parenthood in Scandinavia*. Bristol: Policy Press.

Ellingsæter, A. L., & K. Widerberg, (Eds.) (2012). *Velferdsstatens familier* [Families of the welfare state]. Oslo: Gyldendal Akademisk.

Epstein, D. (Ed.). (1998). *Failing boys? Issues in gender and achievement*. Buckingham: Open University Press.

Erikson, E. H. (1959). Ego development and historical change. *Identity and the life cycle*. Selected Papers. New York: International Universities Press.

Erikson, E. H. (1968). *Identity: Youth and crisis*. New York: Norton.

Esping-Andersen, G. (1990). *The three worlds of welfare capitalism*. Cambridge: Polity Press.

Esseveld, J. (1988). *Beyond silence: Middle-aged women in the 1970's*. Lund: Lund University.

Fagani, J. (2007). Fertility rates and mother's employment behaviour in comparative perspective: Similarities and differences in six European countries. In R. Crompton, S. Lewis, & C. Lyonette (Eds.), *Women, men, work and family in Europe*. London: Palgrave Macmillan.

Fox Harding, L. (1996). *Family, state and social policy*. London: Macmillan.

Fraser, N. (1997). *Justice interruptus. Critical reflections on the 'postsocialist' condition*. New York: Routledge.

Freud, S. (1925). Some psychical consequences of the anatomical distinction between the sexes. *Standard Edition, 19*, 241–258.

Fromm, E. (1941). *Escape from freedom*. New York: Rinehart.

Frønes, I. (2001). Revolution without rebels: Gender, generation, and social change. In A. Furlong & I. Guidikova (Eds.), *Transitions of youth citizenship in Europe: Culture, subculture and identity* (pp. 217–234). Strasbourg: Council of Europe Publishing.

Frosh, S. (2011). *Feelings*. New York: Routledge.

Frosh, S., & Baraitser, L. (2008). Psychoanalysis and psychosocial studies. *Psychoanalysis, Culture & Society, 13*, 346–365.

Frosh, S., & Emerson, P. (2005). Interpretation and over-interpretation: Disputing the meaning of texts. *Qualitative Research, 5*(3), 307–324.

Frykmann, J. (1988). *Dansbaneeländet: Ungdommen, populärkulturen och opinionen*. Stockholm: Natur & Kultur.

Gamles, R., Lewis, S., & Rapoport, R. (2007). Evolutions and approaches to equitable divisions of paid work and care in three European countries: A multi-level challenge. In R. Crompton, S. Lewis, & C. Lyonette (Eds.), *Women, men, work and family in Europe*. Basingstoke: Palgrave Macmillan.

Giddens, A. (1992). *The transformation of intimacy*. Oxford: Polity Press.

Goldner, V. (1991). Toward a critical relational theory of gender. *Psychoanalytic Dialogues, 1*(3), 249–272.

Griffin, C. (2000). Absences that matters: Constructions of sexuality in studies of young women's friendships. *Feminism & Psychology, 10*(2), 227–245.

Gullestad, M. (1996). *Everyday life philosophers*. Oslo: Scandinavian University Press.

Haavind, H. (1982). Makt og kjærlighet i ekteskapet. In R. Haukaa, M. Hoel, & H. Haavind (Eds.), *Kvinneforskning: Bidrag til samfunnsteori*. Oslo: Universitetsforlaget.

Haavind, H. (1984a). Fordeling av omsorgsfunksjoner i småbarnsfamilier. In I. Rudie (Ed.), *My start, hard landing* (pp. 161–191). Oslo: Universitetsforlaget.
Haavind, H. (1984b). Love and power in marriage. In H. Holter (Ed.), *Patriarchy in a welfare society* (pp. 136–168). Oslo: Universitetsforlaget.
Haavind, H. (1987). *Liten og stor*. Oslo: Universitetsforlaget.
Hagemann, G. (1999). De stummes leir? 1800–1900. In I. Blom & S. Sogner (Eds.), *Med kjønnsperspektiv på norsk historie*. Oslo: Cappelen Akademisk Forlag.
Hagemann, G. (2010). Kjøkkenet som samfunnsprosjekt. *Tidsskrift for kjønnsforskning, 4*, 290–311.
Hagemann, G., & Åmark, K. (1999). Fra "husmorkontrakt" til "liketillingskontrakt". Yvonne Hirdmans genusteori. In F. Engelstad (Ed.), *Om makt. Teori og kritikk*. Oslo: AdNotam Gyldendal.
Hansen, T., & Slagsvold, B. (2012). *Likestilling hjemme, NOVA rapport*. Oslo: Norsk institutt for forskning om oppvekst, velferd og aldring.
Harris, A. (2002). Gender as contradiction. In M. Dimen & V. Goldner (Eds.), *Gender in the psychoanalytic space* (pp. 91–115). New York: Other Press.
Harris, A. (2008). "Fathers" and "Daughters". *Psychoanalytic Inquiry, 28*(1), 39–59.
Hartman, H. (1981). The family as the locus of gender, class and political struggle: The example of housework. *Signs, 3*(6), 366–394.
Hernes, H. (1987). *Welfare state and woman power: Essays in state feminism*. Oslo: Norwegian University Press.
Hirdman, Y. (1988). Genussystemet—Reflexioner kring kvinnors sociala underordning. *Kvinnovetenskapelig tidsskrift, 9*(3): 49–63.
Hirdman, Y. (1990). Genussystemet. In *Demokrati och makt i Sverige. Maktutredningens huvudrapport* (p. 44). Stockholm: Almänna förlaget, SOU.
Hobson, B. (Ed.). (2002). *Making men into fathers*. Cambridge: Cambridge University Press.
Hobson, B. (Ed.). (2003). *Recognition struggles and social movements*. New York: Cambridge University Press.
Hochschild, A. (1997). *The timebind. When work becomes hime and home becomes work*. New York: Metropolitan Books.
Hollway, W. (1984). Gender difference and the production of subjectivity. In J. Henriques et al. (Eds.), *Changing the subject*. London: Methuen & Co.
Hollway, W. (2015). *Knowing mothers. Researching maternal identity in change*. London: Palgrave Macmillan.
Hollway, W., & Jefferson, T. (2000). *Doing qualitative research differently*. London: Sage.

Holst, C. (2009). *Hva er feminisme.* Oslo: Universitetsforlaget.

Holter, Ø. G., & Aarseth, H. (1993). *Menns livssammenheng.* Oslo: AdNotam.

Holter, Ø. G., Egeland, C., & Svare, H. (2009). *Gender equality and quality of life. A Norwegian perspective.* Oslo: Nordic Gender Institute.

Illouz, E. (2007). *Cold intimacies. The making of emotional capitalism.* Malden, MA: Polity Press.

Jalmert, L. (1984). *Den svenske mannen.* Stockholm: Tiden.

Jamieson, L. (1998). *Intimacy. Personal relationships in modern societies.* Cambridge: Polity Press.

Jensen, U. H. (2001). Unges politiske univers. In A.-D. Christensen & B. Siim (Eds.), *Køn, demokrati og modernitet. Mod nye politiske identiteter.* København: Hans Reitzel.

Johnson, L. (1993). *The modern girl: Girlshood and growing up.* Buckingham: Open University Press.

Josselson, R., & Lieblich, A. (1993). *The narrative study of lives* (Vol. 1). Newbury Park, CA: Sage.

Kamminga, H. (1990). What is this thing called chaos? *New Left Review*, 181.

Kavli, H. C. (2012). Verdier på vandring. Arbeidsdeling i innvandrede familier. In A. L. Ellingsæter & K. Widerberg (Eds.), *Velferdsstatens familier* [Families of the welfare state]. Oslo: Gyldendal Akademisk.

Kessler-Harris, A. (2003). In pursuit of economic citizenship. *Social Politics, 10*(2), 157–175.

Kitterød, R. H. (2009). Vaskehjelp vanligst i høystatusgrupper. *Samfunnsspeilet, 23*(1), 58–62.

Kitterød, R. H., & Rønsen, M. (2012). Kvinner i arbeid ute og hjemme. Endring og ulikhet. In A. L. Ellingsæter & K. Widerberg (Eds.), *Velferdsstatens familier* (pp. 161–190). Oslo: Gylkdendal.

Kjeldstad, R., & Lappegård, T. (2009). Mest fornøyd med (delvis) likestilling. *Samfunnsspeilet, 1*, 29–35.

Kjeldstad, R., & Lappegård, T. (2010). Holdninger til kjønnsroller og likestillingspraksis hjemme. Mindre samsvar blandt kvinner enn menn. *Samfunnsspeilet, 4*, 62–72.

Kjeldstadli, K. (1994). *Et splittet samfunn: 1905–35.* Oslo: Aschehoug.

Kleven, K. V. (1992). *Jentekultur som kyskhetsbelte.* Oslo: Universitetsforlaget.

Kleven, K. V. (1993). Deadly earnest or post-modern irony: New gender clashes. *Young. Nordic Journal of Youth Research, 1*(4), 40–59.

Knudsen, K., & Wærness, K. (2001). National context, individual characteristics and attitudes on mother's employment: A comparative analisis of Great Britain, Sweden and Norway. *Acta Sociologica, 44*(1), 67–79.

Knudsen, S. V., & Sørensen, A. D. (2006). *Unge, køn og pronografi i Norden.* København: Nordisk Ministerråd.

Kohut, H. (1977). *The restoration of the self.* New York: International Universities Press.

Korpi, W. (2000). Faces of inequality: Gender, class, and patterns of inequalities in different types of welfare states. *Social Politics, 7*(2), 127–191.

Korsvik, T. R. (2011). Childcare policy since the 1970s in the 'most gender equal country in the world': A field of controversy and grassroots activism. *The European Journal of Women's Studies, 18*(2), 135–153.

Kristiansen, H. W. (2008). *Masker of motstand. Diskré homoliv i Norge 1920–1970.* Oslo: Unipub.

Krohg, H. H. (1996). *Middelklassepikers utdannelse og dannelse. Oslo 1890–1940.* Oslo: Universitetet i Oslo.

Lange, E. (1998). *Samling om felles mål:1935–1970.* Oslo: Aschehoug.

Laplanche, J., & Pontalis, J.-B. (1973). *The language of psychoanalysis.* London: Karnac.

Lasch, C. (1979). *The culture of narcissism.* New York: Norton.

Lavik, R., & Borgeraas, E. (2015). *Forbrukstrender 2015.* Oslo, Statens Institutt for Forbruksforskning/SIFO. 5.

Lawler, S. (1999). 'Getting out and getting away': Women's narratives of class mobility. *Feminist Review, 63*(Autumn), 3–24.

Lawler, S. (2000). *Mothering the self: Mothers, daughters, subjects.* New York: Routledge.

Layton, L. (1998). *Who's that girl, Who's that boy? Clinical practice meets postmodern gender theory.* Northvale, NJ: Jason Aronson.

Layton, L. (2002). Cultural hierarchies, splitting, and the heterosexist unconscious. In S. Fairfield, L. Layton, & C. Stack (Eds.), *Bringing thr plague. Toward a postmodern psychoanalysis.* New York: Other Press.

Layton, L. (2004). Relational no more. Defensive autonomy in middle-class women. In J. A. Winer, J. W. Anderson, & C. C. Kieffer (Eds.), *Psychoanalysis and women* (pp. 29–42). Hillsdale, NJ: Analytic Press.

Layton, L. (2010). Irrational exuberance: Neoliberal subjectivity and the perversion of truth. *Subjectivity, 3*(3), 303–322.

Leira, A. (2002). *Working parents and the welfare state: Family change and policy reform in Scandinavia.* Cambridge: Cambridge University Press.

Leira, A. (2012). Omsorgens institusjoner, omsorgens kjønn. In A. L. Ellingsæter & K. Widerberg (Eds.), *Velferdsstatens familier* [Families of the welfare state]. Oslo: Gyldendal Akademisk.

Lewis, J. (1992). Gender and the development of welfare regimes. *Journal of European Social Policy, 2*(3), 159–173.

Lewis, J. (2001). The decline of the male breadwinner model: Implications for work and care. *Social Politics, 8*(2), 159–173.

Leys, R. (2011). The turn to affect: A critique. *Critical Inquiry, 37*(3), 434–472.

Loewald, H. (1980). *Papers on psychoanalysis*. New Haven, CT: Yale University Press.

Lorentzen, J. (2012). *Fra farsskapets historie i Norge 1850–2012*. Oslo: Universitetsforlaget.

Lorenzer, A. (1986). Tiefenhermeneutische Kulturanalyse. In H. D. König (Ed.), *Kultur-Analysen*. Franfurt am Main: Fischer Verlag.

Lucey, H., Olsvold, A., & Aarseth, H. (2016). Working class fathers and daughters: Thinking about desire, identification, gender and education. *Psychoanalysis, Culture and Society, 20*(2), 128–146.

Lynne, A. (2000). *Nyansenes makt—En studie av ungdom, identitet og klær*. Oslo: SIFO.

Mahler, M. S., Pine, F., & Bergman, A. (1975). *The psychological birth of the human infant*. London: Hutchinson.

Mahony, P., & Zmroczek, C. (1997). *Class matters: "Working-class" women's perspectives on social class*. London: Taylor & Francis.

Mannheim, K. (1952). The problem of generations. In K. Mannheim (Ed.), *Essays on the sociology of knowledge*. London: Routledge & Kegan Paul.

McNay, L. (2004). Agency and experience: Gender as lived relation. In L. Adkins & B. Skeggs (Eds.), *Feminism after Bourdieu*. Oxford: Blackwell.

McRobbie, A., & Garber, J. (1975). Girls and subcultures: An exploration. In S. Hall & T. Jefferson (Eds.), *Resistance through rituals*. London: Hutchinson.

Melby, K. (1999). Husmorens epoke: 1900–1950. In I. Blom & S. Sogner (Eds.), *Med kjønnsperspektiv på norsk historie*. Oslo: Cappelens akademiske forlag.

Melby, K., Ravn, A.-B., & Wetterberg, C. C. (Eds.). (2008). *Gender equality and welfare politics in Scandinavia: The limits of political ambition?* Bristol: Policy Press.

Modell, J. (1989). *Into one's own. From youth to adulthood in the United States 1920–1975*. Berkeley, CA: University of California Press.

Morgan, D. H. J. (1999). Risk and family practices: Accounting for change and fluidity in family life. In E. Silva & C. Smart (Eds.), *The new family*. London: Sage.

Myhre, J. E. (1994). *Barndom i storbyen: Oppvekst i Oslo i velferdsstatens epoke*. Oslo: Universitetsforlaget.

Nadim, M. (2012). Mellom familie og arbeid. Moralske forhandlinger blant kvinnelige etterkommere. In A. L. Ellingsæter & K. Widerberg (Eds.), *Velferdsstatens familier*. Oslo: Gyldendal Akademisk.

Nash, K. (2002). A movement moves ... Is there a women's movement in England today? *European Journal of Women's Studies, 9*(3), 311–328.

Nielsen, H. B. (1995). Seductive texts with serious intentions. *Educational Researcher, 24*(1), 4–12.

Nielsen, H. B. (1996). The magic writing-pad: On gender and identity work. *Young. Nordic Journal of Youth Research, 4*(3), 2–18.

Nielsen, H. B. (1998). Sophie og Émile i klasseværelset. *Pædagogik—en grundbog til et fag*. In J. Bjerg (Ed.). København: Hans Reitzels forlag.

Nielsen, H. B. (1999). 'Black Holes' as sites for self-constructions. *The Narrative Study of Lives, 6*: 45–75 (Making Meaning of Narratives).

Nielsen, H. B. (2003). Historical, cultural, and emotional meanings: Interviews with young girls in three generations. *NORA—Nordic Journal of Women's Studies, 11*(1): 14–26.

Nielsen, H. B. (2004). Noisy girls: New subjectivities and old gender discourses. *Young—Nordic Journal of Youth Resarch, 12*(1), 9–30.

Nielsen, H. B. (2013). Gender on class journeys. In C. Maxwell & P. Aggleton (Eds.), *Privilege, agency and affect. Understanding the production and effects of action*. London: Palgrave.

Nielsen, H. B. (2015). The arrow of time in the space of the present: Temporality as methodological and theoretical dimension in child research. *Children & Society, 30*(1), 1–11.

Nielsen, H. B., & Davies, B. (2008). Discourse and the construction of gendered identities in education. In N. H. Hornberger (Ed.), *Encyclopedia of language and education* (Vol. 3, pp. 159–170). New York: Springer Science+Business Media.

Nielsen, H. B., & Rudberg, M. (1989). *Historien om jenter og gutter*. Oslo: Universitetesforlaget.

Nielsen, H. B., & Rudberg, M. (1994). *Psychological gender and modernity*. Oslo: Universitetsforlaget.

Nielsen, H. B., & Rudberg, M. (2000). Gender, love and education in three generations. *European Journal of Women's Studies, 7*(4), 423–453.

Nielsen, H. B., & M. Rudberg. (2006). *Moderne jenter. Tre generasjoner på vei* [Modern girls: Three generations on their way]. Oslo: Universitetsforlaget.

Nielsen, H. B., & Rudberg, M. (2007). Fun in gender—Youth and sexuality, class and generation. *NORA—Nordic Journal of Women's Studies, 15*(2/3), 100–113.

Nilsen, A., Brannen, J., & Lewis, S. (Eds.). (2012). *Transitions to parenthood in Europe. A comparative life course perspective*. Bristol: The Policy Press.

Noack, T., & L. T. Hovde. (2012). Samlivsrevolusjonen. In A. L. Ellingsæter & K. Widerberg (Eds.), *Velferdsstatens familier* [Families of the welfare state]. Oslo: Gyldendal Akademisk.

NOU 15. (2012). *Politikk for likestilling. Norges offentlige utredninger*. Oslo: Barne-, likestillings- og inkluderingsdepartementet.

Oakley, A. (1990). *Housewife*. Harmondsworth: Penguin Books.

Pateman, C. (1989). *The disorder of women: Democracy, feminism and political theory*. Cambridge: Polity Press.

Pedersen, E. (2012). "Trange" fødsler? Tidsplassering av foreldreskap i livsløpet. In A. L. Ellingsæter & K. Widerberg (Eds.), *Velferdsstatens familier* [Families of the welfare state]. Oslo: Gyldendal Akademisk.

Pedersen, W. (2005). *Nye seksualiteter*. Oslo: Universitetsforlaget.

Pedersen, W., Samuelsen, S. O., & Wichstrom, L. (2003). Intercourse debut age: Poor Resources, problem behavior or romantic appeal? A popuylation-based longitudinal study. *The Journal of Sex Research, 40*(4), 333–346.

Pfau-Effinger, B. (1998). Gender cultures and the gender arrangement—A theoretical framework for cross-national gender research. *Innovation: The European Journal of Social Science Research, 11*(2), 147–166.

Plantin, L., Månsson, S.-A., & Kearney, J. (2003). Talking and doing fatherhood: On fatherhood and masculinity in Sweden and England. *Fathering, 1*(1): 3–26.

Plummer, K. (1995). *Telling sexual stories: Power change and social worlds*. London: Routledge.

Prokop, U. (1996). *Cultural pattern of the feminine—On the construction of the ideal woman in Rousseau*. Oslo: University of Oslo, Centre for Womens Studies. 7.

Ravesloot, J., Dubois-Reymond, M., & Te Poel, Y. (1999). Courtship and sexuality of young people in the fifties and nineties—An intergenerational study from the Netherlands. *Young, 7*(4), 2–17.

Reay, D. (2005). Beyond consciousness? The psychic landscape of social class. *Sociology, 39*(5), 911–928.

Reay, D. (2015). Habitus and the psychosocial: Bourdieu with feelings. *Cambridge Journal of Education, 45*(1), 9–23.

Ricoeur, P. (1991a). Life in quest of a narrative. In D. Wood (Ed.), *On Paul Ricoeur: Narrative and interpretation*. London: Rouledge.

Ricoeur, P. (1991b). What is a text. In M. J. Valdes (Ed.), *A Ricoeur reader: Reflexions and imaginations*. New York: Harvester/Wheatsheaf.

Ringdal, K. (2010). Sosial mobilitet. In K. Dahlgren & J. Ljunggren (Eds.), *Klassebilder. Ulikhet og sosial mobilitet i Norge*. Oslo: Universitetsforlaget.

Rosaldo, M. Z., & Lamphere, L. (1974). *Woman, culture, and society*. Standford: Standford University Press.

Rose, J. (1986). *Sexuality in the field of vision*. London: Verso.

Roseneil, S. (2006). The ambivalence of Angel's 'arrangement': A psychosocial lens on the contemporary conditions of personal life. *The Sociological Review, 54*(4), 847–869.

Roseneil, S. (2007). Queer individualization: The transformation of personal life in the early 21st century. *NORA—Nordic Journal of Women's Studies, 15*(2–3), 84–99.

Rosenthal, G. (2004). Biographical research. In C. Seale, G. Gobo, J. F. Gubrium, & D. Silverman (Eds.), *Qualitative research practice*. London: Sage.

Rudberg, M. (1983). *Dydige, sterke, lykkelige barn. Ideer om oppdragelse i borgerlig tradisjon*. Oslo-Bergen-Stavanger-Tromsø: Universitetesforlaget.

Rudberg, M. (1995). A bloody story? On construction of bodily gender among girls. *NORA, 3*(1), 32–44.

Rudberg, M. (2009). Paradoxes in schooling gender—A messy story. *Young—Nordic Journal of Youth Research, 17*(1), 41–58.

Rudberg, M., & Nielsen, H. B. (2005). Potential spaces—Subjectivities and gender in a generational perspective. *Feminism & Psychology, 15*(2), 127–148.

Rudberg, M., & Nielsen, H. B. (2011). Gender in three generations: Narrative constructions and psychological identifications. In K. J. de Lopéz & T. G. B. Hansen (Eds.), *Development of self in culture* (Vol. 1). Aalborg: Aalborg University Press.

Rudberg, M., & Nielsen, H. B. (2012). The making of a 'new man: Psychosocial change in a generational context. *The Journal of Psycho-Social Studies, 6*(1): 55–74.

Rydström, J. (2011). *Odd couples: A history of gay marriage in Scandinavia*. Amsterdam: Amsterdam University Press.

Sainsbury, D. (2001). Gender and the making of welfare states: Norway and Sweden. *Social Politics, 8*(1), 113–143.

Sandvik, H. (1999). Tidlig moderne tid i Norge. 1500–1800. In I. Blom & S. Sogner (Eds.), *Med kjønnsperspektiv på norsk historie*. Oslo: Cappelen Akademisk Forlag.

Segal, L. (1994). *Straight sex. The politics of pleasure*. London: Virago Press.

Silva, E. B. (2005). Gender, home and family in cultural capital theory. *The British Journal of Sociology, 56*(1), 83–103.

Simonsen, B., & Ulriksen, L. (1998). *Universitetsstudier i krise: Fag, projekter og moderne studenter*. Roskilde: Roskilde Universitetsforlag.

Simpson, M. (1994). *Male impersonators: Men performing masculinity*. New York: Routledge.

Skeggs, B. (1997). *Formations of class & gender*. London: Sage.

Skeggs, B. (2003). *Class, self, culture*. London: Routledge.

Skeggs, B. (2005). The making of class and gender through visualizing moral subject formation. *Sociology, 39*(5), 965–982.

Skilbrei, M.-L. (2005). Making paid work into housework: Conformity and opposition in "traditional" femininity. In G. Hagemann & H. Roll-Hansen (Eds.), *In Twentieth-century housewives: Meanings and implications of unpaid work*. Oslo: Universitetsforlaget.

Skrede, K. (1986). Gifte kvinner i arbeidslivet. In L. Alldén, N. R. Ramsøy, & M. Vaa (Eds.), *Det norske samfunn III*. Oslo: Gyldendal.

Skrede, K. (1996). Levekår i tre generasjoner. Kjønn, generasjon og forandring. Universitetet i Oslo, Senter for kvinneforskning. A-notat 8.

Skrede, K. (1999). Shaping gender equality—The role of the state: Norwegian experiences, present policies and future challenges. In B. Palier & D. Bouget (Eds.), *Comparing social welfare systems in Nordic countries and France* (Vol. 4, pp. 169–199). Paris: Maison des sciences de l' Homme Ange-Guépin. MIRE.

Skrede, K., & Wiik, K. A. (2012). Forsørgelsesstruktur og inntekstfordeling: Mer likestilling og større ulikhet? In A. L. Ellingsæter & K. Widerberg (Eds.), *Velferdsstatens familier*. Oslo: Gyldendal.

Skugge, L. N., Olsson, B., & Zilg, B. (Eds.). (1999). *Fittstim*. Stockholm: Bokförlaget DN.

Slettan, D. (1984). Barnearbeid i jordbruket. In B. Hodne & S. Sogner (Eds.), *Barn av sin tid. Fra norske barns historie*. Oslo: Universitetsforlaget.

Søland, B. (2000). *Becoming modern: Young women and the reconstruction of womanhood in the 1920s*. Princeton, NJ: Princeton University Press (se littpersp tregen).

Solberg, A., & Vestby, G. M. (1987). *Barns arbeidsliv*. Oslo: NIBR.

Solheim, J. (2007). *Kjønn og modernitet*. Oslo: Pax.

Solheim, J. (2012). Den nordvesteuropeiske modellen. Familie og hushold i historisk og komparativt perspektiv. In A. L. Ellingsæter & K. Widerberg (Eds.), *Velferdsstatens familier*. Oslo: Gyldendal Akademisk.

Sørensen, A. D. (2002). Pornografi ad bagdøren. *Ungdomsforskning, 2*: 31–37.

Stormhøj, C. (2003). Den politiserede tokønnethed. *Grus, 24*(69), 118–137.

Stormhøj, C. (2013). Queer theories, critiques and beyond. *Kvinder, køn og forskning, 13*(1), 61–72.

Telste, K. (2002). Den unge piges by. *Kvinneforskning, 26*(1): 5–21.

Therborn, G. (1993). The politics of childhood: The rights of children in modern times. In F. G. Castles (Ed.), *Families of nations: Petterns of public policy in Western democracies*. Aldershot: Dartmouth.

Thompson, P. (1997). Women, men, and transgenerational family influences in social mobility. In D. Bertaux & P. Thompson (Eds.), *Pathways to social class*. Oxford: Clarendon Press.

Thomson, R., Kehily, M.J., Hadfield, L. & Sharpe, S. (2011). *Making modern mothers*. Bristol: The Policy Press.

Thorsen, L. E. (1993a). A room of one's own? Farmer and working-class girls in Norway during the 1930s and 1940s. *Young, 1*(1), 29–38.

Thorsen, L. E. (1993b). *Det fleksible kjønn: mentalitetsendringer i tre generasjoner bondekvinner 1920–1985*. Oslo: Universitetsforlaget.

Thorsen, L. E. (1997). Skis, skates and language: Traits of Norwegian urban young girl's culture in the 1930s. *Ethnologica Scandinavica, 27*, 48–64.

Trondman, M. (2010). Ubegripelige ting. Når livsbaner stiger og faller. In K. Dahlgren & J. Ljunggren (Eds.), *Klassebilder. Ulikhet og sosial mobilitet i Norge*. Oslo: Universitetsforlaget.

Usdansky, M. L. (2011). The gender-equality paradox: Class and incongruity between work-family attitudes and behaviors. *Jorunal of Family Theory & Review, 3*(3), 163–178.

von der Lippe, A. (1988). Mødre som modeller for døtres yrkesorientering. *Tidskrift for Norsk Psykologforening, 25*(Supplement nr.4), 149–159.

Walby, S. (1997). *Gender transformations*. London: Rouledge.

Walkerdine, V. (1990). *Schoolgirl fictions*. London: Verso.

Walkerdine, V. (1997). *Daddy's girl*. London: Macmillan.

Walkerdine, V., & Lucey, H. (1989). *Democracy in the kitchen*. London: Virago.

Walkerdine, V. J., & Jimenez, L. (2012). *Gender, workand community after de-industrialisation. A psychosocial approach to affect*. Basingstoke: Palgrave Macmillan.

Wengraf, T. (2001). *Qualitative research interviewing : Biographic narrative and semi-structured methods*. London: Sage.

Wennhall, J. (1994). *Från djäkne til swingpjatt: Om de moderne ungdomskulturenes historia*. Uppsala: Etnolore.

Wetherell, M. (2012). *Affect and emotion. A new social science understanding*. Los Angeles, CA: Sage.

Williams, R. (1977). *Marxism and literature*. Oxford: Oxford University Press.

Williams, R. (2011). *The long revolutiosn*. Cardigan: Parthian.

Winnicott, D. W. (1971). *Playing and reality*. London: Tavistock.

Wolf, N. (1997). *Promiscuities. A secret history of female desire*. London: Chatto & Windus.

Woodward, K. (2015). *Psychosocial studies*. London: Routledge.

Øia, T. (2011). *Nordisk ungdommers holdninger til likestilling*. NOVA-report. Oslo: NOVA. 25/11.

Öhrn, E. (2002). *Könsmönster i förändring? En kunnskapsöversikt om unga i skolan*. Stockholm: Skolverket.

Permissions

All chapters in this book were first published in FGAGPA, by Springer by Harriet Bjerrum Nielsen; hereby published with permission under the Creative Commons Attribution License or equivalent. Every chapter published in this book has been scrutinized by our experts. Their significance has been extensively debated. The topics covered herein carry significant information for a comprehensive understanding. They may even be implemented as practical applications or may be referred to as a beginning point for further studies.

We would like to thank the editorial team for lending their expertise to make the book truly unique. They have played a crucial role in the development of this book. Without their invaluable contributions this book wouldn't have been possible. They have made vital efforts to compile up to date information on the varied aspects of this subject to make this book a valuable addition to the collection of many professionals and students.

This book was conceptualized with the vision of imparting up-to-date and integrated information in this field. To ensure the same, a matchless editorial board was set up. Every individual on the board went through rigorous rounds of assessment to prove their worth. After which they invested a large part of their time researching and compiling the most relevant data for our readers.

The editorial board has been involved in producing this book since its inception. They have spent rigorous hours researching and exploring the diverse topics which have resulted in the successful publishing of this book. They have passed on their knowledge of decades through this book. To expedite this challenging task, the publisher supported the team at every step. A small team of assistant editors was also appointed to further simplify the editing procedure and attain best results for the readers.

Apart from the editorial board, the designing team has also invested a significant amount of their time in understanding the subject and creating the most relevant covers. They scrutinized every image to scout for the most suitable representation of the subject and create an appropriate cover for the book.

The publishing team has been an ardent support to the editorial, designing and production team. Their endless efforts to recruit the best for this project, has resulted in the accomplishment of this book. They are a veteran in the field of academics and their pool of knowledge is as vast as their experience in printing. Their expertise and guidance has proved useful at every step. Their uncompromising quality standards have made this book an exceptional effort. Their encouragement from time to time has been an inspiration for everyone.

The publisher and the editorial board hope that this book will prove to be a valuable piece of knowledge for students, practitioners and scholars across the globe.

Index

A

Adult Informant, 300-301

Agrarian Family, 82, 128, 276-277

B

Bedrocks Of Gender, 274, 292

Bisexual, 16, 197, 294

Bourgeois, 66-67, 69, 97, 273

C

Childcare Facilities, 6, 236

Collective Class, 14-15

Commercialisation, 84-85, 88

Cultural Patterns, 25-26

D

Degendering, 144-145, 153, 173, 176, 179, 189, 191, 194, 196, 198, 202, 205, 256, 272, 274, 276, 281, 287-288, 295

Demanding Career, 228, 234

Different Generations, 14, 22, 29, 35, 45, 52, 58, 63-64, 235, 237, 282-283

Distant Fathers, 128, 136, 245

Divorce Rates, 4, 117

E

Economic Structures, 25, 290

Educational System, 15, 73-74, 134, 205, 256, 280

Eldest Generations, 50, 125, 192

Emotional Links, 243, 277-278, 282-283

Equal Pay, 76, 80, 172

Equity, 7, 125, 169, 283

F

Family Forms, 66, 254

Farmer Girls, 102, 104, 108, 141-142

Female Care, 116-117, 123, 133

Feminine Personalities, 38, 265

Femininity, 8, 37-38, 49, 87, 101-102, 111, 118, 121, 153-155, 168-169, 171, 191, 193, 200, 202, 204-205, 217, 246-247, 251-252, 256, 258, 260-263, 265-266, 271, 275, 278-281, 291, 295, 315

Feminist Politics, 17, 166

G

Gender Ambiguity, 263, 267, 269, 273-274

Gender Contracts, 7-9, 276-277

Gender Differences, 5, 37-38, 134, 153, 155-157, 169-170, 191, 199, 202, 204-205, 215, 217, 225, 264-265, 269, 286-287, 289, 291

Gender Discrimination, 115, 215, 218, 227, 231, 286

Gender Equality, 4, 7, 12, 15, 17, 22, 45, 53, 68, 76-77, 80-81, 125-128, 130, 147, 154-155, 158, 167-172, 174, 177-178, 180, 182, 191, 204, 206, 209, 212-218, 220-235, 238-240, 276-277, 283-289, 304, 309, 311, 315

Gender Gaps, 4, 75, 286

Gender Identity, 10-11, 37, 244, 247, 252-253, 261-263, 265-266, 268-269, 271-272, 275, 287

Gender Radical, 228

Gender Relations, 3-7, 13, 17, 66, 81, 118, 150, 158-159, 261, 275

Gendered Psychologies, 270, 274

Gendered Subjectivities, 2, 10-11, 22, 36, 240, 243, 252-253, 261, 263, 274, 278, 281

Generational Patterns, 13, 49, 51, 62, 220, 243, 270

H

Hardworking Mothers, 49, 103, 117, 123, 126

Heterosexuality, 205, 263, 280, 293

High-powered Job, 225, 287

Homosexuality, 46, 170, 197, 250, 271

I

Idealisation, 34, 60, 98, 104, 106, 116, 123-124, 144, 257-258, 264, 268, 271-272, 278

Identification, 9, 27, 35, 37-38, 60, 99-102, 104-107, 109, 136-139, 141, 152-153, 181, 183-184, 186, 198, 228-230, 232-234, 240-241, 244-245, 250-252, 254-256, 258, 260-261, 264, 267-269, 273, 275, 280, 288, 304, 311

Individual Rights, 66, 70, 228

Individuality, 33, 36, 81, 88, 154-155, 167, 173, 198, 200, 205, 215, 217, 233-234, 256, 260, 263, 282, 290-292

Intergenerational Transmission, 9, 12, 51, 303

Intimacy, 2, 56, 66, 149-150, 167, 179, 187, 195-196, 253, 259, 265-267, 269, 272, 307, 309

Intrapsychic World, 271

L

Labour Market, 4, 7, 15, 58, 69, 75, 78-79, 118, 174, 240, 253, 277, 282, 285

M

Masculine Sides, 232, 262

Menstruation, 109, 147, 191-192, 259

Middle Generation, 6, 13, 44, 47, 49-50, 52-55, 57-58, 72-73, 78-80, 88-89, 131-136, 144-145, 158-160, 169, 176, 185-186, 196, 199-200, 221-222, 225-226, 228, 237-241, 257-260, 271-272, 279, 284-285, 287, 290, 292, 297-298

Modernisation, 5-6, 15, 42, 47, 66-68, 70, 81-82, 240, 242, 291

Moral Obligation, 216

Mother's Position, 241, 300

Mother's Proficiency, 102, 104, 254

P

Political Issue, 12, 86, 206

Post-war Period, 84, 87, 132, 235, 277

Psychoanalysis, 18, 25, 39, 62, 165, 303, 305, 307, 310-311

Psychology, 2, 29-30, 39, 58, 157, 243, 270, 289, 305, 307, 314

Public Sector, 175, 217, 224, 227, 229, 235

R

Regendering, 276, 287-288

S

Self-esteem, 33, 157, 256, 260, 262, 267, 271

Sex Education, 70, 82, 86

Sexual Debuts, 86, 195

Sexual Difference, 38, 155, 170, 197-198, 225, 234, 262, 290-291, 293, 303

Sexuality, 5, 11, 15, 17, 21, 37-38, 45, 48, 64-65, 85-86, 88-89, 107, 109, 111, 121, 146, 150-152, 157, 171, 189, 194, 196, 243, 250-252, 259-261, 264, 271-273, 279-281, 291-292, 294, 305, 307, 312-314

Social Differences, 53, 76, 236

Social Mobility, 5, 15-16, 47, 52, 63, 74, 96, 136, 235, 241, 286-287, 303, 316

Social Patterns, 2, 16, 22-24, 36, 60, 98

Social Transformation, 1-2, 13, 16, 52, 274, 276

Socialisation, 9, 26, 29, 31, 270

Socially Patterned, 24-25

Stay-at-home Dad, 165, 210, 212

Subdued Mother, 129, 184

Subject Formation, 30, 33-34, 315

Subjectivity, 1, 10-11, 21, 25-27, 35, 61, 118, 244, 247, 252-253, 256, 260, 262-263, 266, 272, 275, 308, 310

T

Taxation, 6, 73

U

Unemployment, 73, 75, 92, 235

Universalism, 38, 40

Unmasculine, 189, 202, 273

Unpaid Work, 6, 69, 315

W

Work Division, 117, 162, 177, 198, 206, 211, 213, 228-229, 287

Work-family Balance, 206, 221-222

Working-class, 20, 42, 47, 52, 55, 64, 71, 74, 77, 79-80, 82-83, 100, 102, 104-105, 124-125, 135-137, 139-140, 171, 173-174, 188, 195, 198-200, 202, 223-224, 232, 241, 246, 248-249, 254, 257-259, 261, 273, 286-287, 292, 311, 316

Y

Younger Generations, 49, 237, 258, 270

www.ingramcontent.com/pod-product-compliance
Lightning Source LLC
LaVergne TN
LVHW080642210926
848485LV00003B/309